Ultimate Ember.js for Web App Development

Leverage Convention Over Configuration Paradigm to Develop, Build, and Deploy Complex Applications Using Ember.js

Aswin Murugesh K

www.orangeava.com

First published: March 2024

Published by: Orange Education Pvt Ltd, AVA™

Address: 9, Daryaganj, Delhi, 110002, India

275 New North Road Islington Suite 1314 London,

N1 7AA, United Kingdom

ISBN: 978-81-97081-92-7

www.orangeava.com

Dedicated To

My Beloved Wife:

Dr. Sowndharya Meera
and
My Family and Friends

About the Author

Aswin Murugesh K holds a Bachelor degree in Information Technology from the College of Engineering, Guindy, Chennai, India. He has worked as an intern and employee in top MNCs like Amazon, Oracle and also has experience working in startups of different stages, thus having an overall knowledge of the industry. He then started his own company back in 2019, focusing on developing quality products for their customers. He started Kuriyam.io as a service-based company and has recently transformed it into a product-based company in 2023 with their first in-house product, Pinaippu, that focuses on WhatsApp marketing and automation.

Through his company, Aswin helps nurture college students by providing internships for them to learn hands-on about working in a nimble startup environment and learning different technologies. He is an active contributor to Stack Overflow and also provides paid mentorship for Python and JavaScript based projects through online platforms like Codementor.

Right from his college days, Aswin has been a part of the Free and Open Source (FOSS) community and has been interacting with students from colleges across Tamil Nadu to teach them the importance of open-source software and tools in the software community. He also conducts sessions teaching different programming languages like Python, JavaScript, and different frameworks like Ember.js, React.js, Django and Flask. He always insists on students learning the "How" in everything instead of just the "What". His teachings always focus on making people understand how things work, and not just what they do. This will enable the students to become thinkers instead of just doers.

Apart from his technical career, Aswin is an internationally rated Chess player. In his free time, he plays Chess and reads a lot of books. He is reachable in LinkedIn at https://linkedin.com/in/aswinmurugesh.

About the Technical Reviewer

Yamuna is a seasoned professional with 14 years of extensive experience in front-end development. Holding the position of Technical Lead at HappyFox, she boasts over 13 years of comprehensive web development expertise alongside a robust background in physics. With a passion for problem-solving and analytical thinking, Yamuna excels in crafting high-quality, secure, and user-friendly features using Ember, a cutting-edge JavaScript framework. Her enthusiasm for embracing new technologies is only rivaled by her dedication to imparting knowledge to others.

In her role as Technical Lead, Yamuna undertakes a multifaceted approach, encompassing code review, release management, and seamless coordination with backend teams. Notably, she has spearheaded the implementation of generic solutions addressing critical web application security concerns, including XSS, CSRF, and CSP. Yamuna's proficiency extends to end-to-end feature development, leveraging Python and Ember, while her skill set encompasses HTML5, CSS, Javascript, and Jquery, among others.

A pivotal member of the development process team, Yamuna has played a pivotal role in establishing best practices for REST APIs and elevating code efficiency and quality. Her commitment to fostering teamwork, collaboration, and innovation is evident in her efforts to cultivate a positive and inclusive work environment for her team members.

Having made significant contributions during her tenures at Zoho and HappyFox, Yamuna is now eagerly seeking a new and exciting role where she can continue to leverage her expertise, drive, and passion for excellence in web development. With a proven track record of success and a steadfast commitment to professional growth, Yamuna stands ready to make a meaningful impact in her next endeavor.

Acknowledgements

My experience writing *Ultimate Ember.js for Web App Development* has been a wonderful journey, and I am grateful to everyone in my life who have played a role in shaping my technical skills and guiding me in my constant pursuit of knowledge. This book wouldn't have been possible without the support and expertise shared by many.

Firstly, I would like to thank the Ember.js community and all collaborators involved in creating this wonderful framework. The official documentation of Ember.js, available at https://guides.emberjs.com/release/ has been a very valuable resource in helping me stay true and accurate to the excellence of the framework.

I thank my family for their ever-present support. Especially, I wish to thank my wife Meera, who has been a source of strength throughout the journey of writing this book, my parents, teachers, relatives and friends who have always encouraged me in my endeavors in life. Special thanks to my mentors Vysakh Sreenivasan and Yamuna Subramaniam (the technical reviewer for this book) for being a vital part of my journey with Ember.js.

I would like to extend my appreciation to the publication house for providing me with the opportunity to showcase my knowledge in such a way as to contribute to the community by helping fellow developers learn web development. It was their constant support and guidance that made me achieve my goal of writing my first book.

Finally, to the readers, thank you for choosing this book as your source of knowledge. May it be a valuable companion on your journey to mastering Ember.js and navigating the dynamic world of web development.

Preface

In this fast-evolving world of web development, there are so many new frameworks being released that choosing the right framework for your project is of utmost importance. Introducing Ember.js, the battle-tested frontend framework that can help you build your applications with speed, in the right way. In *Ultimate Ember.js for Web App Development*, we will take you through the journey from being a beginner to becoming a master of the Ember.js framework.

This book consists of 10 chapters. Each of the chapters covers a specific module or topic about the framework, from the basics of Web Development to the detailed internals of Ember.js and also the process involved after the development is complete, like the testing and deployment steps. From beginners to developers who already have knowledge of Ember.js, this book has something for any developer eager to learn something new.

Chapter 1 Introduction to Ember.js: In the first chapter, we will take you through the basics of JavaScript and Web Development, the types of Web Applications available, the different components of a web application, and so on. We will list some of the popular frontend frameworks widely used in the market and discuss the advantages of Ember.js and why it can be a right fit for your project.

Chapter 2 Ember CLI and Local Setup: This chapter talks about Ember CLI, a Command Line Interface that is a package used to interact with and manage your Ember application. We will discuss in detail about the wide variety of options presented by the tool, and we will also take you through the process of setting it up locally and creating your first Ember.js application.

Chapter 3 Ember.js Routing: In this chapter, we will discuss in detail about Ember Routes. We will show you the different types of Routes that can be setup in the application, how you can create dynamic URLS and load specific data based on the URL, and display it to the end user through Templates.

Chapter 4 Ember.js Components Templates: Components are the basic building blocks of your Ember application, and we will dig deeper into building Components, adding dynamicity to the Templates and handling interactions between the Components and Controllers and between Components themselves. We will also learn about creating helpers that facilitate calling dynamic JavaScript functions from within Templates.

Chapter 5 Ember Data and Services: Ember Data is the gateway for connecting your Ember application with a persistent data source and loading and modifying the data the user sees in the application. We will discuss the various functionalities offered by the Ember Data Store for authenticating and interacting with APIs, and we will also look at Services in Ember, a special type of singleton object that can be called from anywhere in the application.

Chapter 6 Configuring your Ember App: In this chapter, we concentrate on the post development activities of an application, the modifications or enhancements you can do to make your application ready for deployment.

Chapter 7 Testing Ember.js Apps: Testing is a vital piece in the Software Development lifecycle, as it helps you keep your application secure and up-to-date with requirements. This chapter talks in detail about the basics of testing, the kinds of testing in Software Development. Then we discuss testing in Ember.js, in particular, the different types of tests you can write for each module present in the framework.

Chapter 8 Ember Inspector: This chapter is about Ember Inspector, a tool used to monitor the performance of your application and to debug issues with your code. We will dive deep into the features available in this tool, how you can use it to gain knowledge of the different objects present in your application, the data that is loaded in the application, and so on.

Chapter 9 Build and Deployment: This chapter shows the steps involved in generating a build for your application and then deploying your application to different cloud hosting providers for everyone to access the application.

Chapter 10 Conclusion: The final chapter concludes the journey by summarizing the concepts we have learned so far in this book. We discuss some of the best practices recommended by the framework and also guide you through the process of creating an Ember addon. We will then provide information on how you can contribute as a developer to this great framework.

This book contains live examples of building a sample project to learn the concepts by doing as and when you learn about them. We have also provided exercises at the end of each chapter to encourage you to validate your understanding of the chapter and tickle your brain with questions that encourage you to research further on certain topics. The live examples and the application built through the process of this book are available at https://github.com/aswinm/sample-ember-application. Happy coding!

Get a Free eBook

We hope you are enjoying your recently purchased book! Your feedback is incredibly valuable to us, and to all other readers looking for great books.

If you found this book helpful or enjoyable, we would truly appreciate it, if you could take a moment to leave a short review with a 5 star rating on Amazon. It helps us grow, and lets other readers discover our books.

As a thank you, we would love to send you a free digital copy of this book, and a **30%** discount code on your next cart value on our official websites:

www.orangeava.com

www.orangeava.in (For Indian Subcontinent)

☑ **Here's how:**

Leave a review for the book on Amazon.

Take a screenshot of your review, and send an email to **info@orangeava.com** (it can be just the confirmation screen).

Once, we receive your screenshot, we will send you the digital file, within 24 hours.

Thank you so much for your support – it means a lot to us!

Downloading the code bundles and colored images

Please follow the links or scan the QR codes to download the
Code Bundles and Images of the book:

https://github.com/ava-orange-education/Ultimate-Ember.js-for-Web-App-Development

The code bundles and images of the book are also hosted on
https://rebrand.ly/dc9a41

In case there's an update to the code, it will be updated on the existing GitHub repository.

Errata

We take immense pride in our work at **Orange Education Pvt Ltd,** and follow best practices to ensure the accuracy of our content to provide an indulging reading experience to our subscribers. Our readers are our mirrors, and we use their inputs to reflect and improve upon human errors, if any, that may have occurred during the publishing processes involved. To let us maintain the quality and help us reach out to any readers who might be having difficulties due to any unforeseen errors, please write to us at :

errata@orangeava.com

Your support, suggestions, and feedback are highly appreciated.

DID YOU KNOW

Did you know that Orange Education Pvt Ltd offers eBook versions of every book published, with PDF and ePub files available? You can upgrade to the eBook version at **www.orangeava.com** and as a print book customer, you are entitled to a discount on the eBook copy. Get in touch with us at: **info@orangeava.com** for more details.

At **www.orangeava.com**, you can also read a collection of free technical articles, sign up for a range of free newsletters, and receive exclusive discounts and offers on AVA™ Books and eBooks.

PIRACY

If you come across any illegal copies of our works in any form on the internet, we would be grateful if you would provide us with the location address or website name. Please contact us at **info@orangeava.com** with a link to the material.

ARE YOU INTERESTED IN AUTHORING WITH US?

If there is a topic that you have expertise in, and you are interested in either writing or contributing to a book, please write to us at **business@orangeava.com**. We are on a journey to help developers and tech professionals to gain insights on the present technological advancements and innovations happening across the globe and build a community that believes Knowledge is best acquired by sharing and learning with others. Please reach out to us to learn what our audience demands and how you can be part of this educational reform. We also welcome ideas from tech experts and help them build learning and development content for their domains.

REVIEWS

Please leave a review. Once you have read and used this book, why not leave a review on the site that you purchased it from? Potential readers can then see and use your unbiased opinion to make purchase decisions. We at Orange Education would love to know what you think about our products, and our authors can learn from your feedback. Thank you!

For more information about Orange Education, please visit **www.orangeava.com**.

Table of Contents

CHAPTER 1

Introduction to Ember.js

Introduction

In this chapter, we will go over the basics of JavaScript, why frontend frameworks are required and the popular web frameworks used in the market. This will give us a perspective of what Ember.js is and how it is different compared to other frameworks to build **Single Page Applications**. Understanding the basics will help you build applications efficiently using the framework. After that, we will be discussing the basics of Ember.js and the structure of an Ember application.

Whether you are a beginner in JavaScript, or an experienced frontend developer, the goal of this book is to help you become competent to individually develop, build and deploy complex Ember.js web applications following the best practices of the Ember.js community.

Structure

In this chapter, we will discuss the following topics:

- An Overview of Web Development
- JavaScript
- Frontend Applications
- Popular Frontend Frameworks
- Ember.js
- Anatomy of an Ember.js Application

An Overview of Web Development

In recent times, we can see most of our day-to-day activities being moved online. Right from purchasing groceries and clothes, to doing your banking transactions from the comfort of your home, anything and everything is now online. We also spend a lot of time scrolling through social media posts, watching movies on OTT platforms, and more. All these activities can be done online either via a browser like Google Chrome, Firefox, or Internet Explorer, or through different mobile applications.

For all these online activities, the data is not stored in your computer or mobile alone, but in some remote server under the control of the owner of the program. For the scope of this book, we will discuss only programs that you access through browsers. Those are called *websites or web applications.*

Websites versus Web Applications

The programs you access through browsers can be categorized into websites and web applications. There are a few differences between the two types.

A website is simply a collection of related pages, where a visitor will see text, images, videos, animations, and more. Any code execution happens only on the browser and there are no server-side actions/logic for a website. The pages will be static and read-only, and the content might differ only based on the region/ language of the visitor. For example, your personal profile site, or a restaurant's website that showcases their business timings and menu are websites.

A web application, on the other hand, is more complex and more dynamic. It usually involves authentication. Users who log in will see content based on their history or their user access level. A web application requires a server to handle requests from the client and respond accordingly. Code executions happen both on the server and the browser. For example, social media platforms where the feed is personalized for the user, or a customer support portal where every user sees data only based on their access level, are examples of web applications.

Defining Web Development

Web Development refers to the process involved in developing, building, and maintaining websites and web applications. It is the creation of an application that is accessible through the internet.

A web application involves the following components:

- Frontend/Client Side
- Backend/Server Side

The following figure depicts a typical architecture of a Web application. This is how the client-side and server-side work together to store and retrieve data that is shown to the user:

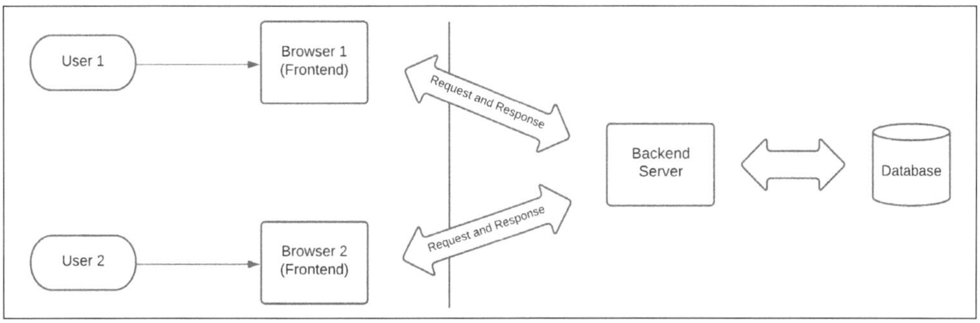

Figure 1.1: *Architecture of a Web application*

Frontend/Client Side

The client side is the part of the application that the end user sees in a browser. It handles the user interface and user interactions. This allows for a responsive and interactive user experience, as the client-side code can handle events, make requests to the server, manipulate the page content, and update the user interface in real-time. Frontend uses the following languages:

- **Hypertext Markup Language (HTML):** HTML is used to define the base structure of a web page using a series of elements called HTML tags.
- **Cascading Style Sheets (CSS):** CSS is used to style the web page. It enables the separation of the structure of the page and presentation of the page and defines how each component of the web page should look.
- **JavaScript:** JavaScript is a scripting language that is used to make web pages interactive and dynamic. JavaScript is used to dynamically alter the elements of an HTML page, also called a Dynamic Object Model (DOM) in the runtime. We will look into detail on JavaScript later in the chapter.

Backend/Server Side

The server side is the part that the end user does not see or interact with directly. The frontend part of the web application connects with the backend through an Application Programming Interface (API). APIs can be understood as a contract of services between the frontend and backend, which allows them to communicate with each other through requests and responses. The server side receives the requests, processes them, executes business logic required by the application, and also takes care of connecting and interacting with the database for storage and retrieval of data.

It is common practice that databases are accessible only via the backend and not directly from the frontend, due to security reasons. The server side concentrates on efficiently executing the business logic and securing the data from the outside world. Some of the common languages and frameworks used for the backend are:

- JavaScript
  - Node.js
  - Express.js
- Python
  - Django
  - Flask
- Ruby
  - Ruby on Rails

JavaScript

JavaScript is the language of the web. It is an interpreted language released in 1995 by the networking company Netscape. Initially, JavaScript engines were used only in browsers. However, in recent times, it has developed to be a full-fledged programming language and is now the most popular programming language, according to GitHub. From the end users' point of view, every time a browser does something other than display static content, it uses JavaScript. Studies state that almost 97% of websites and applications use JavaScript.

Considering the scope of the book, we will be discussing the role of JavaScript in just the front end (Client side). JavaScript consists of a variety of inbuilt functions and APIs for manipulating the HTML DOM. First, let's look at what DOM is.

Document Object Model (DOM)

The DOM is the Object Model for HTML. DOM is a data representation of the HTML page in a tree format. When a browser loads an HTML document, it generates a DOM of the page, which makes it easier for JavaScript to understand

and manipulate the HTML elements on the page. Without DOM, JavaScript will not have an idea of the structure of the web page or its contents.

Key Features of DOM

Here are some of the key points that you should know about the DOM:

- **Tree Structure**: The DOM represents the HTML or XML document as a tree structure, where each element is a node in the tree. The topmost node is called the "**document**" node, which represents the entire document. Elements, attributes, and text nodes are represented as child nodes of their parent nodes.
- **Node Objects**: Each node in the DOM tree is represented by an object with properties and methods. For example, an HTML element node has properties like `tagName`, `className`, and methods like `appendChild()` to manipulate the node.
- **Cross-Browser Compatibility**: The DOM provides a standardized way to interact with web documents, ensuring compatibility across different browsers and platforms. While some browser-specific differences exist, the core concepts and methods of the DOM are consistent.

Consider the following simple HTML code:

```
<html>
    <head>
        <title>My Web Page</title>
        <link rel="stylesheet" href="/link-to-my-css-file.css">
    </head>
    <body>
        <h1 id="page-title">My First Web Page</h1>
        <div class="parent-div">
            <div class="childdiv-1">
                Child Div 1
            </div>
            <div class="childdiv-2">
            </div>
        </div>
    </body>
</html>
```

When the preceding HTML page is loaded on the screen, the browser generates the following DOM:

```
└HTML
 ├HEAD
 │├#text:
 │├TITLE
 ││└#text: My Web Page
 │├#text:
 │├LINK rel="stylesheet" href="/link-to-my-css-file.css"
 │└#text:
 ├#text:
 └BODY
  ├#text:
  ├H1 id="page-title"
  │└#text: My First Web Page
  ├#text:
  ├DIV class="test-content"
  │├#text:
  │├DIV class="subdiv-1"
  ││└#text:
  │├#text:
  │├DIV class="subdiv-2"
  ││└#text:
  │└#text:
  └#text:
```

Figure 1.2: *Example of a DOM*

In the preceding example, you can see how a DOM is mapped from the HTML code provided to the browser. This parsed structure helps JavaScript to select specific elements and manipulate them. There are a few ways to select DOM elements through JavaScript. Here are a couple of examples:

Selecting element by Id

The `id` attribute of an HTML element should be unique across the page. So, when selecting an element by id, JavaScript expects only one element to be returned. Here is how you select an element by its id:

```
document.getElementById("page-title")
```

This line will return the JavaScript version of the h1 element from the page as shown in *Figure 1.2*.

Selecting elements by Class Name

The `class` attribute can be used to specifically target elements that are assigned to the same class. There can be multiple elements with the same class name. So, this function returns a list of matching elements.

```
document.getElementsByClassName("parent-div")
```

The preceding code will return a list of all DOM elements that are associated with the class **parent-div**.

Selecting elements by Tag Name

Instead of the preceding two options, there would be a need to select all elements of a particular tag. This function can be used in such cases.

```
document.getElementsByTagName("div")
```

This line will return all the div elements present in the HTML page (the parent **div** and the child **divs**).

Manipulating the DOM

Now that we've seen different ways to select elements from the DOM, here are a couple of functions that we can use to manipulate the selected elements. Once you have access to an element through the DOM, you can modify its content, attributes, and style. For example, you can change the text inside an element, add or remove CSS classes, or modify attribute values. In order to update the text of a particular element, we can use the following line:

```
document.getElementById('page-title').textContent = 'Changed Web
Page Title'
```

This will update the text that we see in the title section to "Changed Web Page Title". Similarly, basic JavaScript can update the content, styling, position, and more, for any element on the page. For example, in order to change the color of the title text using JavaScript, the following line of code can be used:

```
document.getElementById("page-title").style.color = "green"
```

There are many other capabilities of basic JavaScript, which can make the page very interactive and make the user's experience pleasant.

Event Handling

Another aspect of JavaScript is to listen for certain events to occur and execute functions on the occurrence of those events. The DOM enables event handling, allowing you to respond to user interactions like clicks, key presses, or mouse movements. You can attach event listeners to elements and define functions to be executed when an event occurs.

For example, let's say when a user clicks a button, we need to show the current date as an alert to the user. The following JavaScript function will take care of it:

```
document.getElementById('page-title').onclick = function() {
    window.alert(new Date());
}
```

The preceding code asks JavaScript to listen for a **click** event on the element with the id **page-title** and executes the associated function when that event occurs. Similarly, there can be multiple functions associated with the same event for the same element. JavaScript executes each of those functions in the order in which they are registered. This allows validation of form elements, tracking user activity on the screen, and more, through JavaScript.

JQuery

When JavaScript started becoming popular, it was used in a variety of websites for different purposes, like validating user forms, updating the CSS styles of the elements dynamically, and most importantly, loading dynamic data from a backend server into the browser using Ajax requests.

"**John Resig**", a developer who was working on multiple JavaScript projects, felt that the syntax of plain JavaScript was too redundant and frustrating. So he released the jQuery library in 2006. **jQuery** offers easy-to-access APIs for DOM tree traversal and manipulation, creating animations, handling events, and making Ajax requests.

For example, selecting an element based on its **div** (the equivalent of the previous example):

```
$('#page-title')
```

We can see that the code is a lot simpler compared to normal JavaScript. The preceding code indicates that we are selecting the element with the id **page-title** (# denotes that we are accessing the element by its id). To access all elements that have a particular class, the jQuery syntax is:

```
$('.parent-div')
```

Here the **.**(dot) in front of the selector indicates that we are accessing the element based on the class. Similarly, updating the DOM elements is also easier in jQuery compared to JavaScript. The equivalent of updating the text of the **page-title** div is:

```
$('#page-title').text("Updated Title")
```

Event handling syntax for the same event we added earlier, in jQuery format, is as follows:

```
$('#page-title').click(function() {
  window.alert(new Date());
});
```

A huge advantage of jQuery is that it enables cross-browser support, handling the differences between JavaScript engines in different browsers. The development of jQuery was a very important step in simplifying the loading of data from different API/server sources. It caused a very important leap to the level where JavaScript is being used now, compared to when it was initially developed.

Frontend Applications

Traditional server-rendered pages require the browser to contact the server with every click. The server generated the HTML code and the browser then rendered the page. It started affecting the user experience as users had to wait for the entire page to reload before they could access the new content/link. Though JavaScript was able to pull data from APIs and update the data through Ajax requests without refreshing the page, it is very difficult to maintain the states of those variables, keep the UI updated based on the variables changing, and more. When there are multiple pages in a web application, even with the support of jQuery, the browser tab has to be refreshed every time the user clicks on a link to navigate to another page in the same application. Every single request had to reach the server, and the server had to process and render the HTML for each request. This impacts the server's performance and increases the waiting time for the user.

Over time, when web applications became large and complex, it became very difficult to maintain and manage all the code using plain JavaScript or jQuery. So, people wanted an efficient way to manage the complexity on the client side and reduce server dependency for rendering HTML, CSS, and JS, which are all browser-oriented. This led to the development of Web Application frameworks that develop "**Frontend Applications**". Frontend applications can be classified into three types: client-side rendering or single-page application, server-side rendering, and static site generation.

Client-Side Rendering /Single-Page Application

A client-side rendering (CSR) application or a Single-Page Application (SPA) is a web app implementation that loads the HTML, CSS, and JavaScript contents of the application for the first time when the user loads the page. Once the contents are loaded, any navigation within the application is automatically handled and the framework itself rerenders the contents of the browser without requiring a page reload. This means that once the app is loaded into the browser, the server has to be contacted only for fetching and updating data. This made the server-side applications to be reduced to being pure API services or data services.

In most of the applications, the same UI elements are reused across different pages. Consider any social media app or any email app that you have used. You can see that the layout of the site remains the same for all pages, be it the logo on top, the menu items, search bar, and others, remain the same, and only the content in the middle of the screen changes based on the links you navigate to. A single-page application takes advantage of this fact and loads the data from the server only based on what needs to be changed when the user navigates between links.

Advantages of SPA

Here are some of the reasons why SPAs became popular and why we need them:

- **User Experience:** The main advantage of a SPA is the pleasantness the user feels when using the site. They would not face the pain of waiting for the entire page to load whenever they click a link within the site. Lesser data being loaded from the server means the changes are seen by the user way faster than in a traditional application. Since only some parts of the HTML elements are replaced for every action, the browser rendering time is reduced drastically.
- **Reduced Server Queries:** Since the server-side applications need not render the HTML every time now, the overall traffic to the backend reduces even if the number of users remains the same. This means that the companies can save a lot of money while providing a better experience to their users.
- **Independent Development Streams:** SPAs decouple the client-side and server-side applications to work independently. The client-side application can concentrate on the user experience and aesthetics, while the server side can concentrate on optimally fetching and storing data. It helps reuse the same backend APIs for both a web application and a mobile application, which was not possible with the traditional architecture.

Disadvantages of SPA

Even though it provides a lot of advantages, there are some cons to the SPA architecture:

- **SEO:** Many search engines lack the ability to execute JavaScript when crawling across the web. This means that SPAs will not be indexed by the engines properly since all the data is not rendered from the backend. Google has optimized its crawlers to handle SPAs recently, but SEO remains a problem to be solved for SPA sites. A quick solution to this is to use server-side rendering in our SPAs.
- **JavaScript dependency:** SPA is heavily dependent on JavaScript. So if someone has disabled JavaScript in their browser, they will not be able to access the contents of the site at all.
- **Browser resources:** Though it is a relief that SPA reduces the load on servers, it instead transfers the execution load to the browsers, which is limited by the configuration of the client system. Loading large applications in older machines might cause a poor experience for the users.

Server-Side Rendering

With single-page applications, there were a couple of problems:

- The site did not get good SEO rankings because of the crawling issues.
- For large applications, the compiled CSS and JS files become very heavy. So initially, the user has to wait for the entire JS/CSS to load before they can see content on the screen.

The page load time is an important factor for SEO. In order to avoid such delays, "Server-Side Rendering" (SSR) came into existence. When a user visits a web page, SSR apps fetch the information required for the page, render the HTML and return the rendered HTML, instead of the basic plain HTML returned by the CSR apps. So, now the user need not wait for the JS to be loaded before seeing any content on the page. The content is rendered as HTML by the server and sent to the browser. So, when the JS files are loaded in the background, the user can still see the contents of the page, which were returned from the server. Once the page is loaded for the first time, the framework then takes control of the tab and takes care of further navigation or API calls. The only difference is the extra effort of rendering the page on the server before giving it to the browser.

This approach also solves the SEO issue, as crawlers will parse the full contents of the page returned from the server. Because of this, all the popular frontend frameworks have the option of setting up Server-Side Rendering.

Advantages of SSR

- **Fast Loading**: When the user initially visits a page, they see content almost immediately, as the loaded HTML itself contains all the contents, instead of having to wait for the JS files to load and then paint the content on the screen.
- **SEO**: SSR apps are great for SEO, as you can optimize it for SEO similar to optimizing a traditional application.

Disadvantages of SSR

- **Server Dependency:** On the first page load, the contents are rendered twice: once on the server, and once more on the browser. This requires an optimally configured server to handle the load, which will also incur monetary costs.
- **UI Compatibility:** SSR is not fully compatible with some UI libraries, which rely upon the *window* and *document* objects of the browser, since those are not available in node servers.
- **Caching:** Since every page returned from the servers is different, SSR app HTML files cannot be cached in CDN services. So, the user cannot enjoy the luxury of loading cached files from the CDN.

Static Site Generation

Static Site Generation (SSG) is a third option, which is best suited for sites displaying static content that does not change based on the user who is accessing the page. For example, a personal profile website, where you list your expertise, projects, and more, or a corporate company's website that describes the company, team members, contact details, and so forth. The content of these sites always remains the same. Hence, they are best suited for static rendering.

SSG renders the HTML pages on the server, but they are rendered and stored as individual files during the build time itself. So, when the user loads a page, they will get the pre-rendered HTML page directly on the screen. Whenever the content of the page changes, we have to rebuild the app and the rendered pages get updated.

Advantages of SSG

- **Speed:** The individual HTML files are generated and stored during the build time. Hence, the pages are cached and loaded from CDNs pretty fast. It accounts for a pretty good user experience.

- **No Server needed:** Unlike SSR apps, SSG apps do not need any servers and can be served from any content delivery network or static file storage service like Amazon S3, Google Cloud Storage, and so on.

Disadvantages of SSG

- **No support for dynamic content:** The scope of static-generated sites is very limited and when the app becomes a bit complex, requiring dynamic content, it goes out of hand for SSG.
- **Longer build time:** Since all the pages are rendered during the build, the time to generate a build increases proportionally to the number of pages and the size of the pages.

Popular Frontend Frameworks

Before looking into Ember, we will look into similar frameworks in the market and how they work, which will help you understand how Ember is different from the others. Comparing multiple frameworks will also give you an idea of different ways things can be handled in solving user problems.

React

React.js is the most widely used framework in recent times. It was initially released in 2013. It was built and, to date, maintained by Meta (Facebook) and a community of developers. React is known for its performance, which targets optimally rerendering only the specific part of the screen which needs change, using its Virtual DOM concept. It keeps a copy of the DOM in memory, known as virtual DOM. When there is something to be changed in the webpage, it creates a copy of the virtual DOM first and compares it with the existing virtual DOM. Now, only the elements that are different from the current virtual DOM are updated in the actual DOM, reducing the effort of repainting the screen. It is also endorsed for its development speed. It uses JSX, which allows writing HTML code directly into JavaScript functions. It is both an advantage and a disadvantage, considering the initial time taken for beginners to learn JSX. It uses the **Flux pattern**, which is a unidirectional data flow pattern that passes data/variables from parent to child components. Since JSX binds HTML and JS together, there is no Model/View pattern here, as everything is written in the same file.

However, react does not have a strict convention on the architecture of the application, so there is no uniformity in the structure of the app and hence it is difficult to maintain large apps. Popular apps like Atlassian, Airbnb, Facebook, Instagram, and more, have all been built using React. React is suitable for applications that require high user interaction. A simple state management system within React allows you to smoothly rerender pages, which involve a lot of interactive and dynamic elements.

Next.js

Next.js is a framework created by a company named Vercel. It helps to provide support for *server-side rendering* and *static site generation* for react-based applications. It is not a standalone framework, but only a framework written on top of React.js. It offers a huge boost in page load time, and SEO, along with better development speed due to its SSR and SSG capabilities. Websites like Loom, HBO Max, and Hulu have been built using Next.js. Next.js can be used when you want to enable SSR or SSG in your React application.

Angular

Angular is the second attempt at a successful framework by Google. They initially released AngularJS in 2010, which was one of the earliest SPA frameworks. They then rewrote and released Angular in 2016, which is built on top of Typescript. Typescript is a superset of JavaScript developed by Microsoft. It offers a type system that does type checks for variables and functions. JavaScript allows you to pass any data type to any variable/function. However, in Typescript, you have to specify the type of parameters passed to a function, and Typescript ensures that the code does not pass data of any other type. It reduces the risk of bugs caused by unexpected data-type behaviors of JavaScript. Angular follows the **Model-View-Controller** pattern similar to ember, which we will discuss later. Most of the Google websites like Google, Gmail, and other popular sites like PayPal, Forbes, and UpWork are built using Angular.

Vue.js

Vue.js is a lightweight framework developed by Evan You, who was a developer for Google. He mentioned that he wanted to take all the things he liked in Angular and create a lightweight framework from it. It has a lot of similarities to Angular and is easy to develop and deploy because of its lightweightedness. Popular websites like NBC Sports, BMW, and Adobe use Vue.js for their websites. Vue.js is your ideal choice when you want to build simple web applications that need to be built fast.

Backbone.js

Backbone.js is one of the frameworks offering a bit different approach. Unlike Angular/Ember, Backbone uses the **Model-view-viewmodel** pattern. It aims toward separating the development of business logic from the user interface by creating an intermediate "**ViewModel**". The **ViewModel** is the abstracted version of the View (UI components) which handles the communication between the view and the data model, using a binder. Sites like Trello, Bitbucket, and **FourSquare use** the backbone or one of its extended versions built by them. You can use **Backbone.js** in your application to add a structure to your JavaScript code with its MVVM pattern. It is lightweight and easily built and deployed.

Ember.js

Having seen the different popular frameworks available in the market, let's look into detail about Ember.js. Ember.js is an open-source JavaScript framework that helps build large-scale web applications. It was created by Yehuda Katz, a member of the core team in jQuery, Ruby on Rails, and SproutCore. It is available under the MIT License. Here is the logo of Ember.js:

Figure 1.3: *Ember.js Mascot*

This is called a "**Tomster**" and it is the alternative to using the Ember logo. It has been customized by different regions for mascots of their own, but this is the base mascot provided by Ember.js.

History

It was in 2007 that a company named **Sproutit** created a framework for their mailroom application and named it **SproutCore.** It was one of the earliest frameworks that introduced the MVC model, which was incorporated in Ember, and other frameworks like Angular too.

When they developed the second version of the same, **SproutCore2.0,** in May 2011, they decided that to cater to a larger audience with an easy-to-build web framework, they had to make a lot of changes to the existing SproutCore framework. So, they decided to create a new framework with SproutCore as the base and named it **Amber.js.** Immediately after announcing this change, they received feedback about the name conflict with an existing application - "Amber Smalltalk". Hence, after receiving feedback on the web, they decided to go with the name "**Ember.js**".

The original intention of SproutCore was to help build native-looking applications (desktop applications). But Ember is about building web applications.

Popularity

Ember.js is being used by top software development teams in the world to build large-scale web applications that serve millions of users at a time. To name a few, the following websites have been built using Ember: LinkedIn, Heroku, Cloudflare, Netlify, Intercom, and Apple apps.

At the time of writing this book, the framework has 22.5k stars and 4.3k forks on GitHub. The technology is being used by around 31.6k developers on GitHub. The repository has over 800 active contributors developing the application for a better experience. It has a weekly download rate of 175k and is the most preferred framework for building complex large-scale single-page applications.

Key Features

Here are some of the important features of Ember.js you should know before you start building applications with it.

Convention over Configuration

Ember follows the convention over the configuration pattern. It helps reduce the number of decisions the developer has to make, without reducing the flexibility. It means that Ember generates all the basic codes and connections using the simple inputs provided by the developer, and the developer has to write additional code in specific cases where the convention does not work. There are a couple of advantages to this:

- It gives a well-defined structure to the application so that even a beginner developer cannot stray too far away from the recommended architecture.
- With many AI assistants emerging in the market, it becomes easier for them to suggest/generate code based on patterns of this convention.

We will look into detailed use cases in the later chapters.

Component-Service Framework

Component-Service Framework is a strategy adopted by companies to build large-scale applications by breaking them down into smaller and reusable components. Components are one of the core features of Ember, which help:

- Reusing code in multiple parts of the application.
- Finding bugs is easier since the code blocks are small enough to zero down precisely on the issue.

Two-Way Data Binding

Data binding is a way to keep the data displayed in the UI and the data in the JavaScript in sync. This means that if there is an update in one of the variables of the component, it should reflect automatically in the UI, and similarly the other way around. Ember also offers a strong binding between variables, such that when one variable changes, the other dependent variable changes automatically.

Anatomy of an Ember.js App

In this section, we will look at the core concepts in Ember, what they stand for, and how they work in sync. It is better to know how Ember works before starting to build applications with it. An Ember application consists of the following core concepts:

Router

The router contains the direct mappings to the path entered by the user in the browser. It determines which part of the code Ember should execute, to return the relevant data for this particular URL. It contains a list of mappings that decide what Route Handler should be called based on the URL entered in the browser. A path is part of the URL entered after the domain. For example, If you enter the URL *https://facebook.com/feed*, *https://facebook.com* is the domain that decides what website/webpage should be loaded. The remaining part of the URL - */feed* is the path (or) route. The router decides which route handler to call based on the path. A router is an inbuilt feature in Ember.js (It has to be included via a third-party library in React).

Route Handler

A route handler is called by the router. The function of the route handler is as follows:

- Load the template associated with this route
- Define the model for this route, which will be used by the template or controller

Route handler can load the model for the route dynamically based on the parameters passed in the URL. For example, When viewing someone's profile on Facebook, the URL looks like *https://facebook.com/<fb_username>*. The *fb_username* part is dynamic, and it can contain the username of any user on the platform. The router takes care of parsing this dynamic element and sending the information to the route handler. The route handler then loads the model data using this dynamic parameter.

Models

Models represent the persisted data. The data may either come from a local storage, or a backend server, or maybe even hardcoded in the code. A model is a representation of any data that can survive page reloads. Ember has a data library called "**EmberData**", which contains the model layer for communicating with backend/server environments. For example, On Facebook, when you load a profile, the data about the user, namely name, email, and phone number are all represented via a **User** model.

Templates

Templates manage the HTML part of the application. Templates define the structure of the page and the elements to be displayed on the page. In previous versions, Ember used an inbuilt engine of "**Handlebars.js**", a library that supports adding dynamic content into HTML by using the curly braces `{{ }}` syntax. Now Ember supports templates by default, and we can use the same handlebars syntax to introduce all the dynamicity we want to the HTML files. Templates call for different components to promote the reusability of code. By default, the curly braces syntax handles output encoding, which prevents malicious JavaScript code from being inserted/executed accidentally. This has to be handled specifically when using plain JavaScript or jQuery, but Ember has this security feature enabled by default.

Components

Components are the broken-down reusable parts of the application. A template can call multiple components, each having its own functionality. You can consider components to be an Ember way of writing your own custom HTML tags. Adding just the component name in the template will display the HTML of the component. Components can either contain just HTML code or can contain both HTML and JavaScript code, making them modular and self-contained to be easily called from anywhere. For example. If you want a **UserAvatar** component that displays the name, email, and profile picture of the user, you can create that as a component and it can be used anywhere with a single line to embed the details exactly in the same style.

Controllers

Controllers are objects that act as mediators between the route handler and the templates/components. The model data fetched by the route handler is passed to the templates via the controller. By default, controllers are not generated when creating a route and are implicitly created by the route handler when the route is instantiated. We can generate the controller only when we want to customize the model data being passed from the router or have to maintain page-level attributes/functions that are passed to multiple components via the templates. To put it in other words, controllers are the state maintenance area for a route, which keeps track of the model and other variables, and in some cases, even functions. A controller is a singleton instance. This means that only one instance of the controller is generated when the application is loaded, and every time a route is called again, the same instance of the controller is used instead of creating a fresh instance.

Services

Services are independent utilities or objects that are alive for the entire duration of an Ember application, and they can be shared or used across all the components in the application. A service can be used in any controller or component by *injecting* the service. Services are used to keep track of global data for the application or for doing asynchronous tasks. For example, an **authentication** service can keep track of whether the user is logged in and the details of the logged-in user. A **socket** service can maintain web socket connections with the server. This way, the same piece of code can do all the work, and the data is unanimously shared across the application.

The preceding are the different sections of Ember that work together to run the application.

Overall Architecture

Figure 1.4 shows the architecture of an Ember application:

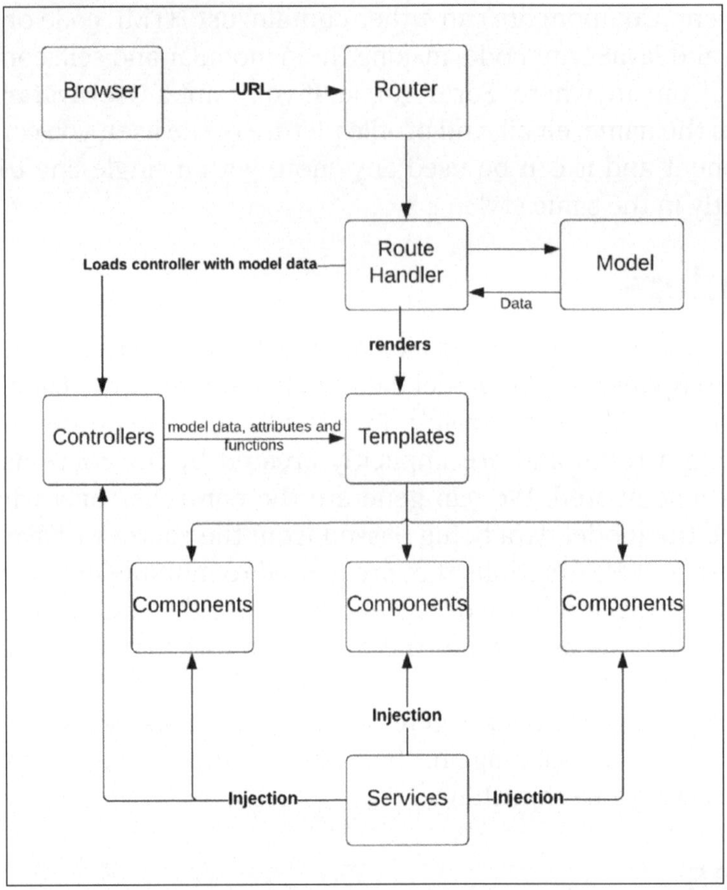

Figure 1.4: *Ember Architecture*

Based on the preceding figure, here is what happens when you enter a URL in the browser and it loads the Ember application:

- Router decides which route handler to call based on the URL.
- Route Handler fetches the model data, sets up the controller, and renders the template.
- Controller is used to pass the model data and other attributes or functions to the template.

- Template renders the HTML content of the page, uses variables from controllers, and calls multiple components.
- Components are self-contained modularized code that has HTML and the core JavaScript logic related to that HTML.
- Services can be injected into both components and controllers on demand.

Tests

Tests are a very important part of an application, especially when the app grows large. Tests are a definite requirement to ensure that the functionalities are working as expected and are not affected by any recent changes made to the code. Tests are an integral part of Ember, which helps make your application robust and secure. We will cover in detail about writing tests later in the book.

Addons

Even though Ember contains so many inbuilt functionalities, there can be cases where we need additional functionality or features to be integrated into the app. Ember has a large collection of addons that can be easily integrated into your application. Functionalities like CSS scripting using SASS/SCSS are perfect examples of Ember addons.

Conclusion

In this chapter, we are now familiar with the concepts of HTML, CSS, and JavaScript, and what each of them is used for. We discussed why there was a need for front-end applications and the types of client-side applications. You are familiar with different frontend frameworks in the market and how they are different from each other. Most importantly, you understand how Ember.js works and the individual concepts of the framework that combine to provide an amazing experience to the user. The knowledge attained so far will help you make efficient decisions when you build applications later in the book. In the next chapter, we will discuss the "**Command Line Interface**"(CLI) provided by Ember to set up, run, and build Ember applications. We will also start our hands-on development process in the next chapter by creating an Ember application and generating different components using the CLI.

Points to Remember

- HTML defines the layout of the page.
- CSS is used for styling the page.
- JavaScript makes the page dynamic by manipulating DOM elements.
- Frontend frameworks were introduced to improve user experience and to reduce the server load by preventing page reload when moving to different pages.
- Ember follows the **convention over configuration** pattern that reduces the number of decisions the developer has to make without affecting the flexibility of the application.
- Ember has a router, route handler, controllers, components, models, templates, and services that work together.
- Ember has an integrated test framework that makes the application robust and secure.

Multiple Choice Questions

1. Which of the following is used to define the layout of a web page?
    a. HTML
    b. CSS
    c. JavaScript
    d. Python
2. Which of the following ways can we select a DOM element using JavaScript?
    a. By tag name
    b. By element id
    c. By element class
    d. All of the above
3. What is the type of request that fetches data from the API without refreshing the page?
    a. Poll request
    b. MQTT request

   c. AJAX request
   d. Socket request
4. What pattern does Ember follow?
   a. Flux pattern
   b. MVC Pattern
   c. MVP Pattern
   d. MVVM Pattern
5. Ember is preferred for building large-scale applications.
   a. No
   b. Yes

Answers

1. a
2. d
3. c
4. b
5. b

Questions

1. What are the various types of Frontend applications? How do they differ?
2. What is two-way data binding and how does it work?
3. How are components and controllers different?
4. How is dynamic data introduced into templates?
5. How are dynamic parameters handled by the router?

Key Terms

- **Browser:** Tool used to view websites and applications.
- **Server:** Handles the requests from the browser and takes care of storage, fetching of data, and the business logic.
- **Frontend Frameworks:** Application frameworks that execute on the browser to provide a pleasant experience to the user.
- **Single-Page Applications:** Frontend applications that do not reload the page every time a new link is clicked.
- **Convention over Configuration:** Reduces the effort of the user by creating boilerplate code based on user input, and allows configuring further only when needed.

CHAPTER 2
Ember CLI and Local Setup

Introduction

In this chapter, we will look at the developer side of things on the "**Command Line Interface**" (CLI) features provided by Ember. We will understand the installation process, the different commands it offers, the folder structure of an Ember application, and other different concepts of the CLI. By doing this, the developer will have a full idea of interacting with an Ember application and make complete use of the interface to efficiently build the application.

We will look at installing addons for the application to support additional features we want in the application. We will also look at integrating CSS extensions and managing styles and assets for the application.

Structure

In this chapter, we will discuss the following topics:

- Ember CLI
- Ember Folder Structure
- Assets and Styling

Ember CLI

Ember CLI is the official way to create, manage, test, and build an Ember application or an Ember addon. The Ember CLI takes care of creating the folder structure, adding the internal connections to make the app functional, and running the server required to render the application on the browser. It contains a dependency package manager, local server, and test runner all rolled into a single package. You can start all this with just a single command and zero configuration.

Installation

Installing Ember CLI is simple. It requires you to install the node package in your system. Node.js is the base for running any kind of JavaScript engine or server on your system, be it for backend applications or frontend applications. It allows you to run/execute JavaScript outside the browser. You can install the node by using the following commands:

- **Windows:** For Windows, you can download the `.msi` of the node package from here: https://nodejs.org/en/download
- **Linux:** For Linux systems, you can use the package manager of your specific Operating System like **`apt`** or **`yum`**. The command is:

```
sudo apt install nodejs
```

- **Mac:** You can download the **`.dmg`** file of nodejs from here: https://nodejs.org/en/download or if you are using brew, you can install it with the following command:

```
brew install node
```

This is one of the easiest ways to install node.js. Depending upon the operating system, node.js can be installed in different ways, such as compiling from the source or downloading the package file for the OS.

To ensure that nodejs is installed properly, you can try the following command: **`node -v`**

If the node is installed and working, you will get the following output:

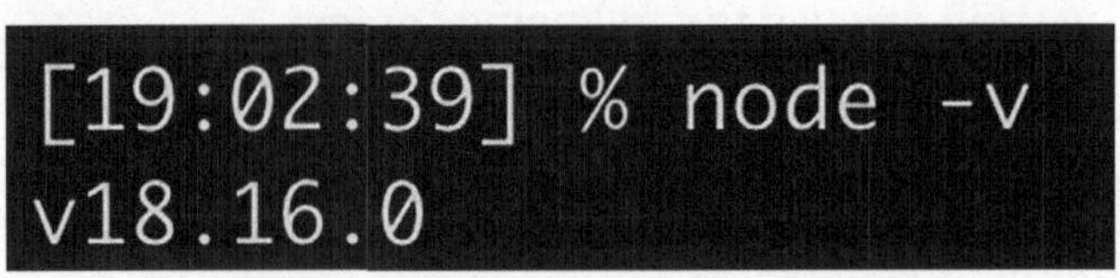

Figure 2.1: *Node.js Version command*

When you run the **`node -v`** command, it returns the version of node.js installed in your system. If it returns the version, it means the node library is installed properly and ready to use. When running multiple projects at the same time, there can be cases where each project requires a different version of node.js. Node.js supports cases like that and we can use the **Node Version Manager**

(NVM) to maintain multiple versions of node.js in your system and switch between versions based on the project you want to work on.

Tip: *If you get an error stating* **`node: command not found,`** *it means either that the library is not installed or the terminal is not able to locate the installed library. This usually happens in Windows when it is installed on a different path. You can overcome that by adding the node path to your environment variables by going to the* **`Start`** *menu -> Search for* **`Environment Variables`** *-> Go to* **`PATH`** *-> click on* **`EDIT`** *-> Add the node installation path.*

Now that the node is installed and ready to use, we will next install Ember CLI using the Node Package Manager(`npm`). Ember CLI can be installed using the following command:

```
npm install -g ember-cli
```

The **`-g`** in the preceding commands denotes *global*. Usually, npm creates a folder called **`node_modules`** inside the current folder (from where the **`npm install`** command is run) to download and store the npm libraries/dependencies. Those libraries are accessible only by projects within the folder containing the **`node_modules`**. However, the **`-g`** flag ensures the library is installed globally and is accessible from anywhere. The **`ember-cli`** installation command will download and install the Ember source code and some of the addons required by the Ember CLI for running its commands.

To ensure that Ember CLI is installed, you can use the following command: **`ember version`**

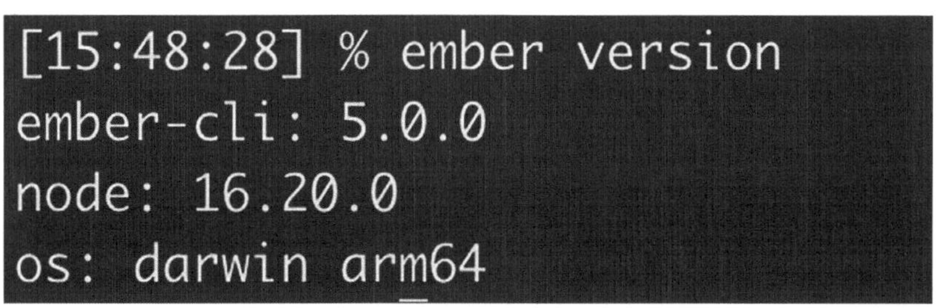

Figure 2.2: *Ember version command*

`ember version` returns the version of the CLI installed, the node version installed the system, OS details, and more.

Similar to npm, there is another package manager named YARN, which we will use inside the Ember project to manage the dependencies for the project. **Yet Another Resource Negotiator** (YARN) was built by Facebook to overcome some performance and security issues in npm. Whenever you install a package in npm, it always reaches a repository called the npm registry to fetch the source files before installation. However, yarn creates a local cache of the libraries and fetches the libraries from the cache when you try to install them. This makes the installation step way faster since there is so much time saved when fetching packages. There have been a lot of security updates done by npm after the release of yarn. Yarn has an edge, though, with its `yarn licenses list` command, which shows the licenses provided by all the packages that have been installed, which is useful to ensure we haven't violated any copyrights by installing a package that does not follow an open-source license. Yarn can be installed manually too with the following command:

```
npm install -g yarn
```

Though these are two different package managers maintained by different communities, they follow the same procedure for installing and maintaining packages. They both read a file named `package.json` in your project for getting the list of dependencies in the project, download and place the dependent libraries inside a folder named `node_modules` folder in the project. The `package.json` can contain relative versions of the packages. For example, a package can have version `<2.0.0` , which means this project requires any version of the package less than `2.0.0`. Using this approach, depending upon when the package is installed, the versions might vary as the latest version following the condition `<2.0.0` will be installed. This can cause conflicts, as different versions can be installed in different machines/environments, causing conflicts in library usage. In order to avoid this issue, both the package managers maintain a lock file, which denotes the exact version of the package installed in this project. If this lock file is present, the version specified in the lockfile will be installed when it meets the version conditions mentioned in the `package.json` file. If there is a conflict in the versions mentioned, the version specified in the `package.json` file would be given preference to provide uniformity on the packages installed across different machines. There is just a small difference between the two package managers: npm names this file as `package-lock.json`, whereas yarn names this file as `yarn.lock`. However, the flow and the purpose are the same for both.

Functionalities

Let's look at what the multi-functional CLI can do. If you run the command `ember --help`, you will get a list of all available options in the cli. Let's look at them one by one.

Ember new

`ember new` is used to create a new Ember application. This command can be executed in two different ways. The first way is to call **`ember new`** without any parameters to it. In this method, it will ask for different parameters asking you if you are going to create a new app or addon, a name for your project, the default language used in the contents of your app, whether you would like to use npm or yarn as the package manager, the CI/CD pipeline you would like to use, and more. Here's what the output looks like once you've created the app using **`ember new`**:

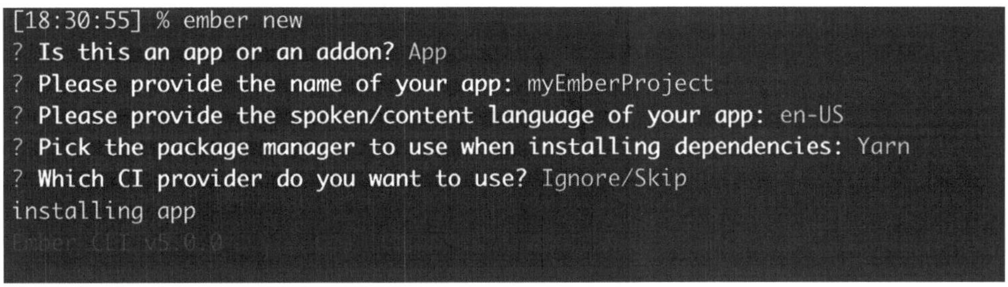

***Figure 2.3**: Ember new command*

You can see from the preceding image that we are creating an Ember app with the name **`myEmberProject`**, with the default language as English and Yarn as the package manager. We're skipping the CI provider for now. As the output of this command, you can see a folder named **`myEmberProject`** in the same directory, which is our new Ember application. We can look into the files present in this folder in detail after looking at all the functionalities of the CLI.

An easier method to create an app is to provide the app name when calling the ember new command, as follows:

```
ember new myEmberProject
```

By doing this, we can skip the questions previously asked by Ember and create the application with all the default settings. The command supports a lot of configurable parameters , such as **`--skip-npm`** and **`--skip-git`**, which will skip the steps of initializing the npm packages or creating a git repository inside the app folder. The other parameters are all self-explanatory.

Ember addon

This command is used to generate a new addon. An addon is a plugin that can be imported into other Ember applications. An addon is a reusable component that can be imported by any project to reduce the effort of coding the same component again. You can call the addon command with the name of the addon to create the folder structure.

```
ember addon myNewAddon
```

The addon command creates a folder structure similar to an Ember project. We will look into the folder structure of an addon later as well. The addon command also supports the same parameters as the new command, which allows you to choose between npm or yarn, setting the CI provider, and so on.

To try out all other commands, we will need to go inside the project folder. You can do that using the **`cd`** command:

```
cd myEmberProject
```

Ember init

The **`init`** command is used to reinitialize an existing Ember app. It supports all the parameters supported by the **`ember new`** command, and it prompts and resets the code to the initial state when the app was created. Ember new command creates the project folder and internally runs the Ember **`init`** command inside the project folder.

Ember install

`Ember install` is the Ember CLI equivalent of **`npm install`**. This is used to add additional addons to the project. It internally uses the ember or yarn to add the package to the application. One additional step that the install does is it runs customized blueprints configured in the installed package.

An **Ember blueprint** is a customized piece of code that will be executed when a package is installed. It can be about generating a required set of code files inside the client app or installing additional packages required by this addon. They are used to generate and share a common pattern for a particular package to be used across the community.

Ember generate

We spoke about Ember blueprints and how they are used by packages. Ember itself has its own set of blueprints that generate different types of files in Ember. The following are the blueprints available by default:

- Route
- Component

- Controller
- Model

For example, running the following command will create a new route in the app with the given name:

```
ember generate route home
```

Once run, you can see the output as follows:

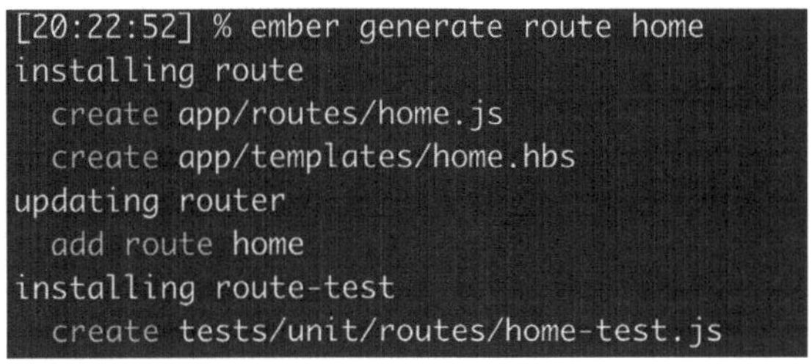

Figure 2.4: *Ember generate command*

What did we do with the preceding command? We generated a new route with the name **`home`.** We used the Ember blueprint named ***`route`*** to do that (The blueprint name is usually the name we specify after the word generate). This command did the following:

- Created files for your route and template
- Updated the router to add a mapping for this route
- Adding a test file for this route

You can open any of the newly created files and you can see that they are not empty. Ember has placed some predefined code in the file. That's the advantage of an Ember blueprint. It creates a set of files, adds the basic boilerplate code required for each of the files to function, and also updates certain files necessary to include the newly generated route. We will be looking into what each of the blueprints does in detail in the corresponding chapters related to the functionality of the blueprint.

Ember destroy

If you want to destroy all the hard work done by an Ember blueprint using the generate command, destroy is the go-to person for you. If you have generated any element by mistake or want to undo the generated route, you use the destroy command. Let's destroy the home route we created now using the following command:

```
ember destroy route home
```

The output of the command will look like this:

```
[20:35:51] % ember destroy route home
uninstalling route
  remove app/routes/home.js
  remove app/templates/home.hbs
updating router
  remove route home
uninstalling route-test
  remove tests/unit/routes/home-test.js
```

Figure 2.5: *Ember destroy command*

In *Figure* 2.5, you can see that destroy does the exact opposite of what generate does.

Ember serve

Ember serve runs the code and makes it accessible from a browser through a port. By default, Ember uses **`port 4200`** to run the server. We can configure that using the **`--port`** Parameter. This is a self-sufficient server that allows for configuring many things like the listening host, and serving the app through an SSL (https connection). The Ember serve command will throw an error if there is some syntax error or import issue in the code. If it runs successfully, the output will look like this:

```
[20:38:39] % ember serve

Build successful (1841ms) – Serving on http://localhost:4200/

Slowest Nodes (totalTime >= 5%)                               | Total (avg)
--------------------------------------------------------------+-------------
ember-auto-import-webpack (1)                                 | 920ms
Babel: @ember/test-helpers (1)                                | 202ms
Package /assets/vendor.js (1)                                 | 159ms
Rollup (2)                                                    | 97ms (48 ms)
```

Figure 2.6: *Ember serve command*

You can see from the output that Ember is serving the app in port 4200. It also shows some of the slowest actions in the process of building the app. This will be useful when we are looking to optimize the build performance of the application. Next, let's go to the browser to see what we have in the app so far. You can go to the browser and hit the URL http://localhost:4200 to access the application. The output will look something like this:

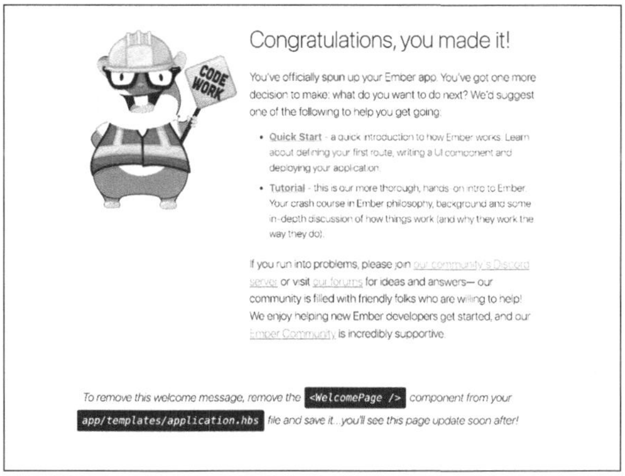

Figure 2.7: *Ember default page*

Any changes made to the code will be reflected on the web page automatically. *Figure* 2.7 shows the output based on the default blueprint code generated by Ember.

watchman

When you run **`ember serve`**, it runs a server locally. The server keeps running indefinitely unless we decide to close it. Whenever you make any changes to the code, the browser is automatically notified of it and the page is reloaded to serve the new code. Ember CLI (or watchman) keeps listening for changes done to files inside the Ember project, and if there is a change detected, it sends a web socket notification for the browser to reload the page, thus updating the latest code in the browser. Through this, we can see our changes immediately on the browser, or get to know as and when some change breaks the code.

In certain versions of Mac and Linux, there are some inconsistencies with the auto-restart mechanism. So, for the smooth working of the autoreload, we recommend Mac and Linux users install the **`watchman`** watcher that resolves these inconsistencies. You can install it using **`brew install watchman`** on a Mac, or **`sudo apt install watchman`** on a Linux machine.

If watchman is not installed, Ember might show a warning message that watchman is not installed. You can ignore the message, but it's better to use watchman as it is smoother to use compared to the default file watcher.

Remote access

We saw how we can access the ember app from your browser. Ember also offers the capability to access the application from another person's browser (provided that the port is accessible from the other machine). You can pass the **--host** with a value of **0.0.0.0**, and Ember will allow accessing the Ember application from a different machine.

Ember test

The test runner in Ember can be used to run all the configured tests in the app or to run only a specific set of tests. It allows you to ensure that the app is secure and works as expected right from day one. Running your test suite is a vital step before deployment to ensure that everything works as expected so that it doesn't break anything to disrupt user experience. The output of **ember test** would look something like this:

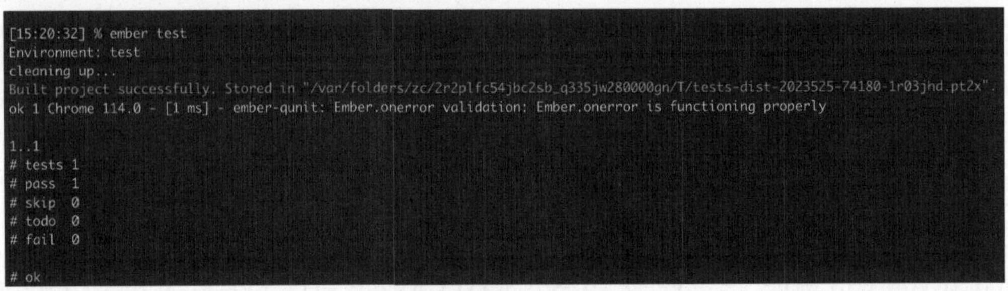

Figure 2.8: *Ember test*

The test command summarizes the test results by providing counts of the number of tests run, number passed, failed, etc. By default, the command runs the test suite only once and publishes the results. Here are a couple of important parameters this command supports:

- **--server** runs the test server. A test server is similar to a development server, but it runs the test suite explicitly whenever there is a change made to the code. It will automatically open a browser window and show the test results.
- **- -module** : When running tests during development, you might not want to run all the tests for each and every change. In that case, you can use the module parameter to specify the specific file or test to run in order to save time.

Ember build

After developing through the serve command, and testing everything by running the test command, we will now build the application. Building the application means compiling the different files present in the application into one JS file, creating one file from all the CSS files present in the application, and combining all the dependencies into a single JS file. This is required to deploy the app in such a way that the browser just loads the static files and executes them rather than pulling each file from the source code.

Building is the process of combining and minifying the different files in the application into a single file, which will be pulled and used to execute the Ember code in the browser. Running the build command is very simple: **`ember build`**. The output will look like this:

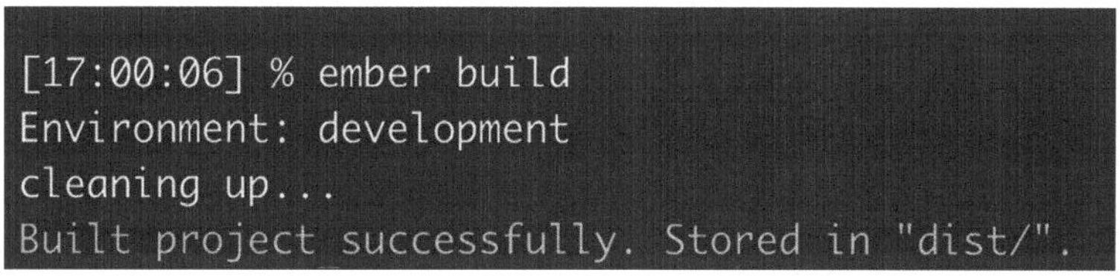

Figure 2.9: *Ember build*

We can see that the build files have been stored in the dist folder. You can configure the output path by passing the **`--output-path`** parameter with the path where you want to store the build files.

Ember asset-sizes

Once we've built the application, one thing to ensure is that the generated output files are compact. Since these files will be loaded from a source every time the user loads the page, it is necessary these files are easily loaded to reduce the waiting time for the user.

For this purpose, we can use the asset-sizes command to see the size of the output files. The output of this command will look like this:

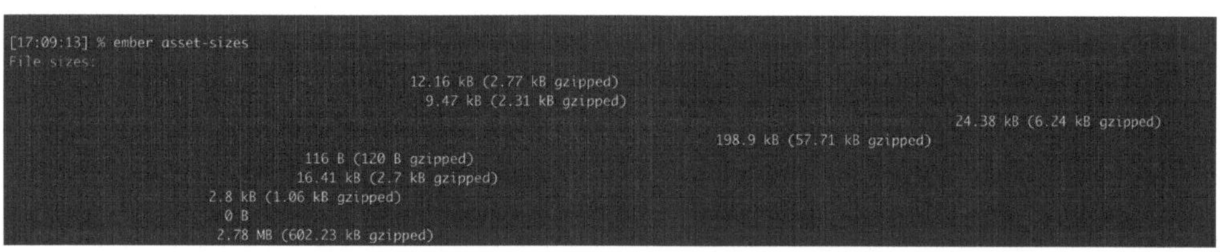

Figure 2.10: *Ember asset-sizes*

You can see the size of each of the CSS/JS files present in the output folder. You can also see that Ember provides the sizes of the files when they are gzipped. Gzipping is a way to compress the CSS/JS files when storing them in the CDN/file storage. This reduces the amount of data that is transferred between the CDN and the browser.

For example, if you look at the **vendor.js** file from *Figure* 2.10, the default size is 2.7M, which when gzipped comes to 602kb. It is reduced to more than 75% of its original size, which means the file is transferred way faster to the browser. The browser then uncompresses the file before executing it. The uncompression time is usually much less compared to the data transfer time. This does not depend upon the internet connection speed of the client. Hence, it is preferred to gzip the files before deployment.

Since the developer/maintainer of the project cannot always keep track of the growing asset sizes, there are addons that can be injected into your CI/CD pipeline that will restrict your output size to a specific amount, and you don't have to manually check and keep track of the sizes anymore.

Short Commands

A cool feature of Ember CLI is that it provides a shorter alternative to popularly used commands. Here are the following commands and their corresponding shorthand mappings:

`ember build`	`ember b`
`ember install`	`ember i`
`ember serve`	`ember s`
`ember test`	`ember t`
`ember version`	`ember v`
`ember generate`	`ember g`
`ember destroy`	`ember d`

***Table 2.1**: Ember CLI commands*

Ember Folder Structure

Now that we've looked at all the functionalities offered by the CLI, let's explore what **ember new** has done. If you look at the folder structure of the newly created **myEmberProject**, it will look like this:

```
.
├── README.md
├── app
│   ├── app.js
│   ├── components
│   ├── controllers
│   ├── helpers
│   ├── index.html
│   ├── models
│   ├── router.js
│   ├── routes
│   ├── styles
│   │   └── app.css
│   └── templates
│       └── application.hbs
├── config
│   ├── ember-cli-update.json
│   ├── environment.js
│   ├── optional-features.json
│   └── targets.js
├── ember-cli-build.js
├── package.json
├── public
│   └── robots.txt
├── testem.js
├── tests
│   ├── helpers
│   │   └── index.js
│   ├── index.html
│   ├── integration
│   ├── test-helper.js
│   └── unit
└── yarn.lock
```

***Figure 2.11**: Folder structure*

Let's look at what each of the folders/files does.

README.md

README file will be a part of any open-source repository you see. This file will contain all the documentation required for the repository. It is the first file anyone sees when they visit the home page of the repository. Usually, this file contains the setup and installation instructions for the repo, its licensing details, and more. You can open the **README** file in the current project to understand how you can set up and run this project locally.

app

The **app** folder is where you write all your application's code. As you can see from *Figure* 2.11, it contains a folder each for routes, controllers, components, templates, models, and also helpers. It contains the base **index.html** that is loaded in the browser during the build time. It also contains a **router.js** file, which has the details of all route mappings in the application.

config

The **config** folder contains two important files - **environment.js** and **targets.js**. **environment.js** is where you specify different configuration settings to be applied to different environments, namely development, staging and production. You will want to enable specific features only in production, and enable some debugging features only in staging. These configurations go inside the environment file.

The **targets.js** file is where you specify the list of browsers supported by this application. Ember backs this file with popular website usage tracking sites like **Browserlist** and **CanIUse**. Using this, you can target browsers based on their usage statistics. For example, if you want to support only browsers that have more than 10% market share in the US, you can specify **> 10% in the US** inside the *browsers* section of the targets file, and the targets will be applied accordingly. This setting will help Babel to support the latest JavaScript format like ES6.

ember-cli-build.js

This file defines how Ember CLI should build this application. It uses a compilation library named **broccoli.js** to build the app. We can specify options like how to handle CSS files, enable preprocessors like LESS, SASS or SCSS in the application, and more.

Source maps

When Ember generates a build, it combines all the source JS files into one single file. Source maps are mapping files with **.map** extensions, which contain information on how the generated build maps with the source code. This feature is enabled by default in Ember in the development and staging environments, but disabled in the production environment by default. You can enable it in the production build, too, by adding the following line in the **ember-cli-build.js** file to the constructor of the **EmberApp** call present inside the file:

```
{
    ...
    sourcemaps: {
```

```
            enabled: true
        }
    }
```

By doing this, you will be able to view all the source files from the **Network** tab of the browser, which we will look at in detail in a later chapter corresponding to debugging.

package.json

package.json is a generic file you can see in any JS project. It contains details like the project name, description, the licensing of the project, and more. The list of dependencies required by this project can also be found in this file. Also, you can see a scripts section in this file. It defines the list of subcommands that can be run in this project and the subcommands that will be called for the respective commands.

public

The **public** folder contains all asset files that do not need processing. When building the project, Ember copies all the files from the public folder into the build path. This folder is normally used to store image files or font files. By default, you can see a file named **robots.txt** in the folder. **robots.txt** is used by search engines and crawlers to identify which URLs are supposed to be crawled and indexed, which ones should be ignored, and so on.

testem.js

Testem is the test runner that Ember uses internally to run your tests across browsers. This file contains the configurations required for **testem.js**. You can configure the port you want to run the tests on, a list of tests you want to skip, and so on.

tests

The **tests** folder is where you write all your tests for the project. You can write unit tests, and integration tests specifically, and structure them inside this folder.

yarn.lock

yarn.lock is generated by Yarn. If we are using npm, we will have a similar file called **package-lock.json**. A "**lock file**" is typically used by package managers to keep track of all the packages that have been installed. It stores the packages, and the versions installed, locking them into the project. This will ensure that the same version of dependencies will be installed across different machines this project is installed in. It allows maintaining consistency of the packages, to avoid conflicts arising due to version changes in different machines.

node_modules

`node_modules` is where all the dependencies are pulled and stored. This nomenclature is also common across JS projects. This is where JavaScript looks for functions and variables in dependent libraries when running the project.

.ember-cli

This file is used to specify parameters that are dynamically passed when running Ember CLI. For example, instead of passing the port dynamically by calling the `ember serve` command, you can add it to this file, and it will be automatically applied whenever you run the server.

Assets and Styling

We looked at how the public folder is used for storing files that do not need processing, like images or fonts. For CSS, it is by default combined into a single file from all the source CSS files. Combining them into a single file helps the loading time, as the browser needs to load only one file before it applies the styles on the page. However, when the project size grows, the size of the CSS file can also become large and might cause the combined CSS file to be too large for the browser to load. In order to reduce the size of the output CSS file, we follow a process called minification.

CSS minification is the process of removing extra spaces, new lines, comments, and so on, from the output file so that the file size is reduced to a good extent. It also makes the CSS file less readable. So, we usually maintain the full version/ the beautified version for the development process and minify the CSS during the build time. This ensures that the CSS file the browser loads will be smaller. CSS minification is disabled by default in Ember and can be enabled by adding the following line to the **EmberApp constructor** in the `ember-cli-build.js.`

```
let app = new EmberApp(defaults, {
  hinting: false,
  fingerprint: {
```

```
      enabled: true,
      extensions: ['js', 'css']
    },
    minifyCss: {
      enabled: true
    }
  });
```

Once the preceding option is added, Ember will minify your CSS files and generate **a .min.css** instead of just a **.css** file.

CSS Preprocessors

When writing CSS for your project, you might have to write a lot of repetitive code. For example, you would want the padding to be of a certain amount for different objects, like buttons and cards. You would want a couple of colors being used in multiple places in the project. Using plain CSS means you will have to hardcode the values in all the places, leading to a lot of redundancy.

Now, let's say the requirement changes and you have to change the colors in the project to a different shade. This means you will have to go through all the places you've defined the colors before and redo it. Or consider that the client wants you to create a light theme and dark theme where the colors vary depending on the end user's selection. In this case, managing the colors using JavaScript will be a hassle, as you will have a lot of JavaScript overhead to keep the colors updated.

CSS Preprocessors are your solution for these cases. Preprocessors are scripting languages that allow you to extend the capabilities of CSS by adding dynamicity to it. They enable you to insert variables and manage the nesting of elements in the CSS files. You can also use conditionals like if/else, loops, and more, in your CSS code via preprocessors. When using preprocessors, you will have to go through a build process, which will compile the source CSS files and generate a normal CSS file as output, which will be readable by the browser. We will be using SCSS as a preprocessor in our project.

SCSS/SASS

Sassy CSS (SCSS) is a superset of the default CSS syntax, which allows additional configuration. This means all existing CSS code is valid SCSS code. But not all SCSS code is valid CSS code. It follows the same curly braces syntax of CSS to define blocks. **Syntactically Awesome Style Sheets** (SASS) is a more strict version of SASS. It does not use curly braces syntax to identify blocks. It uses indentation to define the blocks (similar to Python syntax). SCSS is the most widely used of the two syntaxes, due to its compatibility with plain CSS code.

You can install SASS/SCSS as an addon in your Ember project by doing: **`ember install ember-cli-sass.`** Once the addon is installed, you can specify the following lines in the EmberApp constructor of the **`ember-cli-build.js`** file:

```
sassOptions: {
      extension: 'scss'
}
```

Now that we've installed it, let's see how SCSS works with Ember. In your **`app/styles`** folder, you can see a file called **`app.css`**. Since we are going to use SCSS instead of CSS, we can rename the file to **`app.scss`**. Now you can write any valid SCSS syntax and Ember will automatically build the **`.scss`** files and create a **`my-ember-project.css`** in the dist/assets folder.

Let's learn a bit of SCSS syntax. On the home page, which you see at https://localhost:4200, let's say we want two changes: The color of the title text should be green and the description text to be bold. Now, the normal CSS syntax would be:

```
  #ember-welcome-page-id-selector h1 {
  color: green;
}
#ember-welcome-page-id-selector p {
  font-weight: bold;
}
```

In SCSS, the same code can be written this way:

```
/* Variables */
$description-font-weight: bold;
$title-color: green;

/* CSS Blocks */
#ember-welcome-page-id-selector {
  h1 {
    color: $title-color;
```

```
    }
    p {
      font-weight: $description-font-weight;
    }
  }
```

There are two main differences between the two syntaxes:

- You have defined a **`title-color`** variable that can be used across the code. Changing the variable in one place will reflect everywhere in the project where this color is used.
- The code blocks are more readable. The nested braces indicate exactly which selector the styling will apply to, and reduce the redundancy of specifying the base selector (**`#ember-welcome-page-id-selector`**) multiple times.

After adding the preceding lines to app.scss, you can see the changes reflected on your screen. Next, you can open the **`dist/assets/my-ember-project.css`** file and see that Ember has generated the plain CSS syntax for you from SCSS, and the code looks similar to the plain CSS example mentioned previously. This is the power of CSS preprocessors.

Conclusion

In this chapter, we learned about Ember CLI, its functionalities, how to create a new application with the CLI, and generate different parts of the Ember project from the predefined blueprints. We also saw the different commands in the CLI for running tests, installing addons, running the local server, building, and finding out the output sizes of the build files. We learned about the folder structure of an Ember project, different files generated and their uses. We also integrated SCSS into our project for CSS preprocessing. In the next chapter, we will look at Ember routes in detail.

Points to Remember

- Ember CLI is the one-stop shop for all commands for your Ember project.
- You can use the ember serve command to run a live server.
- The Ember live server automatically listens to code changes and updates the browser.
- Ember has a set of predefined blueprints, which allow you to generate code seamlessly.

- Ember has an inbuilt test runner that can be activated using the ember test command.
- Even though Ember builds the code into a single JS file, you can still access the individual source files in the browser using the source map feature.
- Ember has a list of optional features that can be activated whenever required.
- Ember has a well-defined folder structure by which files can be automatically generated and placed in the respective folders.
- CSS Preprocessors are used to make the CSS code reusable and readable.

Multiple Choice Questions

1. What is the command to install ember-cli?
    a. `npm integrate ember-cli`
    b. `node install ember-cli`
    c. `npm install -g ember-cli`
    d. `javascript install ember-cli`
2. Which of the following can be generated automatically through Ember blueprints?
    a. Models
    b. Controllers
    c. Components
    d. All of the above
3. Ember has an inbuilt test runner
    a. True
    b. False
4. What is the default output folder of the `build` command?
    a. build
    b. dist

   c. output
   d. None of the above
5. Which of the following is not a valid CSS preprocessor syntax?
   a. `scss`
   b. `sass`
   c. `less`
   d. `pass`

Answers

1. c
2. d
3. a
4. b
5. d

Questions

1. What are the main differences between npm and yarn?
2. What are the alternatives to SASS/SCSS? What is LESS?
3. How do you remove an addon installed via Ember CLI?
4. What is a sourcemap and how do you use it?
5. Where do you store static content like images and fonts in an Ember project?

Key Terms

- **Ember CLI**: A command line tool to develop, run, build and deploy Ember apps.
- **Package Manager**: A program that's used to search and install libraries.
- **Addon**: A dependency or library that can be installed into an Ember application.

- **Blueprint**: An Ember concept that helps generate dynamic boilerplate code or install dependencies inside the project.
- **Preprocessor**: CSS scripting mechanism that allows adding dynamic content to CSS files.

CHAPTER 3
Ember.js Routing

Introduction

In this chapter, we will learn about **Routing** in detail. It is one of the most powerful features of Ember that decides which part of the code should be executed when a URL is loaded by a browser. It is powerful because it can handle any type of dynamic parameters in the URL, handle query parameters, asynchronously load data through the model, and pass them to the templates via the controller, or decide and redirect the user automatically to another route if the user lacks permissions, and so on.

We will also take a look at Controllers and their functionalities. We will look at their advantages and disadvantages that will help you understand when and where to use controllers, or decide to defer the logic to routes or components.

Structure

In this chapter, we will discuss the following topics:

- Introduction to routing
- Setting up Ember routes
- Nested routes
- Route model
- Route hooks
- Asynchronous routing
- Loading and error substates
- Query parameters
- Controllers

Introduction to Routing

Router in Ember is composed of two parameters.

- **Router** is the gateway to an Ember application. When a user enters a URL in the browser, the router decides and loads the appropriate **Route Handler** based on the URL.
- **Route Handler** is loaded by the router and it takes care of fetching the model for the route, rendering the template for the route and setting up the controller and passing the model data to the controller.

You can see a file named **app/router.js** in the project. This file contains the list of all routes present in the Ember application. If you open the file now, the file will look like this:

```
import EmberRouter from '@ember/routing/router';
import config from 'my-ember-project/config/environment';

export default class Router extends EmberRouter {
  location = config.locationType;
  rootURL = config.rootURL;
}

Router.map(function () {});
```

Router.map is the function where all the routes will be defined. Right now since we don't have any routes configured, the function is empty. But even without any routes, we were able to access the home page in the browser with some default code. How is that possible?

This is one of the jobs of the **ember serve**. When creating the new project, it automatically generates the **Application Route** for you. The application route is the default route loaded by the Ember application. It is the base for all other routes in the application. It can contain functions/actions that need to be executed in common for all the routes. If you open the template for the application route (**app/templates/application.hbs**), you can see the default **WelcomePage** component loaded inside it. This is how we saw the predefined home page when we loaded http://localhost:4200 in the browser.

By default, routes load controllers and templates of the same name specified in the same relative path as the route. For example, a route named application will load the template in **app/templates/application.hbs**. A route file present in **app/routes/output-folder/my-route.js** will load the controllers and templates present in the respective controllers and templates folder, in the same sub path, like **app/controllers/output-folder/my-route.js** and **app/templates/output-folder/my-route.hbs**. This is one of the factors of the *convention over configuration* setup in Ember. The default linking between routes, controllers and templates is done as mentioned earlier, which helps beginners to stay in the recommended practices of the framework. Next, let us set up a couple of simple routes for our application.

Setting Up Ember Routes

In our basic Ember application, we saw the default application route created. But one issue with the application route is that the content in the application route will be visible across all the routes in the application. So, the application route usually contains the menu layout, navbar, and more, which is common to the entire application. For the user to see specific content when they visit the home page, we have to generate a separate **index** route.

The index route is a special case, where there is no entry added to the router.js. Indcx mcans thc landing pagc. Lct's run **ember generate route index** and you will see the following output:

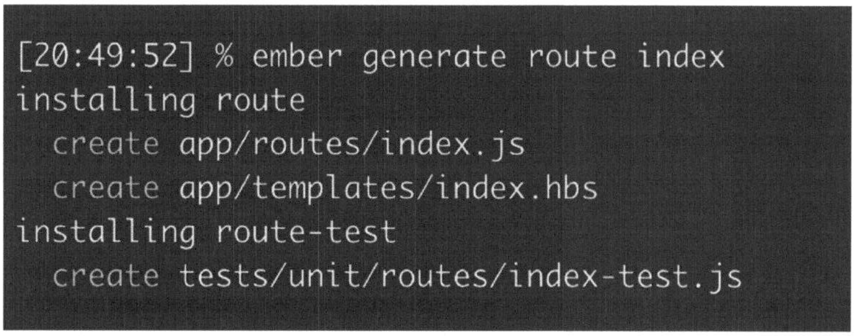

***Figure 3.1**: Ember generate route index*

Comparing the screenshot with *Figure* 2.4, you can note that generating the index route does not update the router file. It only creates the route and template file for the index route.

Let's remove the sample code in the **application.hbs** file by removing the **<WelcomePage />** component. Let's add our own HTML code to it. Let's add our app's name to the **application.hbs** file through the following code:

```
<h1 class=”page-title text-center”>My Ember Application</h1>
```

You can add the corresponding CSS to the **app.scss** file we created in the preceding chapter. Adding the following snippet to the **app.scss** will center the title.

```
.text-center {
    text-align: center;
}
```

You can visit http://localhost:4200 in the browser to see the updated content. Next, let's add some content to the index template. You can add the following line to the **app/templates/index.hbs** file:

```
<p class="text-center">Welcome to our index page</p>
```

Now if you go to the browser, you can see the updated content from both the application template and the index template. Ember server would have automatically reloaded the page with the latest content for you. To understand the difference between the application template and the index template, let's create one more route called about. You can do so by running the command - **ember generate route about**. In the newly created about template, you can add the following line:

```
<p class="text-center">Welcome to our about page</p>
```

After adding the preceding line, when you visit http://localhost:4200/about, you can see the newly created "**about**" route. You can see that it contains the title from the application template and the content from the about route. That's the difference between the application and the index routes. The application route is the base route and the template from that will be visible in all the pages. When you open the application template file, you can see a line with **{{outlet}}**. The outlet is the place used to render sub-templates in Ember. Since the application template is the base of all other templates in Ember, all other templates are loaded in the outlet section of the application route.

Linking Between Routes

Now we have two different routes in our application. How do we allow the user to navigate between the routes? We cannot ask the user to enter the URL every time to switch between routes. So we have to internally add links in the application for easy navigation.

We use the **<LinkTo>** tag to link to another route. Since it's common to all pages, let's add the following lines to the application template file, below the page title:

```
<div class="text-center">
    <LinkTo @route="index">Home</LinkTo>
    <LinkTo @route="about">About</LinkTo>
</div>
```

You can specify the route that you want to link to using the `@route` attribute. You can visit the browser to see the links below the page title. You can click the links to ensure the routing works perfectly between the two routes.

Nested Routes

We saw how you can generate multiple routes in Ember. Also, we saw how each template is rendered at the *outlet* tag of the application template. Similarly, we will have cases in your application where you might want to render a template inside another template. Let's take a simple use case. Let's say we want to build a simple **CRUD** (Create, Read, Update, Delete) operation for managing a list of our clients. Now all these actions can be categorized to be part of the clients module. For the *clients* module, there can be a few common things:

- All URLs of the clients module should start with `/clients`. The routes can be as follows:
    - `/clients` : Shows the list of clients
    - `/clients/new` : Shows the form to create a new client
    - `/clients/:client-id` is a dynamic route that shows details of a particular client
    - `/clients/:client-id/edit` to edit a particular client
- We will have a common template code that we want to display across all the pages or have common functions to be executed in all the routes in this module.
- From the code structure point of view, we will want all code related to the clients module in a single folder so that the entire project is neatly organized.

Nested Routes are Ember's answer for the preceding issues. It creates a structure for URLs, keeps the code related to the nested modules in a separate folder, and renders all templates of the nested routes inside a base route for that block. Let's generate the nested routes for the clients module.

For each nested route, we have to first create an index route. An index route is the default fallback route to load when there is no sub-route specified. For example, in the clients module, **/clients/** is the base URL for the block, and just specifying this URL in the browser will load the index route of the nested block. The index route can be created with the following command:

```
ember generate route clients/index
```

The output of the command will look like this:

```
[15:18:51] % ember generate route clients/index
installing route
  create app/routes/clients/index.js
  create app/templates/clients/index.hbs
updating router
  add route clients/index
installing route-test
  create tests/unit/routes/clients/index-test.js
```

***Figure 3.2:** Ember generate nested route*

As a result of the generate command, you can see the following changes which are a bit different from generating a normal route.

- You have a new record for the *clients* route in the router.js file. However, you can see a function as an additional parameter to this record. It is the indicator that the current record is a nested block, and the sub-routes will be listed inside the function that's passed as the parameter.
- Inside both the templates and routes folders, you can see a *clients* folder and an index file inside it. These are the files pertaining to the specific route. We can write code specific to the clients list page in these two files.

Now that the clients list route is generated, we can add it to the list of links we have in the application template. Add the following line after the About link in the **app/templates/application.hbs file:**

```
<LinkTo @route=”clients.index”>Clients</LinkTo>
```

With this, we can now see the link to the clients list page from anywhere in the application. Let's add some dummy content inside the **templates/clients/index.hbs** file:

```
<table class=”table”>
  <thead>
    <tr>
```

```
            <th>Name</th>
            <th>Company Name</th>
            <th>Email</th>
            <th>Phone Number</th>
            <th></th>
        </tr>
    </thead>
    <tbody>
        <tr>
            <td>John</td>
            <td>John’s Furniture</td>
            <td>+91 98765 43210</td>
            <td>john@example.com</td>
            <td>
                View | Edit | Delete
            </td>
        </tr>
        <tr>
            <td>Robert</td>
            <td>Smart Boutique</td>
            <td>+91 98764 53210</td>
            <td>robert@example.com</td>
            <td>
                View | Edit | Delete
            </td>
        </tr>
    </tbody>
</table>
```

For styling purposes, let’s add the following to the **styles/app.scss** file:

```
.table {
    width: 90%;
    margin: auto;
    border: 1px solid #ddd;
```

```
    margin-top: 30px;
}

.table th,
.table td {
    border: 1px solid #ddd;
    text-align: center;
    padding: 5px;
}
```

After adding the code, you can visit http://localhost:4200/clients to see the table along with the styling added to the css file. The content that we have added is specific to the **clients/index** route. Now, if we want to add some HTML that is shown in all the sub-routes of clients, we have to create a new file at **app/templates/clients.hbs**. This file will have the same name as the nested block, but will be placed outside the folder of the nested route. Let's add the following contents to the *app/templates/clients.hbs* file:

```
<h1 class="text-center">Clients</h1>
<div class="text-center">Manage all your client details in this page</div>
{{outlet}}
```

You can go back to the browser to see the content from **clients.hbs** reflected on the page. The content added will reflect in all the sub-routes of clients.

In the same HTML content we added, you can see the last column had the text **View | Edit | Delete** without any links. We are going to add these routes now. First, let's create the view route.

```
ember generate route clients/view
```

You can view the newly created route in the **router.js** file. You can see that the view route is present inside the clients route, indicating that it is a sub route. However, one issue is that the route doesn't indicate which client is selected. This means that the view route needs to know which client is selected in order to show the details about that particular client.

Dynamic Segments

For identifying which client the user has selected, we will need to add a **dynamic segment** to the route. A dynamic segment is a part of the URL that is not constant and can change based on the item the app has to load. Dynamic segments start with a **:** and go on to define a variable name. For the client view route, we need the client id as a parameter, in order to load the client details accordingly. We can specify the path for a route using the **path** parameter to the route. You can modify the line for the view route to look like this:

```
this.route('view', {path: '/:client_id'});
```

As per Ember conventions, the view route will have the default path as **/clients/view.** This is where Ember's flexibility comes into play. Even though it creates the route based on its convention, we can configure the route to have a different path using the *path* parameter in the route. Next, let's see how we can link to this route from the clients list page. We need to surround the text *View* with the **LinkTo** tag and call the view route with the id as a parameter. Here is how you can do it for the first row:

```
<LinkTo @route="clients.view" @model=1>View</LinkTo>
```

For the second row, we can make the same **View** text look like this:

```
<LinkTo @route="clients.view" @model=2>View</LinkTo>
```

Just like the previous links, we have added a LinkTo tag pointing to the **clients.view** route. We have also added a *model* attribute to the tag, which varies for each row. The model attribute specifies the dynamic part, which will be passed as the **client_id** parameter. Now when you visit the clients list page, you can see that the View buttons are hyperlinked. You can click on the link to visit the client view page. However, when clicking on the link, you can see there is no change in the page. That's because you can see an error in the browser console:

```
▸Error while processing route: clients.view Assertion Failed: You used the dynamic        router.js:1142
segment `client_id` in your route `clients.view` for which Ember requires you provide a data-loading
implementation. Commonly, that is done by adding a model hook implementation on the route
(`model({client_id}) {`) or by injecting an implemention of a data store: `@service store;`. Error:
Assertion Failed: You used the dynamic segment `client_id` in your route `clients.view` for which Ember
requires you provide a data-loading implementation. Commonly, that is done by adding a model hook
implementation on the route (`model({client_id}) {`) or by injecting an implemention of a data store:
`@service store;`.
    at assert (http://localhost:4200/assets/vendor.js:15451:15)
    at Object.find (http://localhost:4200/assets/vendor.js:23369:64)
    at ClientsViewRoute.findModel (http://localhost:4200/assets/vendor.js:23154:46)
    at ClientsViewRoute.model (http://localhost:4200/assets/vendor.js:23134:19)
    at ClientsViewRoute.deserialize (http://localhost:4200/assets/vendor.js:23145:19)
    at UnresolvedRouteInfoByParam.getModel (http://localhost:4200/assets/vendor.js:44154:24)
    at http://localhost:4200/assets/vendor.js:43988:113
    at invokeCallback (http://localhost:4200/assets/vendor.js:45774:17)
    at publish (http://localhost:4200/assets/vendor.js:45760:9)
    at invoke (http://localhost:4200/assets/vendor.js:39979:16)
```

Figure 3.3: *Ember model hook error*

The error message is simple: Ember says you've configured a route with a dynamic segment, but there is no code included in your route handler to handle the dynamic parameter. And it is asking for you to implement a **model** hook to handle the dynamic parameter.

Route Model

Model is a hook in a route handler that loads the data required for the particular route. The data returned by the model is directly accessible from the template. The model hook will have access to the params passed in the URL, with which we can load the data into the page dynamically. Model typically uses the **Ember store** to connect with a backend data source through API. We will look into the store and dynamically load the data in later chapters. For now, we will dynamically return the data based on the **client_id** parameter in the URL. Let's add the following code to the **app/routes/clients/view.js**

```
model(params) {
  let clientId = params.client_id;
  if (clientId === '1') {
    return {
      id: 1,
      name: 'John',
      company_name: "John's Furniture",
      email: "john@example.com",
      phone_number: "+91 98765 43210",
     active: true
    }
  } else if (clientId === '2') {
    return {
      id: 2,
      name: 'Robert',
      company_name: "Smart Boutique",
      email: "robert@example.com",
      phone_number: "+91 98764 53210",
     active: false
    }
  }
}
```

Even though we don't load the data from a backend source yet, the model hook dynamically returns the hardcoded data based on the **client_id** passed as the parameter. To access the returned data from the template, let's add the following code in the **app/templates/clients/view.hbs** file:

```
<div class="text-center">
    <table class="table">
        <tr>
            <th>Name</th>
            <td>{{@model.name}}</td>
        </tr>
        <tr>
            <th>Company Name</th>
            <td>{{@model.company_name}}</td>
        </tr>
        <tr>
            <th>Email</th>
            <td>{{@model.email}}</td>
        </tr>
        <tr>
            <th>Phone Number</th>
            <td>{{@model.phone_number}}</td>
        </tr>
    </table>
</div>
```

You can see that we don't hard code the data, and access the data returned by the model using the **@model** notation. In this example, we have directly returned an object from the model hook. However, the general use case is to make an API call to fetch the data for the model. So, the model hook will return a promise object, which will be resolved by Ember automatically.

Route Hooks

Aside from the model, the route handler provides certain hooks. Hooks are functions that are called at specific points of time in the route lifecycle. They can be used to make checks based on params provided in the URL, based on the response from the model, or pass additional data to the template. Let's look at a few major lifecycle hooks in Ember.js

activate

The **activate** hook is fired when the router enters the route from another route. It does not fire when just the model changes within the same route. This can be used to track some analytics based on the different routes a user visits.

deactivate

The **deactivate** hook is fired when the router leaves the route. This also does not fire when just the model of the route changes.

beforeModel

beforeModel is called as soon as the route is created. As the name suggests, it is called before the model is executed. This can be used to redirect the user to another route based on permissions or data. For example, in our client view route, we will want the dynamic **client_id** parameter to be a number. Hence, in the **beforeModel**, we can add a check to see if the **client_id** is a number. If it is not a number, we know that the id is not valid and can redirect the user to the client list page.

We saw that the model hook is called with the list of URL parameters. Since **beforeModel** is executed as soon as the route is created, it receives a transition object as a parameter. The transition object contains details of the route, which was previously loaded (if the user was transitioning from one route to another). If the user directly entered the URL in the browser, the "from" route will be null. Similarly, it contains a to object, which contains the details of the route it is being transitioned to. Inside this object, we will find the parameters passed in the URL. Let's add a **beforeModel** to our **clients/view** route to check if **client_id** is a number.

For transitioning a user to another route, we will be using the **transitionTo** function in the router service. As discussed earlier, services are Ember objects that live across the duration of the application and can be injected into any route or component. The router is an inbuilt service that handles functionalities like transitioning from one route to another. Let's add the following code into our **routes/clients/view.js** to inject the router and make the redirection in our **beforeModel**.

```
import { service } from '@ember/service';


export default class ClientsViewRoute extends Route {
  @service router;
```

```
    beforeModel(transition) {
      let clientId = transition.to.params.client_id;
      clientId = parseInt(clientId)
      if (isNaN(clientId)) {
        this.router.transitionTo('clients');
      }
    }
    ...
  }
```

From the preceding code sample, you can see that we've injected the router service using the **`@service`** syntax, and referenced the service using **`this.router`** notation to redirect the user to the client list if the id is not a number. Now, when you visit some random URL like http://localhost:4200/clients/asdsdf, and you will be redirected to the clients list page automatically. When you click on the view link of any of the clients in the list, you will be redirected to the client detail page, since the parameter is a proper number.

One advantage of **`beforeModel`** is, it contains the transition object as the parameter. It allows us to identify from where the user visited this page. So, if the user visited the client detail page from somewhere else in the app, we can use this transition object to identify the source route and redirect the user to that specific route, instead of the clients list. This will be needed when you don't want the user to lose context of where they arrived from.

afterModel

As the name suggests, this hook is fired after the model is loaded. This hook can be used to add checks or make redirections based on the data returned by the model. For example, in the model, we have a flag called active, which is true for one record and false for the other. Let's say that we do not want the user to view the client detail page for a client that is not active. So, we will use **`afterModel`** to check if the client is active and redirect otherwise. Let's add the following code to the *routes/clients/view.js* file:

```
afterModel(model) {
  if (!model.active) {
    this.router.transitionTo('clients');
  }
}
```

This function will redirect the user back to the clients list if the particular client is not active. **afterModel** also receives the transition object as the second parameter, which can also be used to redirect the user back to where they came from.

setupController

The **setupController** hook is fired after the **afterModel** hook, once the controller is initialized. We will look into how controllers work later in the chapter, but for now, we can see how we can manipulate/pass additional data to the template via the **setupController** method. We can pass any information through this function. This function is called with the controller for the current route as the first parameter. Let's add some dummy variables by adding this function to **app/routes/clients/view.js**:

```
setupController(controller, model) {
  controller.set('testVar', 'Testing Var');
}
```

By doing this, the variable **testVar** is accessible from the template as **{{this.testVar}}**. You can add the same inside **app/templates/clients/view.js** to see the value displayed on the web page.

An advantage of **setupController** is that you can use this function to pass data to any of the controllers of the parent routes. If we are in the **clients/view** route, the parent routes are **clients/index** and **application** routes. We can manipulate data for any of the routes inside **setupController**. Let's say instead of hardcoding "**Clients**" in the **app/templates/clients.hbs** file, we want to show the name of the selected client when visiting the client detail page. We can do that inside **setupController** like this:

```
setupController(controller, model) {
  controller.set('testVar', 'Testing Var');
  this.controllerFor('clients').set('clientModuleTitle', model.
name);
}
```

We have referenced the base controller for clients, by using the **controllerFor** function and set a variable called **clientModuleTitle** to the name of the selected client received from the model. Next, we can replace the hard-coded word **Clients** in **app/templates/clients.hbs** to **{{this.clientModuleTitle}}**, and you can see the name of the client in place of the title.

willTransition

willTransition is triggered when the router initiates a transition (within the same route or between different routes). This function receives the transition object as a parameter, and based on the destination of the transition or based on the current state of the controller, you can decide if you want to add more data to the transition or redirect the user to another route altogether. For example, let's say we have a form on our page and we don't want the user to transition away from the page without filling out the form, the following function will help us do that:

```
@action
willTransition(transition) {
  if (!self.controller.get('hasCompletedForm')) {
    transition.abort();
  } else if (self.controller.get('someOtherFlag')) {
    this.router.transitionTo('/some-other-route');
  }
}
```

From the preceding example, you can see that we check the state of a variable in the controller, and if the variable is not set to true, we abort the transition. Or if we have some other flag in the controller and we want to redirect the user to some other page based on that (say if the user's subscription has expired, we have to redirect them to the pricing page always). Note that **willTransition** will be fired only when there is no existing transition in progress. So, when we redirect the user to **/some-other-route, willTransition** will not be fired again.

If you want **willTransition** to be fired even for this case, you will need to do **transition.abort()** to exit out of the current transition, and then call **transitionTo**.

didTransition

didTransition is triggered when a transition is completed successfully. It occurs after the **beforeModel, model** and **afterModel** hooks are completed and resolved. This action does not receive any parameters but can be used to track page analytics or collect user activity data.

resetController

We have discussed before that controllers are singleton instances and they are initiated only once when the route is first called, and the same instance is used again and again. For each route, in the **setupController** function, we might set different values for the controller. Those values stay even after the router exits this route. Those values can be reset to default in the **resetController** function.

This function receives three parameters:

- **controller**: The controller object for the current route.
- **isExiting**: This denotes if the router is moving to a different route altogether. If only the model of the route changes, this flag will be passed as false.
- **transition**: The transition object

Let's say we want to set some edit flag in the controller to false when the user moves out of the page. We can do that as follows:

```
resetController(controller, isExiting, transition) {
  if (isExiting) {
    controller.set('isEditing', false);
  }
}
```

redirect

Sometimes in an application, you will want to redirect from a parent route to child routes, or between siblings. In those cases, when we use **transitionTo** to switch between routes, the current transition gets invalidated and all the hooks like **beforeModel, model** and **afterModel** are fired for the parent route again. This is a bit inefficient as they finished executing just now before we initiate the transition.

For this purpose, we use the **redirect** method. This is similar to the **afterModel** hook and is triggered almost at the same time as **afterModel**. The only difference is, if we do a **transitionTo** from inside the redirect function, those hooks are not called again and the router just transitions into the child route.

Asynchronous Routing

Most of the time, in a real-time application we will load the data from a backend source using APIs. In those cases, the data is not immediately available as it might take a few seconds for the browser to make the network call, receive and parse the response. JavaScript supports asynchronous operations, which means that it can run tasks in parallel. So, when the API call is being made, the Ember application can perform other tasks like setting up the templates, showing the skeletal HTML on the screen, and so on.

JavaScript has a concept called **`Promise`** for handling asynchronous operations. A Promise is a proxy for data that is not available yet. When making an API call to fetch data, the function will return a Promise instead. It indicates to the code that it is an asynchronous operation and the data will be loaded later. Once the data is received, the Promise resolves to return the data or rejects it if there is an error in the response. A Promise has the following states:

- **Pending**: When the Promise is created and the data is not received yet
- **Fulfilled**: When the data is received and the operation is completed successfully
- **Rejected**: When the operation has some error or the data is corrupt.

A Promise has two functions, which are called based on its result. It has a **`.then()`** function that is called when the promise is fulfilled/resolved, and a **`.catch()`** called when the promise is rejected. A Promise also has a **`.finally()`** function, which will be called after the Promise is completed, irrespective of whether it is resolved/rejected.

The Ember route handler is **`Promise`** aware. This means that if any of the hooks (**`beforeModel, model, afterModel`**) returns a Promise, it waits for the promise to complete before calling the next hook. So, irrespective of whether the **`model`** hook returns an object or a promise, the **`afterModel`** hook will always receive the actual data from the model. Let's try it out. We will update the model hook of the *clients/view* to return a Promise instead of an object like it does now. The updated model hook will look like this:

```
import { later } from '@ember/runloop';
model(params) {
  return new Promise((resolve, reject) => {
    later(() => {
      console.log("Completing promise");
      let clientId = params.client_id;
      if (clientId === '1') {
        resolve({
          id: 1,
```

```
          name: 'John',
          company_name: "John's Furniture",
          email: 'john@example.com',
          phone_number: '+91 98765 43210',
          active: true,
        });
      } else if (clientId === '2') {
        resolve({
          id: 2,
          name: 'Robert',
          company_name: 'Smart Boutique',
          email: 'robert@example.com',
          phone_number: '+91 98764 53210',
          active: false,
        });
      } else {
        reject({status: 404, detail: 'Client not found'});
      }
    }, 1500);
  });
}
```

In the updated code, we've wrapped the model logic inside the **`later`** function, which executes after 1.5 seconds. **`Later`** is the Ember equivalent of **`setTimeout`,** but internally it helps to use **`later`** when running Ember in a test environment, as Ember identifies **`later`** calls instead of **`setTimeout`** calls better. The **`later`** call is wrapped around a Promise so that the Ember application waits for the Promise to resolve before going further to call the **`afterModel`**. Just like how we've added a **`console.log`** inside *later*, let's add a **`console.log`** inside **`afterModel`** to see the sequence of events. Once the changes are done and saved, you can notice a slight delay before you can see the data. It is because of the 1.5 seconds delay we've introduced in the model. The console output will look like this:

```
DEBUG: -------------------------------
DEBUG: Ember      : 5.0.0
DEBUG: Ember Data : 5.0.0
DEBUG: -------------------------------
Completing promise
In afterModel
```

Figure 3.4: *Promise execution order*

Figure 3.4 indicates that even though we used a Promise instead of directly returning the data, the order of execution remains the same. You can also chain promises, which means returning a Promise from inside a Promise. This is useful when we want to fetch records from multiple places, and one API call depends on the response from the previous API call. In such cases, Ember will resolve all Promises before proceeding further. There can be cases where multiple API calls are made in parallel. Ember can handle that as well.

Loading and Error Substates

Ember route handler allows you to notify the template when the data is loading, or when the model fails with an error.

Loading Substate

Initially, when the page was loading, we could see a small delay since the model took 1.5 seconds to resolve. In that timeframe, we do not want the user to see an empty screen as it will not be a good experience. For this purpose, Ember allows you to set a loading substate to visually inform the user that some data is being loaded. The loading substate is triggered only when the route contains a hook (**`beforeModel, model`**, or **`afterModel`**) that does not resolve immediately.

A loading substate can be provided by adding a loading file, whose name is **`<templatename>-loading.hbs`** or **`<templatename>.loading.hbs`** It can be defined for each template. Ember looks for the loading substate file from the bottom up and looks for loading files till it finds one. For example, when we are loading the client detail route, here is the order of how Ember looks for the loading file:

- **`clients/view-loading`**
- **`clients.loading`** or **`clients-loading`**
- **`loading`** or **`application-loading`**

We can understand the following based on the order:

- Ember looks for the loading file in the bottommost route template and goes up each level to find the loading file.
- It looks for a **.loading** file in the upper levels (like clients or application), but not on the actual route.
- The **.loading** notation can be used for parent routes, whereas the **-loading** notation is prioritized when the template is for the child route.

You can try adding model delays to other routes as well, and add loading files for each template to test their behavior.

Loading Event

Similar to the loading templates, the route also provides an event that will trigger when any of the hooks (**beforeModel**, **model**, or **afterModel**) fails to resolve immediately. Similar to the substate, Ember looks for the loading event handler in the child route and bubbles up to look for the same function in parent routes. This function can be used to set variables in the controller to update the loading state. We can add the following code to set a loading event for the **app/clients/view.js** route:

```
import { action } from '@ember/object';


@action
loading(transition) {
  let controller = this.controllerFor('clients.view');
  controller.set('isLoading', true);
  return true;
}
```

When a loading event is handled, the loading substate is shown only if the loading event returns true. Since the loading event receives the transition object as a parameter, we can use it to identify when the promise holding up the page load resolves. We can do that as follows:

```
@action
loading(transition) {
  let controller = this.controllerFor('clients.view');
  controller.set('isLoading', true);
  transition.promise.finally(() => {
```

```
            controller.set('isLoading', false);
        });
        return true;
    }
```

Here, we use the **finally** function of the promise, which gets executed irrespective of whether the promise is fulfilled or rejected.

Error Substate

Similar to the loading substate, Ember also supports an error substate, which is loaded when the promise is rejected or there is any other error during the transition process. The error substate file follows the same nomenclature as the loading substate, and it uses **error** instead of **loading** in the file name. From the model code we have written, you can see that the model is rejected if the client id is not 1 or 2. That will trigger the error substate in the route.

Let's load the URL http://localhost:4200/clients/3. Since we don't have an error substate now, you can see that the loading state still prevails after a few seconds, and an error in the console after the model promise resolves. *Figure* 3.5 indicates the console error that occurs after the promise is rejected.

```
DEBUG: -------------------------------
DEBUG: Ember      : 5.0.0
DEBUG: Ember Data : 5.0.0
DEBUG: -------------------------------
Completing promise
▶Error while processing route: clients.view
▶Uncaught (in promise) ▶ {status: 404, detail: 'Client not found'}
>
```

***Figure* 3.5:** *Error Substate*

In cases like these, we will want the user to know that there is an error in the transition process. This is where the error substate comes into place. Let's create an **app/templates/clients/view-error.hbs** file with the following line:

```
<h1 class="text-center">Error loading data</h1>
```

Now when you refresh the page, you can see the error substate being loaded once the promise is rejected. The error substate also follows the same pattern, looking for the **-error.hbs** file of the child route, and then for the **.error.hbs** or **-error.hbs** file of each of the parent routes.

Error Event

Similar to the Loading event, there is an error event fired when the promise is rejected. We can use this to redirect the user to another route or show an error message based on the error type. Let's add the error event to the **clients/view.js** route to handle this.

```
@action
error(error, transition) {
  if (error.status == 404) {
    console.log("404 error");
  }
  return true;
}
```

Note that we have returned true at the end because we want to show the error state template on the screen. Usually, an API server returns a 404 response status when trying to access a non-existent object. In those cases, we can have a generic page that is shown when a user tries to access a non-existing object or a non-existent route in the application. Let's generate a route named **fourohfour** (since route names cannot be numeric like 404) to handle this.

```
ember generate route fourohfour
```

This route will be the default fallback when the user enters a URL that doesn't match any route in the application. To denote that, let's edit the **fourohfour** record in the router.js file as follows:

```
this.route('fourohfour', { path: '/*' });
```

Here, we have specified the path as *. It means that this route catches any URL that doesn't match the routes specified above this route. Make sure to place this route at the end of the router block, since all URLs will be caught by this route, and anything below this will become irrelevant. Let's add some sample content to the **templates/fourohfour.hbs** file:

```
<h1 class="text-center">You have reached a dead-end!!
  Go <LinkTo @route="index">Home</LinkTo></h1>
```

In this page, we are just informing the user they've reached the wrong URL, and showing a link for them to go back to the index route. You can now visit any random URL, like http://localhost:4200/some-random-url, and can see this route in action.

With this route in place, we can easily redirect the user to the **fourohfour** page when the error status from the route is **404**. The updated error event at **routes/clients/view.js** will look like this:

```
@action
error(error, transition) {
  if (error.status == 404) {
    this.router.transitionTo('/fourohfour');
  }
  return true;
}
```

Now when you visit the URL *http://localhost:4200/clients/3*, you will be redirected to the **fourohfour** page automatically.

Controllers

Controllers are objects that are bound to a route. Controllers are used for the following purposes:

- Maintain the state of variables in that route that are passed to templates
- Maintain a set of actions that can be passed to components in that route
- Handle query parameters for this route

Controllers are singleton instances that are initialized only once when the route is visited for the first time. After that, the same instance is used again even when the user leaves the route and comes back to the route after some time. You can use controllers mainly for handling/modifying data based on the model or query parameters passed in the URL.

We cannot perform these operations in the route handler because the data from the route handler is not directly passed to the template, and it is passed only via the controllers. Controllers have a direct two-way binding with the templates. Any change to the data in the template is immediately reflected in the controller and vice-versa.

Generating a Controller

A Controller can be generated through the Ember generate command. Let's generate a controller for the clients route.

```
ember generate controller clients
```

Once executed, you can see the controller file generated here: **`app/controllers/clients.js`**, and an empty controller object created inside it. Now, if you visit http://localhost:4200/clients, you can see that the title is empty, because we have used the **`clientsModuleTitle`** variable for displaying the title, and the **`clientModuleTitle`** is not defined yet. But if you click on the **`View`** link and visit the client view page, the name of the client will appear as the title. And when you click on the **`Clients`** link to get back to the clients list page, you can see the client name still present as the title.

When the user loads the clients list page directly, we don't want the title to be empty. So, we can set the **`clientModuleTitle`** value in the controller as follows:

```
export default class ClientsController extends Controller {
  clientModuleTitle = 'Clients'
}
```

Now you can refresh the page and see the **`Clients`** title on the page. However, if you go to one of the client detail pages by clicking the **`View`** link, and then back to the list page using the **`Clients`** link on top, the client name will still be visible and not the title **`Clients`**.

This is evidence that controllers are singleton instances. We set the **`clientModuleTitle`** variable in the controller from the clients view page and since the controller does not reinitialize when going back to the client list page, we still see the title that was set earlier. If the controller had reinitialized, the title would have been reset to **`Clients.`** To work around this, we will have to set the value of **`clientModuleTitle`** from the **`setupController`** of the **`clients/index.js`** route, and it will execute when the user goes back to the clients list page.

Controllers are recommended to be used only for cases where the action/variable is dependent on the model or its query parameters. It is recommended to use Components for other cases, as controllers are bound to a particular route. This restricts code reusability, as the same code cannot be used in another route/controller.

Query Parameters

Query parameters are similar to dynamic segments in the URL, except that dynamic segments are mandatory, while query parameters are optional. The names of the elements in the dynamic segments are predefined in the route path, but query parameters are not predefined. Anything can be passed in the URL.

Hence, query parameters contain both their name and value, separated by the = symbol. For example, if we want to add sorting options to the clients list page, the URL will look like this: *http://localhost:4200/clients?sortBy=name&order=asc.*

The query parameter part of the URL is denoted by the question mark (?). Each query parameter will have the format **`<key>=<value>`**, separated by the ampersand (&) symbol. There can be any number of query parameters in the URL, and the ones that are not handled by the code are simply ignored.

The query parameters can be accessed in the router by specifying them beforehand on the router. Let's add the preceding query parameters in the **`clients/index.js`** route:

```
export default class ClientsViewRoute extends Route {
  queryParams = {
    sortBy: {
      refreshModel: false
    },
    order: {
      refreshModel: true
    }
  }
  model(params) {
    console.log(params);
  }
}
```

We are defining the list of supported parameters using the **`queryParams`** property in the route. If you visit the URL http://localhost:4200/clients?sortBy=name&order=asc, you can see the query parameters parsed and available in the params property in the model. This can be used to send the params to the backend for the server to filter or sort the data based on the parameter. You can also notice the **`refreshModel`** key added to each parameter. This key is used by the route handler to decide whether the model has to be refreshed when a particular query parameter changes.

For using the same query parameters in the templates/controllers, you can define them in the controller file. Let's define both the query parameters in the **clients/index.js** controller:

```
export default class ClientsIndexController extends Controller {
  queryParams = ['sortBy', 'order']

  sortBy = null;
  order = null;
}
```

In the controller, we specify the list of parameters using the **queryParams** property as a list and create them as individual properties in the controller. Note that we cannot dynamically create properties from query parameters.

Routing with Query Parameters

We can pass query parameters through all routing mechanisms in Ember. Let's look at some examples:

LinkTo

LinkTo tag accepts a **@query** attribute to support query parameters:

```
<LinkTo @route="clients.index" @query={{hash sortBy="name"}}>
Clients</LinkTo>
```

We use the **{{hash}}** helper to generate the query parameters during redirection. Multiple parameters can be separated by space.

transitionTo

The router's **transitionTo** function also supports query parameters. We have used **transitionTo** by passing the route name as the parameter. You can pass the query parameters through the second parameter of this function:

```
this.router.transitionTo('clients.index', { queryParams: { sort-
By: 'name' }})
```

If you want to redirect the user to the same route, but just update the query parameters, you can ignore the first parameter in the **transitionTo** function and pass the second parameter alone:

```
this.router.transitionTo({ queryParams: { sortBy: 'name' }})
```

By doing this, we will only update the query parameters of the current route instead of going to another route.

Conclusion

In this chapter, we learned in detail about the Ember router and the route handler. We went through the different functionalities offered by the route handler, about how you can dynamically inject data into the URL and specify the data accordingly through the model. We discussed the different hooks and when they are called during the lifecycle of the route. You also became familiar with displaying the loading state and error states via templates and handling them through the router code as well. Then, we went on to discuss controllers and their advantages and disadvantages. In the next chapters, we will go through Ember components and templates, which are the core building blocks of Ember.

Points to Remember

- Router is the entry point to the Ember application. It decides which code should execute based on the URL specified.
- URL can contain both static and dynamic parameters.
- Routes can be nested. Parent and child routes can share functions and model data.
- Ember uses dynamic parameters in the URL to load the appropriate data into the template.
- You can specify templates to be shown when the data is being loaded, or when there is an error loading the data.
- Router can modify variables in the controller.
- Variables defined in the controller are directly accessible from the templates.
- Controllers are singleton instances and they are bound to a specific route.

Multiple Choice Questions

1. Which of the following parses the URL to decide the route?

    a. Route handler

    b. Router

    c. Controller

    d. None of the above

2. Which of the following tags/functions are used to move from one route to another?
   a. `transitionTo`
   b. `LinkTo`
   c. `<a>`
   d. All of the above
3. By the order of execution, which of the following is triggered at the end?
   a. `afterModel`
   b. `model`
   c. `setupController`
   d. `beforeModel`
4. When a Promise is rejected, which of the following are executed?
   a. `catch`
   b. `finally`
   c. `then`
   d. (a) and (b)
5. Which parameter is used to define the URL associated with a route?
   a. pathname
   b. path
   c. route
   d. url
6. Which function is used to reset the values of the controller when the router exits the route?
   a. `setupController`
   b. `resetController`
   c. `controllerFor`
   d. `deactivate`

Answers

1. b
2. d
3. c
4. d
5. b
6. b

Questions

1. What is the command to generate a nested route?
2. What is the difference between **`setupController`** and **`resetController`**?
3. What are the different ways to specify loading and error substates? How are they prioritized?
4. What is the difference between **`afterModel`** and **`redirect`**?
5. When should we use controllers over components?

Key Terms

- **Route Handler:** An object that contains details about a URL and loads data and template based on that.
- **Controller:** A singleton object associated with the route. It is used to maintain variables and logic related to the route.
- **Route Model:** Function that loads the data related to a route.
- **Transition:** A Promise like object that represents an attempt to move to another route.

CHAPTER 4

Ember.js Components and Templates

Introduction

In this chapter, we will look in detail at Components and Templates in Ember.js. We will learn what components are, how they can be used to build the Ember.js codebase from the bottom up, how routes and templates interact with components, handle events, and so on. We will look at how components can be reused across the code to prevent code redundancy.

We will learn about templates, how we can add dynamic content to them, and add conditions, loops and similar coding practices into Ember.js templates. We will learn about dynamically calculated functions in Ember called computed objects and create reusable tags in templates called `helpers`. At the end, we will discuss how we can make the webpage look more pleasant and aesthetic using the Ember-bootstrap library.

Structure

In this chapter, we will discuss the following topics:

- Introduction to Components
- Component Arguments
- Templates
- Conditional Statements
- Loops
- Helper Functions
- Component State and Actions
- Computed Values
- Designing with Ember-Bootstrap

Introduction to Components

Technically speaking, it is possible to write all the codes related to a template in a single `.hbs` file and all the logic related to it in the controller file. The Ember app will work perfectly fine in that case. However, from a clean code perspective, it poses a couple of problems:

- The code will look too long and it will not be easy to read through the code with ease.
- When the same code (say a dropdown with custom styling) is needed in another route, you will need to copy and paste the code into the other template, which will lead to a lot of duplication in a large application.

Components are the solution to this problem. It helps us define a small modularized block of code in separate files that can be included in any template across the application or into other components as well. This will mean that the code will also look cleaner and smaller when opening the template file, as most of the code is separated into components.

Every component comprises of two elements:

- A template file (`.hbs`)
- A JavaScript file (`.js` or `.ts`)

Similar to controllers and templates, the component template file contains the HTML that the user sees in the interface, while the JavaScript file takes care of all the logic. Similar to controllers, the JavaScript file of the component is optional and, it can be added when custom logic is required for a component.

Generating a Component

Let's generate a simple component to display the client's list. Similar to routes, Ember components can also be nested. Let us generate a component like this:

```
ember generate component clients-table/table
```

You can see the following output:

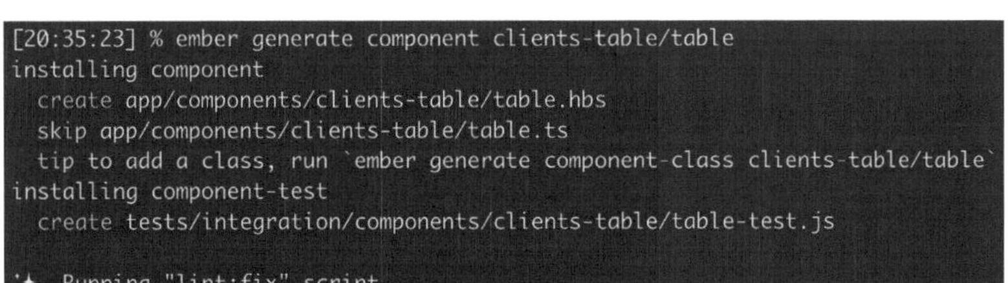

Figure 4.1: *Ember generate component*

You can see from the response that only the template (*.hbs*) has been created and the JavaScript file has been skipped. You can use the **`component-class`** blueprint next to generate the JavaScript file associated with the component.

```
ember generate component-class clients-table/table
```

It will generate the component class, and you can see the file **`app/components/clients-table/table.js.`** Since we do not have any custom logic as of now, we can just move the table HTML into the component **`.hbs`** file (except for the *yield* line at the end of the template file). After moving the code, if you visit https://localhost:4200/clients, you can see the page empty in the place where the table was. Let us call the component from the **`app/templates/clients/index.hbs`** file:

```
<ClientsTable::Table />
```

We can call the component just like any HTML tag. The component name should be in camel case, with the hyphens (-) removed and the next character capitalized. That is why *clients-table* became **`ClientsTable.`** Since the component we are looking for is inside a folder (**`clients-table/table`**), the nested structure is represented by a double colon (::). After adding this line to your client's index template file, the table will be back on the page. Now the **`app/templates/clients/index.hbs`** file looks neat with just one line.

Component Arguments

In templates, we have discussed using the model data and custom variables that are defined in the controllers. The model was automatically passed from the route to the template. However, they are not done between a template and a component. We have to define the list of variables that are passed down to the component from the template.

This will mean that the data the component looks for is predefined, and it only has access to the limited variables we pass in the template, rather than all the information specified in the controller.

Even though we have hardcoded the list of items in the **`clients table/table`** component, we know that the end goal would be to load the list of items in the table from an external API source. That external API source will be queried from the route model hook and will have to be passed from the template to the component. Let us generate a model for the **`clients/index.js`** route resembling the data in the table:

```
model(params) {
  return [{
      id: 1,
      name: 'John',
      company_name: "John's Furniture",
      email: 'john@example.com',
      phone_number: '+91 98765 43210',
      active: true,
  }, {
      id: 2,
      name: 'Robert',
      company_name: 'Smart Boutique',
      email: 'robert@example.com',
      phone_number: '+91 98764 53210',
      active: false,
  }]
}
```

The model is defined and will be passed to the template. We know that we can access the model in the form of **`{{@model}}`** in the template file. We can use the same syntax to pass the variable to the component as an argument:

```
<ClientsTable::Table @clientsList={{@model}} />
```

Let us update the HTML code to reflect the data from the model. We will make changes to the code step by step, refactoring the code when going through new concepts. Now the model is in a list format. So, we need to access list indices when displaying the data according to the existing approach. In Ember, you can access the element in a particular index of a list using **`get`** helper. We will see what helpers are later in this chapter. The **`get`** helper is used to access a specific index/key in an object/list. You can also access a specific key in an element present in an index. The updated code will look like this:

```
<tbody>
    <tr>
        <td>{{get @clientsList '0.name'}}</td>
        <td>{{get @clientsList '0.company_name'}}</td>
        <td>{{get @clientsList '0.phone_number'}}</td>
```

```
            <td>{{get @clientsList '0.email'}}</td>
            <td>
                <LinkTo @route="clients.view" @model="{{get
    @clientsList '0.id'}}">View</LinkTo> | Edit | Delete
            </td>
        </tr>
        <tr>
            <td>{{get @clientsList '1.name'}}</td>
            <td>{{get @clientsList '1.company_name'}}</td>
            <td>{{get @clientsList '1.phone_number'}}</td>
            <td>{{get @clientsList '1.email'}}</td>
            <td>
                <LinkTo @route="clients.view" @model="{{get
    @clientsList '1.id'}}">View</LinkTo> | Edit | Delete
            </td>
        </tr>
    </tbody>
```

From the preceding template code, you can see how we have used the get helper to access the data. Looking at this, you can see that the first row and the second row in the table have almost the same code, except for the index of the element they access. This will cause inefficiency when making a change. For example, if we want to add a class called **phone-number** to the phone number column, we will have to do it in two places now. To avoid redundancy in these cases, we can create a component that displays only a row in the table. We can call this component twice, thus reusing the end code and reducing the number of places you have to update in case of a change. Let us create a new component called **ClientRow**. It can be inside the same **clients-table** folder:

```
ember generate component clients-table/row
```

The component will contain a single row of the table, with the same details:

```
<tr>
  <td>{{@client.name}}</td>
  <td>{{@client.company_name}}</td>
  <td>{{@client.phone_number}}</td>
  <td>{{@client.email}}</td>
  <td>
```

```
    <LinkTo @route="clients.view" @model="{{@client.id}}">View</
LinkTo> | Edit | Delete
  </td>
</tr>
```

You can see we have not used the *get* helper here, as we will just be passing only a single client object to this component instead of a model. The table component can be cleaned up further and updated as follows:

```
<tbody>
  <ClientsTable::Row @client={{get @clientsList 0}} />
  <ClientsTable::Row @client={{get @clientsList 1}} />
</tbody>
```

We have updated the code now to look simpler by using the power of components. Now the code looks even more modular than before, as the table itself is now a component, and we have a separate component for the row, as we want to reuse the same code as much as possible.

HTML Attributes

When passing arguments to components, you can see that we have used **@** as a prefix for each argument. We do this to differentiate Ember arguments from normal HTML attributes that can be assigned to an HTML tag. The attribute can be id, class, or any custom attribute that you want to add to the HTML element. Ember allows us to pass both component arguments and normal HTML arguments that can be applied to the wrapping div inside the component. For example, in the **clients-table/row** component, **<tr>** is the wrapping element. If we want to pass attributes like class from the calling template, we can do so. This is how it will look:

```
    <ClientsTable::Row @client={{get @clientsList 0}} class="-
text-right" />
```

The component calling statement can work like a normal HTML tag and pass default HTML attributes. They can be used by the child component. To use it in the *Row* component, we can do as follows:

```
<tr class="my-custom-class" ...attributes>
```

We use the **…attributes** notation to denote that the attributes passed by the parent component have to be placed here. When the same attribute is defined in both the parent and the child components, we can decide how Ember should prioritize. Any attribute specified before the ...attributes syntax can be overwritten from the parent component. If you do not want an attribute to be updated from the parent, you can define the attribute after the ...attributes call. For example, if you do not want the id of the element to be specified by the parent, you can do this:

```
<tr class="my-custom-class" ...attributes id="client-{{@client.id}}">
```

By defining the id after the attributes, we specify that this attribute cannot be overridden from the parent component. However, you can see the **`class`** attribute being specified from both the parent and the child components. Class is a special case and Ember automatically combines the classes provided in the parent and the child component when rendering the element.

Templates

So far, we have seen how we can modularize the contents of our app by splitting the code into different templates and components. One advantage is that you can use any existing plain HTML code as it is in Ember templates. However, Ember is not required when you want to show simple and plain HTML in your UI. The power of Ember comes into play with the dynamicity. It allows you to add programmatic logic in the templates, just like you do in any language such as JavaScript or Python.

There are only a couple of restrictions in Ember templates:

- Only HTML tags that are valid inside the **`<body>`** tag are allowed. You cannot add tags like **`<meta>`** or **`<link>`** inside a template.
- The **`<script>`** tag is not allowed inside an Ember template.

Other than that, Ember provides you with a lot of options to customize and build a large-scale application in a swift, hassle-free manner.

Comments

Just like comments in HTML, you can add comments to your templates too. Adding comments in HTML format will render the underlying template code and then comment it out on screen, whereas commenting using the template syntax will prevent the process of rendering the code itself. Template comments can be used on big blocks of code instead of just a single line:

```
{{!--
    Multi line
    Ember template comment
--}}
```

The start of a comment block is denoted by `!--` and it ends with `--`, both present between double curly braces (**{{ }}**).

Inserting HTML Directly

In some cases, we might need to display the HTML content returned by the API directly on the screen. This can be for cases like a blog post where the content is loaded via the API. Using the double curly braces will display the HTML content in text format (the user will see the actual HTML syntax instead of the formatted version).

To display the formatted HTML content, you need to use triple curly braces instead of double curly braces.

```
{{{@customHTMLContent}}}
```

The triple curly braces indicate to Ember that the content is HTML and has to be directly inserted as HTML on the page. However, this feature has to be used with a word of caution because it is possible for people to insert malicious HTML/ JavaScript code inside your application through this feature.

It is recommended to not insert data inputted by a user directly through this method, as it can lead to a large number of security issues like XSS attacks. An XSS attack is a process in which an attacker inserts malicious executable scripts into our application, thus executing their code in a trusted manner inside our web application. It can be as simple as a JavaScript code that gets the access token stored in local storage and sends it to someone else, or it could be some script that sends an API request on your behalf through your application itself.

The double braces syntax in Ember handles these problems by default as part of the strong security provided by Ember. However, when it comes to the triple curly braces, Ember does not do that since the custom HTML rendered cannot be validated in that manner. Therefore, it is up to the developers of the application to maintain the sanity and ensure the content rendered within the triple curly braces is secure. The string provided inside the triple curly braces is not encoded or sanitized and is rendered as it is.

Let us say we have a variable in our **app/controllers/clients/index.js** named **dummyHtml**:

```
dummyHtml = '<p style="font-weight: bold">Test Html</p>';
```

Let us see the difference between using double curly braces and triple curly braces. When you render the variable as **{{this.dummyHtml}}** in the template, you will see the following on the screen:

```
<p style="font-weight: bold">Test Html</p>
```

When using the triple curly braces on this variable **`{{{this.dummyHtml}}}`**, you can see that the HTML is formatted and displayed in bold. The HTML is inserted as it is on the page and executed by the browser. That's the difference between double-curly braces and triple-curly braces. It is another example of the **Convention over Configuration** concept of Ember. A beginner developer will not expose the application to be vulnerable to malicious attacks, whereas an experienced developer who knows what they are doing can use the triple curly braces to render the custom HTML they require.

For some reason, if you wish to render custom HTML in your code using the double curly braces itself, Ember offers a solution for that too. There is a function named **`htmlSafe`** that marks an HTML element safe to render directly on screen. You can use it like this:

```
import { htmlSafe } from '@ember/template';


export default class ClientsIndexController extends Controller {
  …
  dummyHtml = '<p style="font-weight: bold">Test Html</p>';
  dummyHtmlSafe = htmlSafe(this.dummyHtml);
}
```

In the preceding example, we have two variables: one a simple HTML and the other marked safe using the **`htmlSafe`** method. When you render both these variables on screen, you can see the first one is plain HTML, whereas the second one is a formatted HTML with just using double curly braces. Please note that passing the HTML through **`htmlSafe`** does not modify the HTML. It only marks the content as safe for rendering and informs the framework that encoding need not be done for this string. It will cause issues if the HTML contains malicious content.

{{outlet}}

We can see the **`{{outlet}}`** tag inside every template that has a child route. In our project, you can see it in the **`app/templates/application.hbs`** and **`app/templates/clients.hbs`** files. The outlet tag specifies the location for rendering the child templates. The outlet tag in the application template is the location where all the route templates will be rendered. And the outlet tag in the **`app/templates/clients.hbs`** denotes the location where all the clients' module templates will be rendered. Since you can have custom HTML code at each level of the template hierarchy, the outlet tag can be placed as per your requirement in an appropriate position.

{{yield}}

When you look at the component template files, you will see a **{{yield}}** tag in all of them. The yield helper is used to transfer content from the parent into the child component and render the same. The difference between passing variables and using the yield block is that the yield block supports handlebar-generated HTML, whereas normal variables can just be dynamic data. When we call a particular child component, notice that we auto-close the HTML tag in the same line, indicating that there are no child HTML elements being passed to the component. However, if we pass any child element to the component, that will be rendered using the **{{yield}}** helper.

Calling a component with a child block will look like this:

```
<ClientsTable::Row @client={{client}} class="client-{{index}}">
  <p>Some Dynamic Element for client {{client.name}}</p>
</ClientsTable>
```

The **<p>** tag passed inside the component will be rendered in place of the yield helper. Similar to the outlet tag, we can position the yield tag anywhere in the component. A yield tag can be placed in multiple places of the component as well. The content provided will be rendered in all the places where the yield tag is specified.

Conditional Statements

In any programming language, conditionals are the first step in implementing programming logic. You can write these conditional statements in Ember templates as well. Here is how you can do it:

if

For beginners, **if** conditions are used to execute a piece of code, only when a particular condition is met. These are used in cases when you want to show some details only when they have a particular permission, or when you want some info to be shown based on information entered by the user, and so on.

You know that we define variables inside double curly braces (**{{ }}**) in the Ember template. For adding block statements like if, unless, each, you add a **#**

after the curly braces, indicating the start of a block. At the end of the block, we add a / after the curly braces followed by the name of the block. For example, this is what an if block looks like:

```
{{#if someCondition }}
    <p>If condition passed</p>
{{/if}}
```

As you can see, the block starts with a **#if**, and ends with a **/if.** In our case, in the client row component, let us say we want to display the email and phone number only if the client is active. We want to hide the contact details of inactive clients. We will wrap the two fields in the **clients-table/row** component with this **if** condition as follows:

```
<tr class="my-custom-class" ...attributes id="client-{{@client.id}}">
  <td>{{@client.name}}</td>
  <td>{{@client.company_name}}</td>
  {{#if @client.active}}
    <td>{{@client.phone_number}}</td>
    <td>{{@client.email}}</td>
  {{/if}}
  <td>
    <LinkTo @route="clients.view" @model="{{@client.id}}">View</LinkTo>
| Edit | Delete
  </td>
</tr>
```

You can visit http://localhost:4200/clients and see that the email and phone numbers are displayed for only one client. The contact details of the client with an active set to false do not show up. However, you can see that the phone number and email columns are not present for the inactive row, and hence the view and delete buttons have come to the third column near the company name. To prevent this, we will need to add either a replacement or an empty column element when the client is not active. That is when an else condition shows up.

else

An **else** block is a backup to the if block. It is executed when the conditions of **if** are failed to be met. An **else** block is always used in combination with an **if** block or each block. The general syntax of an else block is as follows:

```
{{#if someCondition}}
  <p>Condition is met</p>
{{else}}
  <p>Doesn't meet the condition
{{/if}}
```

Note that the else syntax doesn't contain a **#** prefix. It is because else cannot work independently and is only a part of the if block. In our case, we can add the fallback empty columns inside the else block like this:

```
{{#if @client.active}}
  <td>{{@client.phone_number}}</td>
  <td>{{@client.email}}</td>
{{else}}
  <td>-</td>
  <td>-</td>
{{/if}}
```

You can go back to the browser to see the edit and delete buttons back in their original place, with - in place of name and email. This is how the **`else`** block works.

else if

There can be cases where if/else will not suffice for your logic. We will need to check for multiple conditions and have a fallback else when none of these conditions are met. **`else if`** also does not work independently and is only part of an **`if`** block. A typical if block looks as follows:

```
{{#if someCondition}}
  <p>Condition 1 met</p>
{{else if secondCondition}}
  <p>Condition 2 met</p>
{{else if thirdCondition}}
  <p>Condition 3 met</p>
{{else}}
  <p>No Conditions met</p>
{{/if}}
```

As you can see, we can have multiple **else if** conditions in a single if block. There can be as many **else if** blocks as you want.

unless

An unless condition is the reverse block of **if**. It is the equivalent of **if not**. An unless can be used if you want to just write an else block when an if condition is not met. Like this:

```
{{#if someCondition}}
{{else}}
  <p>Condition not met</p>
{{/if}}
```

The **unless** equivalent of the preceding condition is as follows:

```
{{unless someCondition}}
  <p>Condition not met</p>
{{/unless}}
```

For our project, let us say we want to add an **Inactive** tag near the name of inactive users. We can do that as follows:

```
<td>
  {{@client.name}}
  {{#unless @client.active}}
    <span>(Inactive)</span>
  {{/unless}}
</td>
```

This is a sample of how you can use **unless** with Ember.

Inline if

We have seen how an **if** block can be created. That is useful when we want to show blocks of content or text based on conditions. Now, let us say we want to make a small change like adding an attribute or class to an element based on a condition. To say it in terms of our project, let us say we want to add a gray background to the rows of inactive clients. And let's say we are adding a class **bg-gray** to our **app.scss** file as follows:

```
.bg-gray {
    background: #eee;
}
```

This class has to be added to the row only if the client is not active. If this has to be done through the **`if`** or **`unless`** block, we will have to replicate the entire code for the row to just add an extra class. This is because:

- An ember block can only be used within another HTML block, not in the middle of an HTML tag (inside the class attribute). For example, the following code will not work:

  ```
  <tr class="my-custom-class {{#unless @client.active}}bg-gray{{/unless}}" ...attributes id="client-{{@client.id}}">
  ```

  The preceding sample will not work because the unless block is added inside the class attribute instead of within the tag.

- All tags inside a block should be closed inside the block itself. For example, just changing the **`<tr>`** definition as follows will not work:

  ```
  {{#if @client.active}}
    <tr class="my-custom-class" ...attributes id="client-{{@client.id}}">
  {{else}}
    <tr class="my-custom-class bg-gray" ...attributes id="client-{{@client.id}}">
  {{/if}}
  ```

  This example also will not work, as the **`<tr>`** tag is not closed in the if block. All tags have to be closed within a block.

This is where inline **`if`** comes to your rescue. It works for both **`if`** and **`unless`** clauses. You can prevent all this hassle by using a single piece of code:

```
{{if condition value}}
```

Note that there is no **#** prefix before if. It is because we are not creating a block here and the code is just inline. We can achieve what we want in a single line here:

```
<tr class="my-custom-class {{unless @client.active 'bg-gray'}}"
...attributes id="client-{{@client.id}}">
```

Refresh the page to see a gray background on the inactive row in the table.

The inline block supports an else part as well. If we want to differentiate active and inactive clients by adding a gray background to inactive clients and a green background to active clients, here's how you can do it:

```
{{if @client.active 'bg-green' 'bg-gray'}}
```

After these changes, the list page will look as follows:

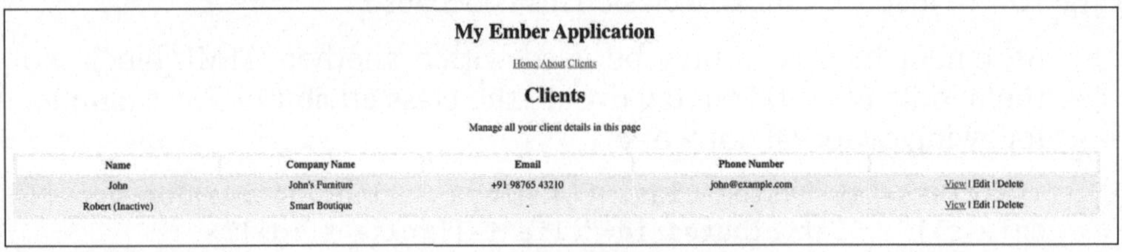

***Figure 4.2**: Clients list page status*

Loops

A loop is for handling repetitive code, which has to be executed multiple times. Whenever you want to display a list of elements in the UI, like the clients list we have in our application, you will have to call the same component multiple times. You can check our code in **app/components/clients-table/table.hbs**, we have the following code:

```
<ClientsTable::Row @client={{get @clientsList 0}} />
<ClientsTable::Row @client={{get @clientsList 1}} />
```

This is okay as long as we know that there are only two clients to be listed in the table. When there are 5 or 10 clients, it will lead to a lot of repetition. In real-time applications where the data is fetched from the backend, we cannot hardcode the component calls like this. So, we will need to use loops in those cases. Ember has an **each** block for handling loops. Let us modify the clients' table as follows:

```
{{#each @clientsList as |client|}}
    <ClientsTable::Row @client={{client}} />
{{/each}}
```

With this approach, it does not matter the number of records being rendered. From the syntax, you can see that we call the **#each** block with the **@clientsList** as the first parameter. We use the **as** keyword to specify the variable name assigned to each item when the code loops through it. The order of the loop is always the same as the order of the list that we iterate over.

index

When looping through the elements of a list, you might want to know the position of the element in the list for multiple purposes. You might want to show some differentiation between odd and even elements or have some specific conditions for the first element of the list. These are achieved by getting the index of the element in the list. index is passed as the second parameter after the **as** keyword. You can use the index as follows:

```
{{#each @clientsList as |client index|}}
  <ClientsTable::Row @client={{client}} class="client-{{index}}" />
{{/each}}
```

This will add the classes **client-0** and **client-1** to the respective rows. The index starts from 0.

Empty lists

Handling empty states is crucial to user experience, as we need to aesthetically inform them there are no records and provide options to take some action accordingly, like a link to create a new record. So, the code that handles empty state should be written separately and cannot be part of **each** loop.

For this purpose, you can use an else block inside **each** block to handle cases when the list we iterate over is empty. The code for handling empty lists will look like this:

```
{{#each @clientsList as |client index|}}
  <ClientsTable::Row @client={{client}} class="client-{{index}}" />
{{else}}
  <tr>
    <td colspan="5">No clients available</td>
  </tr>
{{/each}}
```

Iterating over Objects

The **each** helper is useful when iterating over a list of objects. However, when we want to iterate over an object containing key-value mappings, it will not be useful. For that purpose, ember has an **each-in** helper. It supports and iterates over a set of keys and values. For example, let's consider an object containing the details of clients and the project names associated with them:

```
{
    "John's Furniture": [{name: "Project 1", cost: 100000},
{name: "Project 2", cost: 20000}],
    "Smart Boutique": [{name: "Project 3", cost: 10000}, {name:
"Project 4", cost: 20000}]
}
```

Rendering this type of complex structure will not be possible with the **each** helper. Hence, we will use the **each-in** helper for this purpose. The code looks as given here:

```
{{#each-in @projects as |clientName projectList|}}
  <div class="client-projects">
    <h4>Client: {{clientName}}</h4>
    <ul>
      {{#each projectList as |project|}}
        <li>{{project.name}} ({{project.cost}})</li>
      {{/each}}
    </ul>
  </div>
{{/each-in}}
```

Note that the **each-in** helper provides two parameters instead of one, the first one being the key and the second one the value. You can also see that we can iterate over the list present inside the object using the nested **each** helper. The example provided will transform the object into the HTML as follows:

```
<div class="client-projects">
  <h4>John's Furniture</h4>
  <ul>
    <li>Project 1 (100000)</li>
    <li>Project 2 (20000)</li>
  </ul>
</div>
<div class="client-projects">
  <h4>Smart Boutique</h4>
```

```
    <ul>
      <li>Project 3 (10000)</li>
      <li>Project 4 (20000)</li>
    </ul>
  </div>
```

As you can see, we are able to transform a multi-level object into a beautiful piece of HTML code without redundancy in Ember. We can also add an else block to **`each-in`** for handling empty objects.

Helper Functions

Helper functions are reusable JavaScript functions that can be called from templates. The function can receive parameters, process them, and return the data to be rendered in the template. Compared to components, helpers are lightweight, and they only have a JavaScript component associated with them.

Built-in Helpers

We have already seen a few helpers in our previous chapters. They are:

- get
- if
- unless
- each
- each-in

These helpers are **Built-in** helpers that are available in your Ember app by default. Let us look at some of the other built-in helpers that are commonly used:

concat helper

The concat helper is used to combine multiple strings when displaying them in the template. For example, when we added a class to the **`ClientsTable::Row`** call, we used **`class="client-{{index}}"`** to define the class attribute. Using the concat helper, we can define the same in the following pattern: **`class="{{concat 'client-' index}}"`**. This helper accepts multiple parameters and combines all of them, rendering them in the template.

array helper

The array helper is used to generate a list of elements in the template. If the component that you are calling accepts only a list of elements, you can use the array helper to generate a list and send it to the component, as shown in the following example:

```
<ChildComponent @elements={{array "First Element" "Second Element"
"Third Element"}} />
```

In the child component, you can use the **@elements** parameter considering it to be a list.

hash helper

The array helper is used to generate a list from the template. Similarly, the hash helper is used to generate an object from the template. An example is as follows:

```
<ChildComponent @elements={{hash key1="First Element" key2="Second
Element" key3="Third Element"}} />
```

When sent like this, the keys can be directly accessed from the child component. This can be useful in cases where you need to pass dynamic parameters to a component. It can be accessed as **{{@elements.key1}}** in the child component.

let helper

When you feel the need to use a variable multiple times in a template, and referencing the variable in the structure as returned by the component is too long to be referenced multiple times, you can use the let helper to assign the value to a simple variable name that is bound only within the context of the let block.

```
{{#let @client.name as |name|}}
  <td>{{name}}</td>
{{/let}}
```

In this example, you can see we assigned a simpler variable name to **@client.name**, so that the reference is made simple and easy to understand within the template.

input and textarea helpers

Input and textarea helpers are the extensions of **<input>** and **<textarea>** tags in HTML. The Ember helper supports the two-way binding of the variables, making the changes instantly available in the component/controllers. To demonstrate this, let us add the following to the client view component:

```
{{input value=@model.name}}
```

We are adding an option for the user to edit the name of the client using the input helper. When you visit http://localhost:4200/clients/1, you can see the client's name in both the input box and the existing client details table. When you change the value of the input box, you can see it immediately being reflected in the table.

Creating a Custom Helper

Ember offers a wide variety of built-in helpers to be used by us. On top of that, we will definitely encounter use cases that require us to build custom helpers across the application. Starting from Ember 4.5, Ember has two types of custom helpers:

- Local helpers
- Global helpers

Local Helpers

Starting from Ember 4.5, Ember allows us to use normal JavaScript functions as Ember helpers. This gives developers the ease of defining functions in each component and use them within the component. For example, a simple function that returns a display name of the client as their name and email combined. Let's create a function called displayName in our **`app/components/client-table/row.js`**. We can generate this component class if it does not exist.

```
getDisplayName = (client) => {
  return `${client.name} <${client.email}>`;
}
```

This simple function we have defined in the component can be directly used in the template. Let's replace the name column in the list with the following content:

```
{{this.getDisplayName @client}}
```

The name column will be displayed as the name and the email of the client. This **`getDisplayName`** function is valid only within the **`clients-table/row`** component and cannot be used from outside it. However, this function can be called as many times as you want from the template.

Global Helpers

The other type of helper is the global helper, which is defined separately and can be called anywhere from the application. Let's move the **`getDisplayName`** to be a global helper. You can generate a helper with the following command:

```
ember generate helper get-display-name
```

Helpers are generated inside the **`app/helpers`** folder, and you can now see an **`app/helpers/get-display-name.js`** file for this newly created helper. We can add the same logic to the helper file:

```
export default function getDisplayName(client) {
  return `${client.name} <${client.email}>`;
};
```

The definition in the template will have to be changed as follows, since we are calling a global helper now. You can update the helper call as follows:

```
{{get-display-name @client}}
```

You can visit http://localhost:4200/clients and see that the content remains unchanged. We have simply moved the content from a local helper function to a global helper, making the code reusable throughout the application.

Nested Helpers

Helpers are nestable, meaning that you can call helpers from within other helpers, and the output of the inner helper will be passed as input to the outer helper. For example, we can call the get helper inside concat helper to combine different keys from an object:

```
{{concat (get @client 'name') (get @client 'email')}}
```

Through this, we can nest any number of helpers from one within the other from the template. Helpers can be used anywhere in place of a hard-coded normal value, and Ember will auto-resolve the value of the helper before proceeding to the next step.

Named Arguments

For people who know Python, there is an option to dynamically pass named parameters to a function. They are called keyword arguments, where the parameters are not predefined and can be passed by the calling function as and how they require. Ember helpers also provide such a feature in the form of **Named Arguments**.

Let's say we want to write a helper function that calculates the area of an object. Depending upon the type of the object, the parameters passed will vary, and the formula will vary. We can define it through Ember helpers as follows:

```
export default function calculateArea(objectType, options) {
  if (objectType === 'square') {
    return options.side ** 2;
  } else if (objectType == 'rectangle') {
    return options.length * options.width;
  }
}
```

The calculations change based on the type of the object, and the number of parameters required are also different. This is where the named arguments help us. Receiving the named options and passing them through a single *options* object gives us the power of dynamicity. Now we can call this helper in the following ways:

```
{{calculate-area 'square' side=5}}
{{calculate-area 'rectangle' length=10 width=20}}
```

We've called the same helper but with different parameters each time. This helper can support any number of parameters for calculating areas with different formulae. This serves two purposes:

- From the template perspective, the code is clean and easy to identify what parameters are being passed. **`{{calculate-area 'rectangle' length=10 width=20}}`** is easy to read and understand rather than just **`{{calculate-area 'rectangle' 10 20}}`**
- From the helper point of view, it gives the function the power of dynamicity. Without this, we might have to create different functions for each area type or keep listing so many parameters that it becomes very confusing in the end and the code becomes unreadable.

ember-truth-helpers

By default, you cannot compare two values within an Ember if helper. You can only specify a variable in the helper and Ember decides based on the boolean value of the specified variable. If we need to compare two variables, we will have to write a function that does the comparison and returns the boolean value and use that function inside the Ember template. Ember-truth-helpers is an addon that can be used to overcome this issue. It provides different helpers that can compare two or more variables by using the nested helpers feature of Ember. With this helper, if we want to compare two numbers, we can do it like this:

```
{{#if (gt number1 number2)}}
  {{number1}} is greater than {{number2}}
{{else}}
  {{number2}} is less than or equal to {{number2}}
{{/if}}
```

This operation is possible because of the **gt** helper provided by the ember-truth-helpers addon.

Component State and Actions

A Component behaves like a controller where the state of the object is maintained across the lifecycle of the component. The state variables can be initialized in the component with any default value. You can simply define a variable in the component and use it in the template of the component. Let's create a simple component that maintains a variable to keep track of the number of clicks made to a button in that component. Let's create the component **click-tracker** like this:

```
   ember generate component click-tracker
ember generate component-class click-tracker
```

Tracked Properties

Inside the component, let's create a simple variable called **count**. This will be the state variable that we will display in the template.

```
import { tracked } from '@glimmer/tracking';


export default class ClickTrackerComponent extends Component {
    @tracked count = 0
}
```

The **@tracked** notation identifies that the value of the variable will be changed and hence Ember re-renders the component whenever the value of *count* changes. We can use the variable in the template file of the component by adding the following line to **app/components/click-tracker.hbs**:

```
<p class="text-center">Count: {{this.count}}</p>
```

Let us embed the component inside our home page at **app/templates/index.js**:

```
<ClickTracker />
```

Once added, you can see **Count: 0** on your home page by visiting http://localhost:4200. Now, the default variable set by us in the component (0) is visible on the screen. These values can be updated via actions.

Actions

Actions are the Ember version of event handlers. You can attach an action to any HTML element and the action will be triggered by clicking the element. The actions are usually used to either update variables in the state, make API calls and update models, or show alerts to the user.

An action can be defined using the **@action** decorator. Let us create an action to increment the count variable:

```
import Component from '@glimmer/component';
import { tracked } from '@glimmer/tracking';
import { action } from '@ember/object';

export default class ClickTrackerComponent extends Component {
    @tracked count = 0

    @action
    increaseCount() {
        this.count += 1;
    }
}
```

Next, we need to create a button in our template that calls this action by clicking the button. Attaching an action to a HTML element is simple:

```
<div class="text-center">
    <button {{on "click" this.increaseCount}}>Click</button>
</div>
```

After adding this line, you can go to the index page to see the button and the count automatically increases every time you click on the button. Ember listens for changes to the tracked variable and re-renders the component every time it changes. In order to test the differences between a normal variable and a tracked variable, you can remove the **@tracked** notation in the variable definition and just set it to **count = 0**. After doing that, you can see that clicking the button has no effect. You can even add a **console.log** statement to the action to ensure the action is being called, but there is no change in the screen because the variable is not being tracked by Ember.

Actions with Params

You can also pass parameters to your actions. For example, instead of incrementing the count by just 1, we might want to increase the count by a different number for another button. Let's create a second button that increments the count by 2 on every click. The action will also be updated to receive the count as a parameter and increment by the count instead of a hardcoded 1. The updated action will look like this:

```
@action
increaseCount(increaseBy) {
    this.count += increaseBy;
}
```

And let's update the buttons to pass the increaseBy as a parameter to the action:

```
<button {{on "click" (fn this.increaseCount 1)}}>Click</button>
<button {{on "click" (fn this.increaseCount 2)}}>Double Click</button>
```

We are able to pass parameters to an action through the **fn** helper. Through this method, we can pass as many parameters to the action as required.

Computed Values

Sometimes in the application, there will be cases where a value is not directly entered by a user, but it is calculated based on other values present on the page. To give you a few examples:

- The name of a person is dependent on their first name and last name values
- When creating an order/invoice, the total amount is not directly entered by the user, but it depends on the subtotals and tax amount for the order

For these values, there are two ways to handle it:

1. Create a second variable that stores the computed value, and we update that variable when one of the dependent variables changes.
2. Create a function that returns the computed value, calculating the value based on the current state of the dependent values.

In the first approach, manually handling the second variable and updating its value whenever the dependents are updated is not an easy task. Every time we introduce a new way in which the dependent values are changed, we will need to keep track and update the computed property. This leaves a lot of space for bugs, especially when the number of computed variables increases to a large number, making it a nightmare to manage all of them.

Earlier, Ember was using a variant of the first approach to render computed variables in the template. Ember has a "**computed**" helper that will listen for changes in a list of dependencies and will update the value of the computed property upon a change in dependencies. The resulting computed property can be used in the template, and it will always display the updated value. For example, if we need to display the count multiplied by 2 in our component, earlier notation of using computed variables was something like this:

```
import { computed } from '@ember/object';


multipliedByTwo = computed('count', function() {
      return this.count * 2;
}
```

This computed function listens for changes to the *count* variable and every time it changes, the function is executed and the value of **multipliedByTwo** is updated in the component state. This method has its own issues as listening to changes in a list or an object inside a list was not possible by default and special code had to be written to make that possible. To fix those issues, Ember now uses functions to return computed values. We can create a function named **countDouble** for our use case:

```
get multipliedCount() {
    return this.count * 2;
}
```

The **multipliedCount** function here takes the current count and multiples it by two. This is performed whenever the component is re-rendered, and since Ember is already tracking the count variable to re-render the component on change, the function also recalculates the value to display the updated value on screen.

Combining Actions with Arguments

In the preceding cases, we did not consider the arguments passed by the parent component/template when calling this component. We can use the arguments directly inside the actions/functions using **this.args** notation. If we want the count to be multiplied by some other number than 2, we can pass the number as an argument like this:

```
<ClickTracker @multiplier=4 />
```

And we can use the same in the multipliedCount function as follows:

```
get multipliedCount() {
    return this.count * this.args.mulitplier;
}
```

Here, you can see that using the **this.args** notation, we are able to access the arguments passed from the parent component, and the values are computed accordingly and displayed on the screen.

This is how we introduce dynamicity by directly computing values from within the component or using arguments that are passed from the parent component.

Ember Bootstrap

So far, the custom CSS we have done is to a small extent, and we have not concentrated much on making the application look aesthetically pleasing. However, that is one of the main concerns for a production application, since we want the user to have a pleasant experience when using our **application/product**. To achieve this, we will need to address many aspects, such as:

- Making the design responsive to look good on smaller devices like tablets or mobile phones
- Follow certain predefined specifications on the spacing between objects, and use color combinations that complement each other to prevent odd-looking pages

Bootstrap is a framework that provides a package of all these basic CSS definitions that are required to build a responsive design, with in-built components to reduce the effort required to develop a basic webpage that follows some default styling conventions. It was initially developed by a small team from Twitter and is currently maintained by the founding team along with a large number of independent contributors.

Ember Bootstrap is an addon that integrates the Bootstrap framework with the power of Ember components. You can install it easily with the following command:

```
ember instance ember-bootstrap
```

Once installed, Bootstrap is added to your project with its default blueprint. If you are using a specific preprocessor and want to generate a Bootstrap with that preprocessor, you can use the following blueprint command:

```
ember generate ember-bootstrap --preprocessor=sass --bootstrap-version=5
```

We are generating the blueprint to use the sass preprocessor that we are already using in our project and also specifying the bootstrap version as 5. The default blueprint installs Bootstrap version 4. Once this is done, you can open our *app/styles/app.scss* file to see if there is an import statement at the end that loads the Bootstrap.css file. Any CSS you write below that line will supersede the default Bootstrap code. Any CSS defined above the import statement will have the possibility to be overwritten by the default Bootstrap code.

Immediately after installing, you can restart the Ember server and reload the page to see the changes. You can see the updated fonts for our text and the styling of the buttons. You can visit http://localhost:4200/clients to see the updated design of the table as well. These designs look a lot neater and it is easily portable to mobile and tablets as well.

Built-in Components

Ember Bootstrap has a lot of Ember Components that wrap existing Bootstrap classes to provide a native experience for Ember applications. Let us look at a few of them:

Buttons

Bootstrap provides neat buttons with different varieties of backgrounds. We can use the `<BsButton>` component to style your buttons in accordance with

Bootstrap while enjoying the customizations provided by Ember. Let's update our click buttons to use Bootstrap:

```
    <BsButton @type="primary" @onClick={{(fn this.increaseCount
1)}}>Click</BsButton>
    <BsButton @type="success" @onClick={{(fn this.increaseCount
2)}}>Double Click</BsButton>
```

You can see that we've used two types of buttons: one is primary and the other is success. We've also integrated the **onClick** event into the button. You can refresh the page to see the colorful buttons that look a lot neater. Ember Bootstrap buttons support the following types:

- primary
- secondary
- success
- danger
- warning
- info
- light
- dark

Outlined

The button component supports an *outline* attribute, which can be used to set just the outline and the text color of the button instead of the background. You can try the following code:

```
<BsButton @type="primary" @outline={{true}} @onClick={{(fn this.
increaseCount 1)}}>Click</BsButton>
```

Disabled

Buttons can be disabled by passing the **@disabled** parameter. Here is an example:

```
<BsButton @disabled={{true}}>Disabled Button</BsButton>
```

Promise Support

The Ember Bootstrap Button component can handle Promises. We can set the button text for the default state, when data is being loaded via a promise or when the Promise is completed. This requires the **onClick** event to return a Promise, and the button text can be modified based on the status of the returned Promise object.

```
<BsButton
    @defaultText="Submit"
    @pendingText="Submitting information…"
    @fulfilledText="Data submitted successfully!!!"
    @onClick={{this.onClickAction}}>
      Submit
</BsButton>
```

Navigation

Bootstrap provides a mobile, responsive way to handle navigation buttons. Let us modify our current simple navigation setup to use Bootstrap components. The three links - Home, About, and Clients - will be modified in the following code:

```
<BsNav
  @type="pills"
  @justified={{false}}
  @stacked={{false}}
  @fill={{false}} as |nav|
>
  <nav.item>
    <nav.link-to @route="index">Home</nav.link-to>
  </nav.item>
  <nav.item>
    <nav.link-to @route="about">About</nav.link-to>
  </nav.item>
  <nav.item>
    <nav.link-to @route="clients.index" @query={{hash sort-
By="name"}}>Clients</nav.link-to>
  </nav.item>
</BsNav>
```

You can see that Ember Bootstrap itself provides a version of link-to that replaces the default LinkTo tag. Upon making this change, we can see that the navbar has been moved to the left side of the screen. We can bring the navbar to use the entire width of the screen by setting the **`@justified`** attribute in the **`BsNav`** component to true. Also, by setting the **`BsNav`** type to **`tabs`**, you can see a different UI for the nav buttons. The navbar can also contain dropdowns, which hold multiple links inside them. Here is an example:

```
<nav.dropdown as |dd|>
  <dd.toggle>Dropdown <span class="caret"></span></dd.toggle>
  <dd.menu as |ddm|>
    <ddm.item><ddm.linkTo @route="index">Index</ddm.linkTo></ddm.
item>
    <ddm.item><ddm.linkTo @route="about">About</ddm.linkTo></ddm.
item>
  </dd.menu>
</nav.dropdown>
```

Adding this piece of code within the **BsNav** tag will create a dropdown with two links - to the index and about pages.

Form

Ember Bootstrap provides simple and easy ways to build forms that can align easily in all kinds of devices. Let us create a simple Login route that has a form containing email and password fields:

```
ember generate route login
```

Inside the login route, let us add the form with Email and Password fields, with a submit button. Let us add the following content to the **login.hbs** file:

```
<div class="w-50 mx-auto mt-5">
  <h4 class="text-center">Login</h4>
  <BsForm @formLayout="vertical" @model={{this}} @onSubmit={{this.submit}}
as |form|>
    <form.element @controlType="email" @label="Email" @property="email"
as |element|>
      <element.control placeholder="Email" required />
    </form.element>
    <form.element @controlType="password" @label="Password" @property="-
password" @helpText="Minimum 8 characters, one special character" as
|element|>
      <element.control placeholder="Password" required />
    </form.element>
    <form.submitButton>Submit</form.submitButton>
```

```
  </BsForm>
</div>
```

From this example, you can see that we have created a div that has the following default Bootstrap classes, used for positioning a **`div`**:

- **`w-50`**: This class sets the width of the **`div`** to 50%, which means that the div will occupy only 50% of the screen's width
- **`mx-auto`**: This sets the x margin of the **`div`** to auto, leaving equal space on both the left side and the right side of the **`div`**. This will center the form on-screen since the width of the form is already specified as 50% of the screen width.
- **`mt-5`**: mt is the short form for margin-top. Bootstrap provides classes for 5 levels of spacing for both margin and padding, which can be set like m-1, m-2, m3, p-1, p-2, p-3. The actual spacing depends on the *spacer* CSS variable specified by Bootstrap, which is 1rem by default. Based on the *spacer* value, the spacing class multiplies the following values:
    - 1 - **`$spacer`** * 0.25
    - 2 - **`$spacer`** * 0.5
    - 3 - **`$spacer`** * 1
    - 4 - **`$spacer`** * 1.5
    - 5 - **`$spacer`** * 3

The BsForm component itself has certain interesting parameters:

- **`formLayout`**: This attribute defines how the label and the input box are positioned in the form. The following are the supported values:
    - **`vertical`**: This means the input box is placed below the label.
    - **`horizontal`**: The label and input boxes are placed next to each other, like table columns.
    - **`Inline`**: There is no separate space for the label here. It is mentioned as part of the placeholder in the input box.
- **`model`**: This attribute provides the data values. You can either provide an object defined in the component/passed from the parent or if the variables are individually defined in the current component itself, you can use **`{{this}}`** to notify that the variables required are defined in the current component itself. Based on the object passed as a model, Bootstrap matches the **`property`** value provided for each field to the keys in the object to get the default data and store the updated values.
- **`onSubmit`**: The function to be called when the submit button is clicked.

You can also see that the individual fields of the form are specified using the **form.element** component, which supports attributes like the type of the field, name of the field, label, placeholder, and so on. You can also see that there is a helpText parameter, which displays a description for the field below the text box in a neat manner. The form must look like this when you visit http://localhost:4200/login:

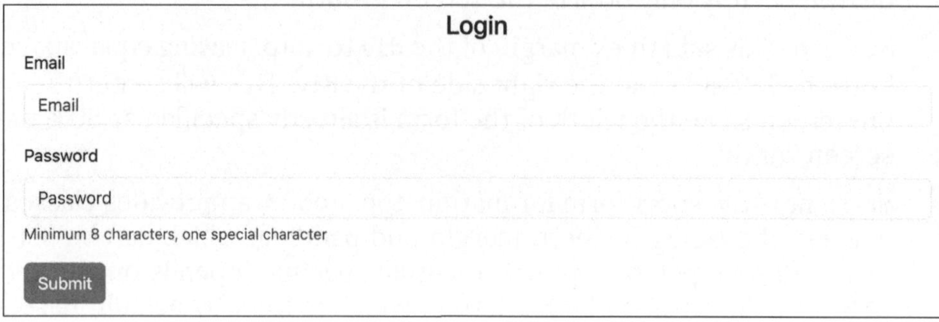

***Figure 4.3**: Login Form*

With just a few lines of code and no CSS, we have designed a pretty form. This is the power of Bootstrap in your application. We will look at how we can add validations to this form later.

Tooltip

Tooltips are used to show some information to the user when they hover over a particular element. Usually, tooltips are used on disabled elements to display the reason why they are disabled, or show labels for a particular icon to inform what it does, and so on.

Ember Bootstrap provides an inbuilt **tooltip** component that you can use:

```
<button class="btn">
  <BsTooltip @title="Title for my Tooltip" />
</button
```

For simple tooltips, you can just pass the **@title** parameter to the component. If you want to display custom HTML inside the **tooltip**, you can pass them as a child to the component:

```
<button class="btn">
  <BsTooltip>
    This is a custom HTML inside the tooltip
```

```
    </BsTooltip>
  </button
```

Carousel

Carousels can be used to show a series of images or slides that automatically loop around, hence making the page interactive and displaying content dynamically to the user. Here is how you can invoke the **BsCarousel** component in your template:

```
<BsCarousel as |carousel| >
  <carousel.slide>
    Carousel Slide 1
  </carousel.slide>
  <carousel.slide>
    Carousel Slide 2
  </carousel.slide>
  <carousel.slide>
    Carousel Slide 3
  </carousel.slide>
</BsCarousel>
```

With these simple lines of code, you can instantly integrate a carousel into your webpage. By default, the slides autoplay one after the other every 5 seconds. You can configure the autoplay mechanism and interval through component properties.

Conclusion

In this chapter, you became familiar with Components – the core building block of an Ember application. We went through what Components are, how you can create one, make them dynamic by passing different parameters to the component, pass dynamic HTML children to the component, and so on. We then got to know how to add dynamicity to the templates using conditionals like if-else, loops, and blocks. Then, we studied in detail about Helpers, and how you can reuse even the smallest of logics by generating dynamic helpers inside your app. We saw how Components maintain a default state with variables that can be updated dynamically using actions. We can combine actions with Tracked Properties to compute values that are dependent on other variables in our system.

At the end, we discussed styling and using Ember Bootstrap, an addon that is an Ember wrapper around the Twitter Bootstrap library. We went through the different built-in components of Ember Bootstrap and how easily you can implement basic components that provide aesthetic elements on the screen. In the next chapter, we will look at communicating with the backend API using Ember Data. API communication will fulfill the application by persisting data and making it dynamic for the user to have a real-time experience. We will also learn how to build services in Ember in the next chapter.

Points to Remember

- Components are the basic building blocks of an Ember application
- It is optimal to split the application into multiple reusable components, thus preventing redundancy in the project.
- Components can support multiple parameters
- You can pass functions and variables to Components
- Templates support dynamic content with conditionals, loops, and blocks
- Helpers are functions that can be used anywhere in templates.
- You can create local and global helpers that can be used across the application
- Component actions can be used to perform API calls or update the Component state
- Tracked properties provide two-way binding, thus updating variable changes immediately on the screen
- Ember Bootstrap is a wrapper around Twitter Bootstrap with custom Ember Components for different Bootstrap components.

Multiple Choice Questions

1. What is the reusable part of an Ember application that can be called from different routes?
   a. Router
   b. Controller
   c. Component
   d. None of the above

2. Which of the following characters is used to denote custom attributes passed to a component?
    a. ?
    b. _
    c. @
    d. !
3. Using triple curly braces(`{{{ }}}`) can be used to insert any HTML into the template.
    a. True
    b. False
4. What do you call a function in Ember that can be reused from templates across the application?
    a. Helpers
    b. Service
    c. Mixin
    d. None of the above
5. Which of the following can be used to update Component state variables?
    a. Tracked properties
    b. Actions
    c. Params
    d. Helpers
6. What are the different types of helpers?
    a. Local
    b. Global
    c. Both a and b
    d. None of the above

7. Which of the following is not a built-in helper?
   a. get
   b. array
   c. list
   d. hash

Answers

1. c
2. c
3. a
4. a
5. b
6. c
7. c

Questions

1. How do you generate a component class?
2. What is the difference between output and yield?
3. What are computed values and how can they be tracked?
4. How do you handle the empty state of a loop?
5. What are global and local helpers?

Key Terms

- **Component:** A reusable block of an Ember application
- **Helper:** A function that can be called from templates
- **Action:** A function that can be bound to events, used to update the state or make API calls
- **Named Arguments:** Dynamic set of arguments that can be passed to helpers

Chapter 5
Ember Data and Services

Introduction

In this chapter, we will discuss Ember Models and how they can connect with backend APIs to persist and store data. We will learn about different interactions with the API, such as creating, updating, retrieving, filtering, and deleting records. We will also explore handling relationships, including foreign keys, many-to-many fields, and more.

Next, you will learn about handling the metadata returned by the API and using the information to paginate records or display details, such as the total count in the template. We will also understand how to use the default Ember data library functions to customize the requests sent to the API and modify the URLs associated with the model using Adapters and Serializers. At the end of the chapter, we will learn about Services and the vital role they play in an Ember Application.

Structure

In this chapter, we will discuss the following topics:

- Introduction to Ember Data
- Setting up Ember Data
- Ember Models
- Setting up a Backend API
- Ways to Make API Requests from Ember
- Ember Store

- Read and Filter Records
- Create, Update, and Delete Records
- Handle Relationships in Models
- Adapters
- Serializers
- Ember Services

Introduction to Ember Data

Ember is a frontend application framework, which concentrates on providing a pleasant user interface that helps users to read and update data using their browsers. However, for storing information, Ember has to contact a third-party backend via API to persist and retrieve data. Ember Data comes into play for this purpose.

It takes care of interfacing with the backend and converting and serving the data in the Ember way, irrespective of the type of the backend. It is the official data persistence library for Ember and is installed, by default, in all new Ember applications created through the Ember CLI. Just like the other modules of Ember, Ember Data also provides a default set of functionalities as follows:

- Create a **Model** that is an object-based representation of the underlying data.
- Interface with the API to create, read, and update data.
- Takes care of authenticating each request by sending the auth token in the header.
- Maps the API response and provides data in the form of a **Model Object**.
- Stores a local copy of the fetched data to prevent multiple API calls and fetch from the API only when required.
- Provides a seamless JavaScript integration, making the application-agnostic of the type of backend used.
- Allows configuring different Adapters to connect with different types of Backend APIs.

Ember Models

Models are the object representation of the data sent and received via APIs. If you want the user to see anything you want when they close our application and open it again, it is recommended that the data be loaded via a Model. A model class will contain a list of attributes associated with the model, along with the type of data associated with each attribute. Specifying the type of attribute helps Ember serialize and deserialize data when communicating with the API. For example, when you specify a **`date`** attribute, you can associate a JavaScript **`Date`** object to that field, and Ember will take care of sending the data in the form of an ISO string to the API. Similarly, the data returned by the API will also be serialized into a **`Date`** object for convenient use within the JavaScript code. This is one of the advantages of using Ember Data, as this default serialization and customizing fields are not part of other third-party API libraries.

Here is the default list of attribute types supported by Ember:

- string
- number
- boolean
- date

Associating a type is not mandatory for an attribute. If we do not specify any type for an attribute, Ember Data will not do any custom processing/serializing on that data. Let us create a model for handling the clients list we have in our application. A Model can be created using the following command:

```
ember generate model client
```

Note that the model name is client (singular) and not plural. It is conventional to name the model according to the data stored in a single object. Here, we store the data of a single client in a record, so the model is named as **`client`** and not **clients**. However, you may note that we always use the plural version in route names and URLs.

With the generation of the model, you can see a new file created at **`app/models/client.js`**. Inside the file, you can specify the attributes of the model using the **`attr`** notation. Here is what our client model will look like:

```
import Model, { attr } from '@ember-data/model';


export default class ClientModel extends Model {
    @attr('string') name;
    @attr('string') company_name;
    @attr('string') email;
    @attr('string') phone_number;
    @attr('boolean') active;
}
```

You can see from the preceding example that we use the **`attr`** notation to denote attributes that will be returned from the API. Only fields that are specified here will be available for use inside the application. Any extra data sent by the API will be ignored by Ember Data.

Default Values

When defining attributes, you can specify a default value to it, which will be used when there is no data sent by the API for that attribute or when you initialize a new object from within the application. Let us create a new field called **`date`,** which you want to be initialized as the current date always. This field does not need to be sent in the API response, you can just set a default value for all objects as follows:

```
@attr('date', {
    defaultValue() { return new Date(); }
}) date
```

Here, we have specified a new field called **`date`**. Whenever a new client object is initialized, Ember Data checks if there is a value for the date provided either by the API or the creating function. If there is no value provided, the **`defaultValue`** function is executed and the response of that function is assigned to that particular field of the object.

getter functions

Most of the time, the data sent in the API cannot be used as it is in the frontend, as it will need many tweaks and changes before presenting it how the user wishes to see the data. For example, the API might have **`first_name`** and **`last_name`** as fields in the Database, but you might need to show both names together or combine any two fields or do some calculation depending on more than one field. Performing these changes/calculations in the backend can lead to the following issues:

- More processing in the backend, which means more bottleneck on the server.
- More redundant data sent from the backend increases the response payload size, which will increase the API load time. It will also be a bad experience for users with slow internet connections.

When using other third-party API libraries, these modifications either need to be applied in every place where an API call is made, or we have to create individual util functions to do these transformations. This can become messy, as you do not always have a context of what each function does, and maintaining many of them is not an easy process.

Enter Ember Data's **getter** functions. These are custom functions you create in a model, which can be accessed like any other variable from the template. For example, let us create a **displayTag** property for our client model, which will contain the name and email of the client. We can add this function to our model as follows:

```
get displayTag() {
    return `${this.name} <${this.email}>`;
};
```

Now, this function will be automatically available for all users from now on, and need not be calculated separately. We can replace the helper we created in the **ClientRow** component with this function. You can see that the function is well-placed inside the client model, so we always know the purpose of this function. From a code maintenance point of view, any developer can clearly identify where this function will exist, even when looking at the project for the first time.

Transforms

We have discussed getter functions and how they can be used to create additional fields that compute values from other fields returned by the API. However, there will be cases where the data from the API will have to be transformed to a different format before being consumed in the frontend. The same data will have to be reformatted before being sent back to the API. For example, a **gender** field may be sending just single-letter references like M, F, or O from the API. The user will not be able to understand what M, F, or O means, so we need to show the expanded version, such as Male, Female, or Other. When sending the request back to the API, we should again send only the single-letter text instead of the full value. This formatting should happen in as many places as we want to use the **gender** field in the application.

Transforms in Models can be used for this specific purpose. You can create a new transform using the following command:

```
ember generate transform gender
```

On running this command, you can see a new folder called **transforms** in your project folder, with the **gender** transform created inside it. If you open the **app/transforms/gender.js** file, you will find two functions inside:

- **serialize**: Serialization is the process of converting the data to the format required by the API. This function is called when you save some data through the store.
- **deserialize**: Deserialization is the process of formatting the data after fetching the base data from the API. This function will be called after the data is fetched from the API, before showing the data to the user.

For our use case, the transform will look as follows:

```
const GENDER_MAPPINGS = {
    'M': 'Male',
    'F': 'Female',
    'O': 'Other'
}

export default class GenderTransform {
  deserialize(serialized) {
    return GENDER_MAPPINGS[serialized];
  }

  serialize(deserialized) {
    var gender = null;
    Object.keys(GENDER_MAPPINGS).map((gndr) => {
        if (GENDER_MAPPINGS[gndr] === deserialized)
            gender = gndr;
    });
    return gender;
  }

}
```

Now that we have configured the transform, using it in the model is very easy. Just like the default data types we set for an attribute, you can use any transform name and associate it with an attribute. Let's add the following line to the client model:

```
@attr('gender') gender;
```

As you can see from the preceding statement, it is very simple to create a new transform and pass it as a data type of a model field.

Setting Up a Backend API

There are different languages like JavaScript, Python, Ruby, and JAVA for setting up backend applications that can be connected to from the frontend via HTTP APIs. Since building a backend application is not within the scope of this book, we will use a way that Ember offers to mock API requests to handle and manage data.

We will use **`Ember CLI Mirage`**, an addon that runs a server to mock the responses of API requests from the Ember application. **`Mirage`** is a generic JavaScript library, which was initially developed with the intention to mock backend APIs so that frontend developers do not need to rely on the backend APIs to build features until they are ready to integrate and test.

To give you an overview of how Mirage works, it is a piece of code that runs on the browser and uses a low-level HTTP interception library called **`Pretender.js`** to intercept AJAX requests made by the Ember application. Mirage uses a custom-built piece of code to provide a mock response that, according to the Ember application, comes from the backend.

This not only provides a transparent way for developers to mock and test the APIs from the frontend but also gives an independent way of developing the Ember application without waiting for the actual APIs to be provided by the backend application. Mirage also provides a mock database to store and retrieve data, simulating the storage and retrieval of data.

Installation

Ember CLI Mirage can be installed just like any other Ember addon. You can run the following command to add Mirage to your project:

```
ember install ember-cli-mirage
```

Once installed, you can see a new folder named **`Mirage`** inside your project. This is where we will add code related to our mock APIs.

Structure of Ember CLI Mirage

Let us look at the structure of Mirage and how it works. Mirage uses a similar structure as other backend frameworks, which makes it easier to mock the functionalities of a backend server. Here are the components of Ember CLI Mirage:

- **Routes**: Just like Ember, routes provide a way for external applications to interface with the Mirage application. Routes handle HTTP requests based on the URL provided.
- **Model**: A Model is a class-based representation of the API data.
- **Database**: A mock database for persisting data.
- **Fixtures**: Fixtures are predefined static data to be populated in the database when the application is loaded.
- **Factories**: Factories are a dynamic way to populate data into the database, which is executed when the application is loaded.
- **Serializers**: Data stored in the database will sometimes be different from the data sent in the API. Serializers can be used to make these transformations or add additional information before sending the object to the frontend.

Creating Routes

Creating routes in Mirage is quite simple. When you open the **`mirage/config.js`** file, you will find a predefined **`routes`** function where all the API routes have to be defined. For our use case, we can define the **`clients`** route to return the list of clients. The **`routes()`** function will look as follows:

```
function routes() {

  this.get('/clients', {} => {
    return {
      data: [
        {
          id: 1,
          name: 'John',
          company_name: "John's Furniture",
          email: 'john@example.com',
          phone_number: '+91 98765 43210',
          active: true,
        },
        {
```

```
                id: 2,
                name: 'Robert',
                company_name: 'Smart Boutique',
                email: 'robert@example.com',
                phone_number: '+91 98764 53210',
                active: false,
            },
        ]
    }
  });
}
```

The routes function looks pretty simple. We define a route called **`clients`**, which returns a hard-coded object containing the two clients. Similar to this, we can define routes to return a specific client when accessed via the ID, just like the backend API. However, since we have hard-coded the data in the list endpoint, we will have to redundantly copy-paste the code to return the specific object based on the ID in the request.

In order to do this efficiently, we need to create a model for the clients object and dynamically store and retrieve the data. Doing so will not only prevent redundancy but also help us dynamically test different cases to make sure that the frontend application is compatible to handle all kinds of use cases.

Models and Database

By default, Mirage provides an in-memory database to store and retrieve information. The data is lost when the application is restarted, but you can use factories and fixtures to create default data when the application loads.

Similar to Ember, you can create multiple models and specify fields and their type for each model. However, since we have already created a model using Ember Data in our application, Mirage will automatically use the model from Ember Data, and we need not create them separately in our Mirage models folder. However, we can directly use them inside the route by updating our routes function as follows:

```
this.get('/clients', (schema, request) => {
    return schema.clients.all();
});
```

This single line will return all the client objects present in the database when an API call is made to the **/clients** API endpoint. Similarly, we can define a route that returns the specific client based on the ID in the URL:

```
this.get('/clients/:id', (schema, request) => {
  return schema.clients.find(request.params.id);
});
```

By doing this, we need not hard-code the data to be returned based on the ID specified in the URL. We have created routes that render data, but we have not populated any data to be rendered. So, let us create a fixture that populates the two records we have already displayed. You can generate a fixture with the following command:

```
ember generate mirage-fixture clients
```

Once created, you can see a new file named **mirage/fixtures/clients.js**. We can add the following code to the fixture file:

```
export default [
      {
        id: 1,
        name: 'John',
        company_name: "John's Furniture",
        email: 'john@example.com',
        phone_number: '+91 98765 43210',
        active: true,
      },
      {
        id: 2,
        name: 'Robert',
        company_name: 'Smart Boutique',
        email: 'robert@example.com',
        phone_number: '+91 98764 53210',
        active: false,
      },
];
```

Adding this piece of code to the fixture file will tell Mirage the exact data that has to be loaded into its database when the application loads. However, we still have not told Mirage to load the fixtures into the database. To do that, we need to alter the **`mirage/scenarios/default.js`** file. You need to add the following line to the default function present in the file:

```
server.loadFixtures();
```

Now we have commanded Mirage to load the fixtures into the database. When the application is started, the data is automatically populated into the in-memory database of Mirage.

Ways to Make API Requests from Ember

We have the data ready to be used. Now, let us look at how we can query it from Ember. In other popular frameworks, we will need to use a separate library to make API calls to fetch/update data from the backend. Some popular choices for these requests are as follows:

- **Fetch API:** https://developer.mozilla.org/en-US/docs/Web/API/Fetch_API
- **Jquery Ajax:** https://api.jquery.com/jquery.ajax/
- **Axios:** https://axios-http.com/docs/intro

These are some of the famous Promise-based libraries that can be used to make API calls. **`Fetch`** is an in-built library available by default in all modern browsers. Considering the Firebase URL for getting the list of users, let us use the Fetch API to make the request and fetch the list of users:

```
const url = 'https://firestore.googleapis.com/v1/projects/ember-back-end-cf576/databases/(default)/documents/users';

const response = await fetch(url);

console.log(response.json());
```

You can see that fetch follows a Promise-based approach, which also supports an **`async/await`** architecture to fetch data.

Advantages of Ember Data

Ember Data is the official data persistence library for the Ember.js framework, and it is designed to work seamlessly with Ember applications. While it is possible to use other data model libraries with Ember, there are several significant advantages to using Ember Data within an Ember application:

- **Tight Integration**: Ember Data is tightly integrated with Ember's data layer, making it easier to work with models and data in an Ember application. It follows Ember's conventions and provides a consistent and familiar API for managing data.

- **Data Modeling**: Ember Data provides a powerful data modeling framework that allows you to define your data models using Ember's object-oriented class system. This makes it easier to represent and manage complex data relationships and schemas.
- **Automatic Data Loading**: Ember Data includes a feature called "**relationship loading**" that allows you to automatically fetch related data when accessing a model. This can reduce the need for custom API requests and simplifies the process of loading associated data.
- **Adapter System**: Ember Data uses adapters and serializers to communicate with various backend APIs. Adapters provide a way to configure how Ember Data communicates with different server technologies, while serializers control how data is transformed between the client and server. This flexibility is useful for working with various backend systems.
- **Data Store**: Ember Data uses a centralized data store to manage the state of your application's data. This means that data is stored in a consistent and organized way, making it easier to work with and manage your application's data.
- **Real-Time Data Handling**: Ember Data includes support for real-time features like WebSockets through its adapters. This can be particularly useful for building real-time or collaborative applications.
- **Ember Inspector**: The Ember Inspector browser extension provides powerful debugging tools for Ember applications, and it is integrated with Ember Data. This makes it easier to inspect and debug the state of your application's data.
- **Community and Ecosystem**: Ember Data has a strong and active community of developers, which means there are many resources, add-ons, and extensions available to enhance and extend its functionality.

While using other data model libraries with Ember is possible, you may lose some of these advantages and may need to write more custom code to achieve the same level of integration and functionality that Ember Data provides. If you are building an application with Ember, using Ember Data is often the recommended choice for a smoother and more productive development experience.

Places to Make API Requests in Ember

We have explored different ways to make API requests. Next, we will examine the different places from where API calls are commonly made in an Ember application :

- **model hook of a route**: This is the most common place for making a request. The model hook is the best place to load data for a particular route and pass it to different components loaded on that page. The model hook provides information about the browser URL, which can be used in the API call. It is also connected to the error and loading substates to provide an aesthetic experience to the end-user.
- **Components**: While data can be easily passed from a model to a component, there are certain cases where we might need to make a call from a component. For example, saving a form and updating data is an example of this.
- **Service**: A service can be used to handle across-the-app use cases, such as authentication or handling third-party requests like payment gateways, single sign-on, and more.

Ember Store

Using existing third-party libraries, there can be different issues that need to be tackled by the developer for each API request made from our application:

- Adding proper headers for each request.
- Sending data to the API in proper format.
- Handling API responses of different types.
- Parsing and returning the data in a model-like format for use inside the application.

Doing this on our own will result in a lot of redundancy and issues to be tackled by the developer. The **Ember Store** is our answer to these questions. The Ember Store is an **Object-Relational mapping** (ORM) interface for our application to coordinate with the APIs. It takes care of making the application layer transparent of the type of backend used, the format of the response from the backend, and more, and returns the data in a specific format based on the model that we are querying. It also stores the queried data in local memory to prevent duplicate API calls for the same record.

The main concept of the Store is to remove the tight coupling between a component and fetching data for the component. According to the principles of good design, it is always better to give only a single responsibility to an object. Following that, a Component is given the responsibility of presenting data to the user and not fetching that data. So, Ember provides a simple Store object that you can inject anywhere into your application: Components, Controllers, and even Routes. Thus, the job of fetching and formatting the data is handed over to a separate service, and we can access the same from anywhere with a single line of code.

Injecting the Store

The store service can be injected into any Component, Controller, Route, or Service in your application. You can do that by using the **`service`** decorator inside your Component as follows:

```
import { service } from '@ember/service';

export default class ClientsViewRoute extends Route {

  @service store;

}
```

You can import the service decorator and use that to inject any existing service into your Object.

Read and Filter Records

With the data being available in the Mirage database and the store service injected into our route, we can replace the hard-coded list of clients in the **`clients/index`** route with a store query to load the data dynamically. There are three kinds of functions offered by Ember Data for reading data of a single type/model from the APIs:

- Fetch all objects
- Filter and fetch certain objects
- Fetch a specific record

Let us look in detail at each of the types.

Fetch All Objects

When displaying a list of all objects of a particular type (say **Clients** in our case), we will want to get all the objects that the API has to offer to show the user. You can use the **`findAll`** method in the Store to do the same. For example, we can update the **model** function of the **clients/index** route as follows, to fetch all the clients from the API and send the list to the template:

```
model(params) {
  return this.store.findAll('client');
}
```

The **findAll** function returns a Promise object, which is handled by the Route as it is Promise-aware. This function makes a network request to fetch all the clients. This findAll query sends a request to the **/clients** URL of the API domain (Ember Data adds the s to make the request to the plural name of the model). We will explore how to configure the API domain and the URL that is mapped to the model later in the chapter.

When calling the **findAll** request from outside the model function, such as in a Controller or inside a Component, we will have to handle the Promise to either store the response in a variable or to handle the error if there is any. The Promise can be handled as follows:

```
let that = this;
this.store.findAll('client')
    .then(function(clients) {
        that.set('clientsList', clients);
    }).catch(function(error) {
        console.log(error);
    });
```

We use the **that** variable because inside the **.then** function, the context is changed, and the **this** inside that does not refer to the Controller/Component object. Whereas defining the context as a separate variable named **that** will help access the Controller object from within the Promise function as well.

Inside the **then** function, we set the **clientsList** variable of the Component/Controller with the list of clients fetched from the API. The **findAll** function returns a list of model objects of the queried type. Since it returns a Promise, you can also use **catch** to handle errors in the request. The error can then either be ignored or displayed to the user in some way.

Another function similar to **findAll** is the **peekAll** function. The difference between find and **peek** in the Ember Store is that **find** makes a network request to fetch the data from the backend API, whereas **peek** does not make a network request to fetch data. It only returns the data that has already been fetched and cached in the Store. **peek** functions can be used when we do not want to make duplicate API calls and want to optimize the application by loading data efficiently from the cache. This can be used when you are doing a **findAll** on a particular type and want to use those same set of records in the same flow, without making an additional network request. A **peekAll** request looks as follows:

```
let clients = this.store.peekAll('client')
```

As you can see, the **peekAll** function does not return a Promise since it does not make a network request. The list of clients that we received inside the **then** function of a **findAll** call will be available as the default response of the **peekAll** function. It is very important to understand the difference between **find** and **peek**, as many times we might interchange the calls, and data will not be available in the application when we try to use **peekAll** before loading data using the **findAll** function.

Filter and Fetch Certain Objects

Oftentimes, we might not need to fetch all the records from the API. When the number of records is very large, loading all the information into the Store will cause memory problems. It is optimal to load only the information that we display on the screen and make additional requests only when the user wants to view more than the initial set of records. There may also be cases where the user will want to see only a portion of the data. For example, let us say we have **Clients** assigned to different **Salesmen** in the company. Now, as a Manager, you might want to see the list of Clients that are assigned to a particular salesman.

For these cases, we can use the **query** function of the Ember store. The query function accepts an object as a parameter, which it translates into query parameters when making the API call. A typical query call looks as follows:

```
this.store.query('client', {
    salesman: 4
}).then(function(clients) {
    // Do something with the clients list
});
```

From this example, you can see that the query function accepts an object, which is translated into query parameters. The above object will be translated into **/clients?salesman=4**. Through this query parameter, the backend will filter out and return only clients that have a salesman with ID 4. Similarly, the query function will handle pagination as well. In order to use the widely available **Page Number Pagination,** you can use the query function as follows:

```
this.store.query('client', {
    page: 1
}).then(function(result) {
    Let clientsList = result.clients
    // Do something with the clients list
});
```

The number of records that are returned on a page are maintained and handled by the backend. We only specify the page number for the list of records to be returned by the API. Unlike the `findAll` function, `query` does not have an alternative that does not make a network request. Since the information queried is bound to change because of the filtering, query always makes a network request to fetch information from the API.

Handling Metadata

You can see from the example that the response of the `query` function is different from the response of the `findAll` function. Typically paginated APIs provide a response in the following format:

```
{
    "meta": {
        "count": 40,
        "next": "https://example.com/clients/?page=3",
        "previous": "https://example.com/clients?page=1"
    },
    "clients": [...list of clients]
}
```

Since pagination returns only a partial set of records, the frontend needs to know the total number of records and the ways to access the previous or next set of records (previous and next pages). This is provided through the `meta` property of the response. It usually contains the following keys:

- `count`: The total number of records that match the provided filter conditions.
- `next`: API URL that points to the next page/next set of records.
- `previous`: API URL that points to the previous page.

With this information, the frontend can decide things such as whether there is a next page of records to fetch, display the total number of records available, and more. This can be accessed through the **meta** property of the response as follows:

```
this.store.query('client', {
    page: 2
}).then(function(result) {
    let meta = result.meta;
    console.log(result.meta.count);
});
```

Fetch a Specific Record

In pages that show the details of a particular client, you might want to fetch a single record alone from the API. The API that returns a single record can sometimes provide detailed information about that record, which will be inefficient to send as part of the list page response. In such cases, Ember Store provides functions for the same.

You can use the **findRecord** function in a similar manner as the **findAll** function. The only difference is that the **findRecord** function returns a single record instead of a list of records.

```
this.store.findRecord('client', 2)
    .then(function(client) {
        console.log(client);
    });
```

findRecord returns a Promise just like **findAll**, as it makes a network request. Similarly, we have a **peekRecord** function that does not make a network request but only returns the data if it is already loaded in the store.

RSVP Hash

In certain routes, we might need to fetch data pertaining to different models. For example, if we have clients and salesmen, we will need to make two API requests in the clients route: one to fetch the list of clients and another to fetch the list of salesmen. We will want the route to continue to the next step (**afterModel** hook) after both the API requests are done.

```
import RSVP from 'rsvp';

model() {
    return RSVP.hash({
        clients: this.store.query('client', {}),
        salesmen: this.store.query('salesman', {})
    });
}
```

In doing this, the model hook is resolved only when both individual API requests are complete. You can access both the clients and salesmen using the notations **`model.clients`** and **`model.salesmen`**.

Create, Update, and Delete Records

Similar to reading data, Ember Store also provides functions and capabilities to create, update, and delete records in the API. Let us look at each of the functions available for the same.

Create Records

The Store provides a **`createRecord`** function that creates model objects in the store. Here is an example of the same:

```
let client = this.store.createRecord('client', {
    name: 'Arjun',
    company_name: 'Modern Bakers',
    email: 'arjun@example.com',
    phone_number: '+91 9876543222',
    active: true
});
```

The **`createRecord`** function gets the object type as the first parameter, and the second parameter is the data for the object.

Persisting Data

Note that the **`createRecord`** function creates the data only in the Store. It does not create the data in the API. Hence, the created record is lost when the page is refreshed and the store is cleared. For Ember to make an API call to the backend, we will need to call the **save** function on the model object. Unless the save function is called, we can create and view records only in the store and the data is valid only for the lifetime of the page.

```
let client = this.store.createRecord('client', {
    name: 'Arjun',
    company_name: 'Modern Bakers',
    email: 'arjun@example.com',
    phone_number: '+91 9876543222',
    active: true
});
client.save()
```

By default, Ember Data automatically takes care of handling newly created records and existing records differently. So, when the **save** function is called on a model object, the backend URL called varies depending upon whether the record exists in the API or not. For example, to create a new client, the API endpoint to call as per the REST conventions is **POST /clients/**.

Updating Records

Making changes to an existing record is as simple as creating them. The save function is the only way to make changes and persist to the API. Here is an example:

```
this.store.findRecord('client', 2)
  .then(function(client) {
    client.name = 'Updated Name';
    client.save();
  });
```

The **save** function is available for all Model objects. Note that the first line, where we assign **client.name**, updates the name field of the client object in the memory/store. However, only when **client.save()**is called, the data is persisted on the API. Even here, Ember Data intelligently makes the API call to update the record instead of the create record API call it does for a new object. As per REST conventions, it makes an API call to **PATCH /clients/<client_id>/**. Both **PUT** and **PATCH** methods can be used to update a record as per REST conventions. The difference is that a **PUT** request expects all the fields of the particular object in the request, just like when you create the record using the **POST** method. In contrast, the **PATCH** method is for partially updating the record and does not expect all the fields in the request; it only updates the fields that are passed in the request data.

Tracking Changes

Ember Data keeps track of the changes made to an object that has not yet been pushed to the API. If you want to know whether a particular record has changes that have not been pushed to the API, you can access it through the **hasDirtyAttributes** attribute of the model. Here is an example of how you can see this variable in action:

```
this.store.findRecord('client', 2)
  .then(function(client) {
    console.log(client.hasDirtyAttributes)
    client.name = 'Updated Name';
    console.log(client.hasDirtyAttributes)
  });
```

When you run this piece of code, you can see in your console that the first console log statement prints false, and the second console log statement prints true because the **name** property of the object was changed in between.

In addition, Ember keeps track of each parameter that has been changed in detail. The model contains a **changedAttributes** function that helps you identify which fields have changed, what their values were initially, and what their values are now. You can try the same with the following code:

```
client.name = 'Updated Name'
client.changedAttributes()
```

Running the preceding code, **changedAttributes** will return an object with the following structure:

```
{
    name: ['John', 'Updated Name']
}
```

The response of **changedAttributes** is an object whose keys are the fields that have changed but have not been pushed to the API yet. For each key, the value is an array. The first value in the array defines the data fetched from the API, whereas the second value is the updated value that is present in the store.

Similar to keeping track of the changes, Ember Data also provides an easy option to rollback the changes that have not been pushed to the API yet. Here is an example:

```
client.name = 'Updated Name'
console.log(client.hasDirtyAttributes) // true
client.rollbackAttributes();
console.log(client.hasDirtyAttributes) // false
console.log(client.name) // John
```

You can see from the example that calling the **rollbackAttributes** function resets the data that has not been pushed to the API yet, and also sets the **hasDirtyAttributes** attribute to false for the particular object. This also sets the **changedAttributes** to an empty object, as the changes have been rolled back. When you call **rollbackAttributes** for an object that was newly created using the **createRecord** function and has not persisted in the API yet, **rollbackAttributes** removes the entire record from the store.

Deleting Records

Deleting records is as simple as creating and updating records through the Ember Data Store. There are two types of deletion functions. The following are the different ways to delete records through Ember Data:

deleteRecord

The first way to delete a particular record is by using the **deleteRecord** function. This function will trigger a **DELETE** request to the endpoint **/clients/<client_id>/** to remove the record from the API.

unloadRecord

Since it is always optimal to reduce the data stored in the frontend storage, Ember Data provides a way to remove a particular record from the store, without affecting the same record in the backend. Normally **unloadRecord** is called when you fetch an object from the API and want to clear the memory after the object does its job. Here is an example:

```
store.findRecord('client', 2)
    .then(function(client) {
        // Do something
```

```
            store.unloadRecord(client);
        });
```

This process does not affect the API and only clears the object from frontend memory.

unloadAll

Instead of removing a single record from the store, **`unloadAll`** can be used to remove all records from the store or remove records of a single type from the store. This will help keep the memory usage of the store in check.

```
this.store.unloadAll();
this.store.unloadAll('client');
```

The first line removes all the records from the store. The second line removes all the **`client`** objects that are present in the store.

Handle Relationships in Models

Databases can have different types of relationships between models. The most common of them are one-to-one, one-to-many, and many-to-many. There are two ways by which all these types are handled.

belongsTo

`belongsTo` is used to handle a scenario of **Foreign Key**, where a field in a particular model points to another model. For example, let us create a new model named **`salesman`** in our application:

```
ember generate model salesman
```

The salesman model will contain only the name for now:

```
import Model, { attr } from '@ember-data/model';


export default class SalesmanModel extends Model {
    @attr('string') name;
}
```

Now, let us say we have a foreign key relationship where each client has a salesman assigned to them. In these cases, **`belongsTo`** comes into play. Here is how you add the **`salesman`** field to the **`client`** model:

```
import Model, { attr, belongsTo } from '@ember-data/model';

export default class ClientModel extends Model {
  @belongsTo('salesman', {async: true}) salesman;
}
```

The common convention to reduce the amount of data transferred from the API is that APIs usually send only the ID of the foreign key object in the response instead of sending the entire foreign key object. The use of **belongsTo** here is to simplify the process of fetching the related element from the API in order to display the details of the foreign key element. For example, let us say the client is assigned to a salesman with ID 3. Note the use of **async: true** in the **belongsTo** section. async is used to determine when Ember should fetch the associated foreign key record. If async is set to true, the associated record will only be fetched from the API when some template or component requests that particular field. If the value is set to false, the data is fetched at the time of fetching the model record itself.

If we want to display the name of the salesman in the client detail route, here is a simple example that doesn't involve the **belongsTo** method:

```
this.store.findRecord('client', 2)
    .then(function(client) {
        var salesman = client.salesman;
        this.store.findRecord('salesman', salesman)
            .then(function(salesman) {
                console.log(salesman.name);
            });
    });
```

We will have to call **findRecord** separately to fetch the salesman associated with the client. With the **belongsTo** relationship, you can directly use **{{client.salesman.name}}** in your template file, and Ember will fetch the related salesman record and show the information on the screen. The Ember function intelligently queries a particular salesman record only once from the API, and the next time when there is another client with the same salesman, the data is peeked from the store and not from the API.

hasMany

Sometimes there can be multiple items referenced to a single model object. For example, we have a salesman assigned to each client in our database. Looking from the other side, it is understood that a salesman can have multiple clients. This relationship can be handled by the **hasMany** method. You can add the following code to the **salesmanmodel** to specify the list of clients:

```
import Model, { attr, hasMany } from '@ember-data/model';


export default class SalesmanModel extends Model {
    @attr('string') name;
    @hasMany('client') clients;
}
```

hasMany works very similarly to the **belongsTo** relationship, with the difference that **hasMany** expects a list of related objects instead of just a single object. Ember Data does a query instead of **findRecord** to fetch the related objects for that field.

inverse

Sometimes multiple fields can map to the same model. In those cases, we need to map which of the fields in the other model map to the current field in the first model. Ember Data provides a way to specify the reverse relationship from one place so that it automatically maintains the mapping, such that when a client is updated, the associated salesman is also updated. Let us create a new field named **backup_salesman**, which will maintain a record of backup salesmen when the associated salesman is not available. We can update the client model to look as follows:

```
@belongsTo('salesman', { inverse: 'clients' }) salesman;
@belongsTo('salesman', { inverse: 'backup_clients' })
backup_salesman;
```

From this, you can see that we have two fields in the **client** model that point to the **salesman** model. Each field has a different name and a different **inverse** value. Just like how we have defined the **clients** field in the **salesman** model, we can define the **backup_clients** field in the **salesman** model. This will keep Ember informed on how to differentiate the two fields in the client model that point to the salesman model.

Adapters

Adapters are the gateways that decide the API domain, URL, headers to send in the API call, and more. Like all other modules in Ember, Adapters also follow a convention, and developers can override the default adapters to configure these parameters for the overall application or, in some cases, to a single model as well. Adapters do not concern themselves with the format of the data sent and received, but it is concerned with the metadata of the request like the URL and headers.

Extending Adapters

In all the Ember applications, the **application adapter** is extended in order to configure the API URL and namespace. Here is how you can extend the application adapter:

```
ember generate adapter application
```

You can see a new file named **app/adapters/application.js** in the project. Any configuration to this adapter will reflect on all the requests made by Ember Data.

Host and namespace

It is a normal convention to specify the API domain and the namespace in the application adapter. It can be added as follows:

```
import JSONAPIAdapter from '@ember-data/adapter/json-api';


export default class ApplicationAdapter extends JSONAPIAdapter {
    host = 'https://exampleapi.com'
    namespace = 'api/v1'
}
```

We have defined two parameters in this Adapter as follows:

- **host**: The domain associated with the API.
- **namespace**: The prefix to be added to the URL for all API calls.

The API URL is generated in the following format: **{domain}/{namespace}/{model-name-plural}**. Given that, the API call for clients will go to the following URL: https://exampleapi.com/api/v1/clients.

Model-URL Mapping

The adapter also takes care of defining the URL name associated with the model. By default, the URL path is considered as the plural form of the model name. The plural format is assumed by adding a s to the model name. Thus, the URL path for a model named **`client`** becomes **`clients`**.

But this does not work in all cases. For example, according to Ember Data, the URL path for our **salesman** model is generated as **`salesmans`**. We know that the correct plural form is **`salesmen`**. For customizing this, the adapter provides a **`pathForType`** function where you can configure the URL mapping for a model. Let us implement the same for our use case:

```
import JSONAPIAdapter from '@ember-data/adapter/json-api';
import Ember from 'ember';

export default class ApplicationAdapter extends JSONAPIAdapter {
    host = 'https://exampleapi.com';
    namespace = 'api/v1';
    pathForType: function(type) {
        if (type === 'salesman') {
            return 'salesmen';
        }
        return Ember.Inflector.inflector.pluralize(type);
    }
}
```

By customizing the **`pathForType`** function, we are specifying a custom value only for the specific **`salesman`** model, while following the default format for all other models. This is how the **Convention over Configuration** setup of Ember works.

Headers

You can specify the set of header values to pass in all requests in our application adapter. You can even customize the headers for each model in the adapter of that particular model. Here is how you can add the headers function to your adapter:

```
get headers() {
    const accessToken = localStorage.getItem('accessToken');
    return {
        'Authorization': 'Token ' + accessToken,
        'Content-Type': 'application/json'
    }
}
```

Notice the **get** before the headers function. Getter functions like these are executed on each call. We use a getter function here because it depends on dynamic values, such as the access token, which is taken from the local storage and can expire after a period of time. Adapters can be customized for individual models as well. Let us say our client model alone requires the data to be sent in **form-data** format instead of JSON, we can generate a separate adapter as follows by generating an adapter with the name of the model:

```
ember generate adapter client
```

Once the adapter is created, you can add the following piece of code to your adapter to differentiate the Content-Type header for the requests to **client** model alone:

```
import ApplicationAdapter from './application';

export default class ClientAdapter extends ApplicationAdapter {
    get headers() {
        const accessToken = localStorage.getItem('accessToken');
        return {
            'Authorization': 'Token ' + accessToken,
            'Content-Type': 'multipart/form-data'
        }
    }
}
```

URL Conventions

As per REST conventions, these are the URL translations done for each type of request as follows. Let us take the **client** model as an example:

- **Fetch all/multiple records:** `GET /clients/`
- **Fetch a particular record:** `GET /clients/<client_id>/`
- **Create a new record:** `POST /clients/`
- **Update an existing record:** `PATCH /clients/<client_id>/`
- **Delete a record:** `DELETE /clients/<client_id>/`

Serializers

Adapters take care of all the metadata of the API call, including the domain, URL, API method, headers, and more. On the other hand, Serializers take care of the data sent and received through the request. They define how the data should be formatted before sending it in the API request or how the data should be transformed when it is made available in the Ember store.

You can generate serializers for individual models as follows:

```
ember generate serializer client
```

Once generated, you can configure the serializer to modify and update the data that you send and receive from the API. For a similar functionality, we have seen **transforms** and how they decide what operations to perform on a particular field in the model. However, this similar functionality works on the entire model level rather than just for a single field.

serialize

For our example, let us consider that we need to send the phone number of the client in a different format. Here is how we can use the serialize function in the serializer to modify the data before it is sent to the server. Here is an example:

```
import JSONAPISerializer from '@ember-data/serializer/json-api';

export default class ClientSerializer extends JSONAPISerializer {
    serialize(snapshot, options) {
        let json = super.serialize(...arguments);
        let phone_number = json.data.attributes.phone_number;
        json.data.attributes.phone_number = {
            country_code: phone_number.slice(0, 3),
            phone_number: phone_number.slice(3)
```

```
            }
            return json
        }
    }
```

You can see from the example that we are converting the phone number, which is a single field into an object, where the country code and **phone_number** are keys in the object.

normalizeResponse

Similarly, when getting a response from the API, the **phone_number** field will be an object, and we can use the **normalizeResponse** function to convert the **phone_number** field back to a string to be used by the model and the Ember application.

```
normalizeResponse(store, primaryModelClass, payload, id,
  requestType) {
    const phoneNumber = payload.data.attributes.phone_number;
    payload.data.attributes.phone_number =
  phoneNumber.country_code + phoneNumber.phone_number;
    return super.normalizeResponse(...arguments);
}
```

This is how we control how the data is being passed to and from the server and the differences in format expectations are adjusted.

Identifier

By default, the ID field of any model object will contain the unique identifier for that record, which would usually be the database ID of that particular object. In some special cases, we might not have ID as the primary key field in the database. In those cases, we can specify the **primaryKey** parameter for a serializer and Ember Data will take care of using that **primaryKey** field as the primary key/unique identifier for the records of that model when serializing and deserializing data:

```
export default class ClientSerializer extends JSONAPISerializer {
    primaryKey = 'identifier';
}
```

Attribute Name Mapping

When it comes to variable naming, there is always a conflict on what kind of conventions to follow when naming our variables. The convention depends on the language we use. For example, it is always recommended to use camel case in JavaScript, while Python supports snake case (using _ between words in variable names). The backend API obviously sends data in a format that supports their own language, but in JavaScript, we might be tempted to use our own conventions.

Handling this in Ember Serializer is an easy job. You have a **keyForAttribute** function in the serializer that can be used to make such general changes or provide specific changes, such as when a particular field is renamed in the backend, and changing the same in our Ember code might need too many changes.

Let us say we have an attribute named **modified_at** in the client model and the API decides to change the field name to **updated_at**. It might be difficult for us to find all the occurrences of this field and rename it everywhere. In such case, we can use the **keyForAttribute** function as follows:

```
keyForAttribute(attr) {
    if (attr === 'modified') {
        return 'updated';
    }
    return attr;
}
```

This function is used to dynamically determine the mapping. If you need to statically specify the change, you can use the **attrs** attribute of the serializer to specify an updated mapping as follows in the serializer:

```
attrs = {
    modified_at: updated_at
}
```

Ember Services

We have seen before that services are singleton instances that live through the lifecycle of an Ember application. It can be injected into any part of the application, such as Controller, Component, Route, and more. We have seen examples of injecting the session service or the router service. Services are used to store information such as an authenticated user's details, handle a WebSocket connection with the backend, or handle any network requests that are not compatible with Ember Data.

Generating a Service

Ember provides a blueprint for generating services as well. Let us generate a service named user-reports as follows:

```
ember generate service user-reports
```

This will create a file named **`user-reports.js`** in your **`app/services`** folder. We can add different functions and variables inside the service.

Configuring the Service

A service is considered an object similar to a Controller or Component. It can handle variables and functions that alter these variables or make external API requests. In our case, let us say we want to keep track of the number of button clicks the user makes across the application. The service will look something like this:

```
import Service from '@ember/service';

export default class UserReportsService extends Service {

    count = 0;

    incrementCount() {
        this.count += 1;
    }

}
```

The service is simple. It has a variable named **`count`** and a function **`incrementCount`** to increase the count variable. Let us create a button component and call the service to increment the count from there whenever the button is clicked:

```
ember generate component count-button
ember generate component-class count-button
```

We can add the button to the template of the component as follows:

```
<button {{action "incrementCount"}}>Click to increment count</button>
```

In the component JavaScript file, we can add the action to call the service as follows:

```
import Component from '@glimmer/component';
import { service } from '@ember/service';
import { action } from '@ember/object';

export default class CountButtonComponent extends Component {

    @service('user-reports') userReports;

    @action
    incrementCount() {
        this.userReports.incrementCount();
    }
}
```

Notice that since the service name contains a **-**, and it cannot be named as a JavaScript variable, we have imported the service by enclosing it within quotes and providing a JavaScript-compatible name to it. Next, we can call this component from multiple places:

- Home route
- About route

We can add the following piece of code to both the home and about templates as follows:

```
<CountButton />
```

Since the variable can be updated from multiple places, we can display the current count in the application template. You can generate the application controller and inject the **`userReports`** service just like we did inside the count-button component. Once injected, we can access the count from the application template below the page title as follows:

```
<h1 class="page-title text-center">My Ember Application</h1>
<p class="text-center">Total Click Count: {{this.userReports.
count}}</p>
```

Once these are added, you can see the count displayed on the page. Next, we can go to both the home page and the about page, click the button, and see the count changing at the top. The difference between a normal component action and the service is that the value of count does not reset once you move out of a particular route, and the service can be injected anywhere inside the application with ease.

Thus, a service can be a good alternative for actions that affect multiple parts of the application and cannot be tied to a specific component or route.

Conclusion

In this chapter, we discussed connecting our Ember application with the outside world through Ember Data. We explored how Ember itself offers a way to mock API requests through Ember CLI Mirage, allowing us to mock external API calls without making changes to how the application communicates with the actual backend. Then, we discussed models and how it is a JavaScript object description of the data being returned from the API. We learned to configure fields that are returned from the API, add additional fields that are computed based on the other fields, and more. We also saw how we can create custom data types in addition to the predefined data types provided by Ember, in the form of transforms, and how to easily inject them into your models. Furthermore, we examined how relationships between models can be handled through the `hasMany` and `belongsTo` decorators.

We learned about the Ember Data Store, how to use it to connect with the backend, and how to configure different stuff using adapters and serializers to customize the default conventions provided by Ember to make API requests and format the request and response data. In the end, we discussed Ember Services and a few use cases that we can use in our application.

In the next chapter, we will look at configuring our application to make it production-ready, so that it can be deployed to server environments.

Points to Remember

- Ember Data is the recommended way to communicate with the external applications that transfer data to and from our application.
- Even though there are other ways to communicate and make API requests, Ember Data provides a lot of default functionalities that reduce code complexity and redundancy.

- Ember Store is an ORM that is agnostic of the backend involved, containing functions to communicate effectively with the API.
- Foreign key and Many-to-Many relationships can be handled via **`hasMany`** and **`belongsTo`** functions.
- You can create custom data types by creating transforms.
- Adapters are used to configure the metadata of API requests, such as the API domain, the URL prefix for each request, URL mapping for each model, headers to be sent in the request, and more.
- Serializers are used to configure the data. They allow you to decide how to reformat data before sending it to the API or after receiving a response from the API.

Multiple Choice Questions

1. Which of the following is not a method to make API requests to the backend?
   a. **`Axios`**
   b. **`Fetch`**
   c. **`Call`**
   d. **`Ember Data`**
2. Which of the following is not a predefined Ember data type?
   a. date
   b. string
   c. boolean
   d. time
3. What is the function that does not make an API call, but fetches the data from the store?
   a. **`findRecord`**
   b. **`peekRecord`**
   c. **`unloadRecord`**
   d. All of the above

4. Where do we set the domain of the API to make all API calls through Ember Data?
    a. Application router
    b. Any controller
    c. Application adapter
    d. Any component
5. Which of the following persists in the variable values even across routes?
    a. Services
    b. Components
    c. Controllers
    d. None of the above

Answers

1. c
2. d
3. b
4. c
5. a

Questions

1. Why do you need to connect your Ember application to an external API?
2. What are the types of Ember Data Store functions to fetch data and how are they different?
3. What is the difference between `findAll` and `query`?
4. How do you keep track of changes to a particular model object that are not pushed to the store?
5. What is the difference between Adapters and Serializers?

Key Terms

- **Ember Data**: The Ember addon that is used to connect with backend APIs.
- **Store**: An Ember Service that provides the functions for communicating with the API and stores the fetched information in a cache.
- **Model**: A class-based object representation of the underlying data.
- **Serializer**: An Ember module that is used to format the data that is sent and received from the API.

CHAPTER 6
Configuring your Ember.js Application

Introduction

So far in our previous chapters, we have discussed the different components of an Ember Application and the basics of building an Ember Application. In this chapter, we will look at different ways to configure the application and update your settings for different environments that we deploy the application to. We will also look at ways we can pass different parameters to the Ember CLI to customize the Ember server.

We will also look at additional features offered by Ember, enabling additional features that are not part of the official release. Then we will look at handling deprecations that are announced by the Ember community. At the end, we will talk about different build targets you can configure for different environments.

Structure

The following topics will be discussed in this chapter:

- Configuring your App
- Configuring Ember-CLI
- Prototype Extensions
- Handling Deprecations
- URL Types
- Embedded Applications
- Feature Flags

- Optional Features
- Build Targets
- Robots.txt

Configuring your App

As we have seen in our previous chapters, Ember provides a lot of default configurations that help even beginners to build a large-scale application with ease. On top of that, Ember also provides ways to configure those default values to suit our application's requirements. Let us look at a few configuration options provided by Ember and how you can use them.

Build Environments

Build environments are the types of situations we run the application in. There are three environments used in any common application:

- **`development`**: The development environment is the local Ember server that you run. It is used in the Ember development server.
- **`test`**: This environment is when you run your tests using the Ember tests command.
- **`production`**: The production environment is where you host the application on a server or a file system to be accessed from anywhere. This is normally used for all your hosting setups, like staging and production setups.

The environment-based configurations are done from the **`config/environment.js`** file. If you open the file in our existing project, you can see some prefilled values. The file contains a function that gets an **`environment`** variable as a parameter and returns an ENV object. Through this **`environment`** variable passed to this function, we are able to configure the settings of your application. A common example would be that we will want to disable detailed logging in our production environment as it might make the application inefficient due to too much logging.

You can see the if conditions in the **`config/environment.js`** file as follows:

```
if (environment === 'development') {
  …
}


if (environment === 'production') {
```

```
    ...
}
```

We can use these `if` conditions to modify the ENV object before returning it for the application to use.

App Secrets

The environment variable-based configuration is useful for cases where we need different settings for the local environment and other settings for hosted environments (production). But there are certain cases where you have to specify additional parameters like API URL, some third-party API keys, and so on. These values cannot be specified in the environment file because of the following reasons:

- You should not hard-code any API keys or credentials into your code. When you push the code to any third-party Version Control System (VCS) like GitHub, the credentials are accessible to anyone with access to the repository, which is not recommended, as it can lead to security problems. The ENV object in the environment file is set as a Meta tag in the HTML file generated by the build. So placing any credentials in the ENV object makes it wide open for everyone to see the credentials.
- Even with the same build environment - **production**, you might build your staging and production deployments. In these cases, we will have different API URLs for different deployments. Handling such cases with if else conditions will be hectic.

To handle these issues, we will need a way that does not hard-code the credentials in the repository and supply the values during the build time of the application. The common way of doing this is through a `.env` file. A `.env` file contains a key-value syntax used to store sensitive details like passwords, or flags and values that are specific to the particular build of the application. Here is a sample of a `.env` file. You can add this to the root folder of our project:

```
API_URL=https://api.mydomain.com
SOME_API_KEY=TestAPIKey
```

To read the `.env` file into the Node environments object, we will install an addon named `ember-cli-dotenv`:

```
ember install ember-cli-dotenv
```

Once this addon is installed, it automatically finds the `.env` file in the project root directory and adds those values to the `process.env` object, which is a global variable injected into node runtimes to access the environment variables from the shell. Typically, these application-level variables are passed through to the **`APP`** key of the **`ENV`** object. You can update the **`APP`** section of our **`config/environment.js`** file as follows:

```
const ENV = {
  APP: {
    ...process.env
  },
}
```

Once this is injected, you can access the variables from the **`.env`** file anywhere in the application. Since we have entered our API URL in the **`.env`** file, let us see how we can use that value in our **`adapters/application.js`** file. You can update the adapter file as follows:

```
import ENV from '../config/environment';


host = ENV.APP.API_URL;
```

You can do a **`console.log`** of the host or the **`ENV.APP.API_URL`** variable to see the value being fetched from the **`.env`** file. When you pass credentials this way to your application, it is more secure and flexible to configure. There are different ways to pass your secrets to the build using the **`process.env`**. It also depends on the CI/CD system you use. For example, GitHub has **Github Secrets**, Amazon AWS has **Parameter Store** and **Secrets Manager**.

Configuring Ember-CLI

In the previous section, we have seen how we can configure the Ember application to handle things in the run time. Next, we will see how we can configure Ember-CLI to set up the parameters to be called when running the server. There are two ways to handle the Ember-CLI parameters:

- Pass the parameters when running the **`ember serve`** command
- Configure the parameters through the **`.ember-cli`** file in the project with the required parameters

Configuring the **`.ember-cli`** file is preferred because it is a one-time setup and you can just call **ember serve** or **ember s** after that and the parameters are implicitly applied. Even when the project is worked on by multiple developers, this becomes useful as every one might not pass all the parameters when running manually and this might lead to misconfiguration. Let us look at some of the parameters that can be configured through the `.ember-cli` file:

- `port` - The default port Ember uses is 4200. But in certain cases, we might want to use a different port if 4200 has been used by some other process.
- `liveReload` - **Live Reload** is the process of refreshing the browser page automatically whenever a file in the project has changed. This flag is by default true and you can set it to false and the changes are reflected only when you manually refresh the browser.
- `isTypeScriptProject` - Typescript is disabled by default in a new Ember project. When this flag is set to true, any blueprint generator we use in the project will create the objects compatible with TypeScript syntax.
- `disableAnalytics` - If you wish to send your local Ember server stats and information to the Ember community, you can set this flag to true. The data that is sent from your server is completely anonymous and used by the community to keep track of server-level errors, and so on.
- `proxy` - When running the Ember server from your local setup, there might be cases where a direct request from the browser might cause **Content Security Policy (CSP)** or **Cross-Origin Request Sharing (CORS)** errors. To overcome these errors, we can specify the **proxy** with a URL. Whatever requests are sent to the Ember server that cannot be handled by the server will be sent to this Proxy URL. By doing so, the browser has the illusion of sending the request to the same domain and not a different domain.

A sample of the `.ember-cli` file with these values filled will look like this:

```
{
    "port": 4201,
    "liveReload": true,
    "isTypeScriptProject": true,
    "disableAnalytics": false,
    "proxy": "http://localhost:8000"
}
```

Prototype Extensions

We have seen in the previous chapter how Ember keeps track of (observes) changes to tracked variables to update dependent variables or update the values displayed on the screen. This works by default for simple variable types like string, number, or boolean. When it comes to Array elements, the tracking does not work as it is. In order to observe changes done to an Array object, Ember has defined its own versions of the Array object that are observer-friendly.

Ember defines two Array-type objects and recommends using these for storing and manipulating a list of elements:

- `EmberArray`
- `MutableArray`

A `MutableArray` is an Array whose values can be changed/updated once they are created. An Immutable Array's values cannot be changed after creation. Any change you make like adding, removing, or updating elements cannot be done on that object, but only on a copy of that object.

Advantages of Immutability

By default, objects in JavaScript are mutable. But there are some advantages when an Array-like object is made immutable:

- When passing the Array to another function, we cannot be sure that the operations done inside the function do not affect the original array object sent to the function. We might want to ensure the changes are done to a copy of the Array and not disturb the original Array. Immutability achieves this purpose.
- It is easier to track changes to an object when the value does not change unless we manually reassign the value using the same variable name.
- When working with asynchronous programs and multi-threaded processes, mutability can lead to a lot of problems when the value of the object is somehow altered and it can easily lead to data corruption in the object.

Disadvantages of Immutability

Immutability also has the following disadvantages:

- This approach uses more memory as a new object is created every time a change is made to an Array.
- From an efficiency point of view, it is faster to update an existing object rather than create new objects.

Making an Array immutable

As mentioned earlier, Arrays in JavaScript are mutable by default. But there are ways to make an Array immutable. Here is an example:

```
let a = [1, 2, 3];
a.push(4);  // Works without error as the array is immutable.
Object.freeze(a);
a.push(5);  // Throws an error, as a is immutable.

// In order to modify the array, we need to copy it into a new
// object.
let b = a.map(function(item) {
  return item;
});
b.push(5);  // Works as Array b is mutable
```

Disabling Prototype Extensions

Utilizing Ember extensions prevents us from writing a lot of boilerplate code for handling basic scenarios like listening for changes to an Array and updating dependent variables or rerendering the screen, and so on. Even though Ember recommends using these prototype extensions fully in our applications, in some cases, when the Ember Application has to be embedded inside other environments or applications, or author third-party JavaScript that might use an Ember addon in places beyond our control. In such cases, we might have to ensure that the application does not use these prototype extensions, since they may not be supported by the end environments. It will lead the application to break due to conflicting libraries or Array extensions.

You can disable the extensions by passing flags through the **`EmberENV`** section of our **`config/environment.js`** file:

```
const ENV = {
  EmberENV: {
    EXTEND_PROTOTYPES: false
  }
}
```

Ember also allows you to specifically disable only one particular extension instead of disabling all of them together. Here is an example:

```
const ENV = {
  EmberENV: {
    EXTEND_PROTOTYPES: {
      Array: false
    }
  }
}
```

Alternatives to Prototype Extensions

When we disable these extensions in the environment, we will need to handle some cases if we want our data to be consistent. For example, using native JavaScript Arrays, we might display them on screen using a **{{#each}}** helper. However, any change made to the Array will not reflect on the template/screen, as Ember observers do not trigger on changes to a native Array.

For these cases, Ember provides a method that sets up the required interfaces to listen for changes in an Array. It is called **Ember.A** and can be used with any native Array as follows:

```
import {A} from '@ember/array';

let myArray = ['A', 'B', 'C'];
myArray.pushObject('D'); // Does not trigger any re render
A(myArray);

// The below line triggers re render as myArray is passed through
// Ember.A()

myArray.pushObject('E')
```

Handling Deprecations

When new versions of Ember are released, there are always older functions that are marked for removal from the Ember source. These functionalities/APIs are **deprecated** before they are actually removed from the code. **Deprecation** means that the functionality is still present in the code, but usage of that functionality will generate warnings in your console.

This way, we can keep track of items that we are going to have to change when we are going to upgrade to the next version, without the application being affected in the current state. When the application gets older and larger, these warnings get piled up and become hard to manage. The warnings can become large enough to flood your console and overshadow useful log messages that you need in the console. Ember provides a clean and simple way to handle these deprecations and clean them up one by one.

Filtering Deprecations

Whenever new versions of Ember are released, it is better to upgrade the version of your project along with other dependencies. When you wish to upgrade your Ember version, you need to make sure you are not using any APIs/functionalities that are removed in the new version. Over the years, the number of deprecations can increase and it will be an easy option to filter out deprecations that are removed only in the next version you are upgrading to.

Fortunately, Ember provides handlers to decide which deprecations have to be notified and which to ignore. You can add this handler anywhere in the application and it is registered during runtime to override the default deprecation handling behavior. Here is an example of how the handler works:

```
import { registerDeprecationHandler } from '@ember/debug';

export function initialize() {
  registerDeprecationHandler((message, options, next) => {
    if (options && options.until && options.until !== '5.3.0') {
      return;
    } else {
      next(message, options);
    }
  });
}

export default { initialize };
```

Here, we change the if condition with the version that we are going to upgrade next to. So if we upgrade to 5.5.0, we change the version from **`5.3.0`** to **`5.5.0`** and only deprecations that are removed from the code in Ember version **`5.5.0`** will be logged in the console.

Deprecation Workflow

By adding the previously mentioned deprecation handler, we can filter out deprecations that need not be handled immediately and concentrate on items that have to be handled before upgrading to the next version. Even after that, there can be a lot of deprecations, or deprecation warnings, that are triggered only when a certain scenario is met, or when a certain UI flow is triggered. How will we be sure that we have found and updated all the deprecations and the code is clean enough to move to the next version? This is where the addon **ember-cli-deprecation-workflow** comes into place.

The addon once installed, will keep track of all the deprecations encountered from the time the server was started, to the time we generate a dump of the same. You can even run your entire test suite by visiting **http://localhost:4200/tests** and it will ensure all deprecations in the code covered by the test suite are tracked. Once we have gone through the test suite and done manual testing for places not covered by the test cases, we are ready to generate the dump of all deprecations. You can go to your browser console and run the following command:

```
deprecationWorkflow.flushDeprecations();
```

The JavaScript code printed as a response to this command can be copied and pasted into a new file named **`deprecation-workflow.js`** in the project root folder. The response is a JavaScript code and it will look something like this:

```
window.deprecationWorkflow = window.deprecationWorkflow || {};
window.deprecationWorkflow.config = {
  workflow: [
    { handler: "silence", matchMessage: "Ember.Handlebars.
registerHelper is deprecated, please refactor to Ember.Helper.
helper." },
  ]
```

The workflow list will contain one entry for every unique deprecation message collected during the test period. Also note the **`handler: "silence"`**: Once saved in the **`deprecation-workflow.js`** file, this denotes that the corresponding deprecation message will not be displayed and will be suppressed.

When we decide to make changes to the code to remove all usage of the particular deprecated functionality, we will change the `handler` value to `throw` instead of `silence`. Once updated, it will throw an error in the browser whenever that deprecation is encountered. Even after we remove all occurrences, it is better to leave the `handler` value as it is, so that during the runtime of the application, if we encounter this anywhere else, we will get to know immediately. Going through all the items in the workflow list and handling each of them will make your application "**deprecation-free**".

URL Types

We have seen earlier that when we move from one route to another, the URL in the browser gets updated to reference the new route. There are different options for configuring how Ember has to handle URLs when transitioning from one route to another. It is configured using the `locationType` setting present in your `config/environment.js` file. If you open the file you can see that the setting is set to `history`. Here are the options that you can set for `locationType`:

- `history` - This is the default option that uses the `History` API of the browser to track transitions. Using this method, the route URL is appended to the domain part. So the URL for our client detail route is `/clients/1`.
- `hash` - This was a method used by single-page applications to update URLs without triggering a page refresh. This method keeps the URL part of the location constant and updates the route based on the **anchor tag (#)**. So, for example, the URL for the client detail route will be **http://localhost:4200/#/clients/1**. This method uses the `hashchange` event present in the browser to update the anchor part of the URL. Only the part after the **#** changes when transitioning between routes.
- `auto` - Some older browsers do not support the History API. In those cases, we might want to use the hash method in those browsers, but use the History API when it is available. `auto` option takes care of that and switches between the two modes based on the capability of the browser.
- **none** - In cases where we are embedding our application inside another website, we do not want our Ember application to interact with or update the browser URL at all. For such applications, you can set the `locationType` to `none` and then we need not worry about the browser URL being updated by the Ember application.

Embedded Applications

An Ember application is designed to function independently. Even then, there can be cases where we want an Ember application to be embedded into another HTML page and be served from the same domain as the parent page (to prevent issues arising due to embedding a URL from a different domain through an iframe).

Root Element

When embedding an Ember application inside another page, the base page could use plain JavaScript or any other frontend framework for its application. So it is better to restrict all of Ember's activities to a specific root element that we assign to our application. By default, Ember generates the template as HTML and appends it to the **body** tag of the HTML page. We can override that using the **rootElement** property in the **app/app.js** file:

```
export default class App extends Application {
  …
  rootElement: '#ember-application'
}
```

The value of the **rootElement** property can be any valid jQuery selector that we have seen in the preceding chapters.

Root URL

As mentioned earlier, we might have cases where multiple applications are served through the same domain. It is also a common practice to serve both frontend and backend applications from the same domain to prevent CORS issues. In those cases, we will have to specify a sub-URL for Ember application to identify that all the routes will be prefixed with a particular URL path. This can be set in the **ENV** object of the **config/environment.js** file:

```
let ENV = {
  …
  rootURL: '/apps/ember/',
}
```

Once set, all URLs accessed from Ember will need to add the prefix **/apps/ember/**. For example, the client detail route will now look like this: **http://**

localhost:4200/apps/ember/clients/1. If you look at how this works, you can see these values being passed to the `app/router.js` file for the router to parse and update URLs in the browser. You can see the following lines in the `app/router.js` file:

```
import config from 'my-ember-project/config/environment';

export default class Router extends EmberRouter {
  location = config.locationType;
  rootURL = config.rootURL;
}
```

Feature Flags

When new features are built into the Ember framework, before the code is merged into the main branch of the Ember repository, the entire code related to the feature is placed inside `if-else` blocks. It can be conditionally enabled in your project based on the config. It is done so because of two reasons:

- Any issues with newly developed features should not affect planned releases or cause issues in any existing projects.
- The code should be tested by the Ember community before they deem it ready for production use.

Life-cycle of an Ember feature

A freshly merged feature is available only by enabling the feature from your config file. At the start of a release cycle, the Ember community tests each feature and features that pass the testing are enabled and pushed to the beta stage, and become part of the next stable release of Ember. Features that receive negative feedback are disabled until the issues present are resolved.

Ember has an inbuilt package named `canary-features` that exports a list of flagged features in a release, and its status. A newly built feature can be of the following statuses:

- `true` - The feature is present and enabled in this build.
- `null` - The feature is present, but disabled by default. We can enable it from the config file.
- `false` - The feature is completely disabled. It cannot be enabled in this build.

The features with the **null** status are optional and can be enabled from the configuration file. Any developer creating a feature in Ember will add a flag for that feature in a file called **FEATURES.md** in the repository. The entry will contain the flag associated with the feature and a description of what the feature does.

Enabling features in runtime

The features with the status as **null** (present but not enabled) can be enabled at runtime through the **config/environment.js** file. You can see that the file contains a section called **FEATURES** inside the **EmberENV** section of the **ENV** object. Here is how you can enable a feature:

```
const ENV = {
  EmberENV: {
    FEATURES: {
      EMBER_NATIVE_DECORATOR_SUPPORT: true
    },
  },
}
```

This can be used to enable a specific feature in our project. If you want to enable all the canary features instead of specifying them one by one, you can use the catch-all flag as follows:

```
const ENV = {
    EmberENV: {
      ENABLE_OPTIONAL_FEATURES: true
    },
  }
```

Optional Features

Ember has a set of "**optional features**" which can be enabled and disabled at will. It is powered by an addon named **@ember/optional-features**. This addon is automatically installed when the project is created. You can see the list of optional features shipped by default using the following command:

```
ember feature:list
```

This will list all the optional features available by default. The output will look as illustrated in *Figure* 6.2. Let us look at a couple of these features and what they do.

- **application-template-wrapper** - This feature is enabled by default. If enabled, it will add a wrapper around the rendered content of the page with the **`class .ember-view.`** This can be used to target the elements in the page by using the class name.
- **jquery-integration** - Even though Ember has a rich set of features that can manipulate the DOM and its contents, sometimes jQuery is required to manipulate elements directly from inside a component. This can be achieved by enabling this optional feature and then installing an addon - **`@ember/jquery.`** Once done, you will be able to access jQuery from any of the files using `this.$()`.

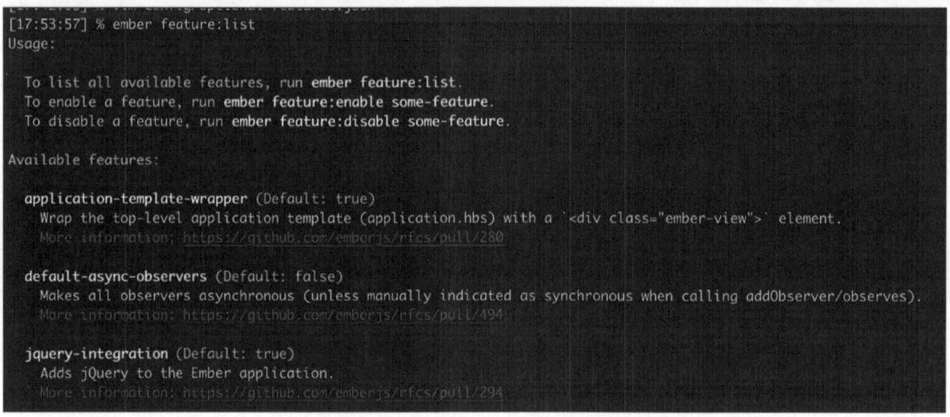

Figure 6.1: *Ember optional features*

Figure 6.2 shows the list of available optional features. You can enable any feature by using the following command:

```
ember feature:enable jquery-integration
```

The command will result in an output as follows:

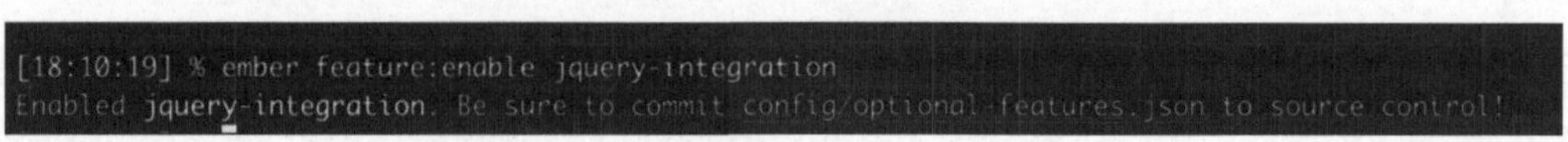

Figure 6.2: *Enabling an optional feature*

You can now see from the message that Ember has created a new file called **`config/optional-features.json`** which tracks the status of each optional feature. The file will look like this:

```
{
  "application-template-wrapper": true,
  "default-async-observers": true,
  "jquery-integration": true,
}
```

It shows that we have all the optional features enabled. To disable a feature, you can use the disable command:

```
ember feature:disable jquery-integration
```

Once disabled, you can confirm that by opening the **`config/optional-features.json`** and making sure the **`jquery-integration`** is set to false. These are a broad overview of the features and functionalities provided by the Ember CLI.

Build Targets

An advantage of a web application is that it can be accessed by the end users from the comfort of their browsers without any additional configurations or downloads. However, when it comes to frameworks like Ember, they are built and compressed before they are used in the browser. As we know, Ember code is transformed into JavaScript code that can be read from the browser. Ember, by default, uses **Babel.js**, a **`transcompiler`** that converts modern JavaScript code into code that can be parsed by the browser.

As technology advances and browsers are upgraded, users move over to new browsers, with support for JavaScript code that can be compressed further, thus reducing the size of our application that is loaded in the browser. Depending on your user base, Ember allows you to specify the browser versions that your application is supposed to support. With this specification, Ember can decide how efficiently it can compress/translate the JavaScript code.

Inside the **`config`** folder, you can see a **`targets.js`** file, with the following code:

```
const browsers = [
  'last 1 Chrome versions',
  'last 1 Firefox versions',
  'last 1 Safari versions',
];
```

```
module.exports = {
  browsers,
};
```

You can see that our application supports the latest versions of the most widely known browsers like Chrome, Firefox, and Safari. Specifying it in a relative manner and not the absolute version will help the application keep updated based on new releases from both the browser side and from Ember releases.

Robots.txt

Have you ever wondered how search engines like Google fetch information about so many websites and give it to you within milliseconds of searching? These search engines have automated bots called **Web Crawlers** that explore the internet. The goal of such a bot would be to learn about any and all web pages in the world wide web, download and index them so that the search engine can filter and show them to people who search with the relevant keywords.

We would usually want our web application/website to show up on the first page of the search results for keywords related to our business. But, we will need some pages of our website to be hidden from search engines so that they are private only for users you want to share it with. Every search engine bot that tries to query your website will first look for a **`/robots.txt`** URL on the website, which tells the bot which pages can be indexed and which cannot. You can go to http://localhost:4200/robots.txt to see the default configuration in Ember, and the same file inside the **`public/robots.txt`** file in the repository.

The **`robots.txt`** file will have the following content by default:

```
# http://www.robotstxt.org
User-agent: *
Disallow:
```

The robots.txt syntax contains the following syntax:

- **`User-agent`**: **`User-agent`** is used to specify the specific bot this configuration is applied to. If you specify a **`*`**, it means it applies to all the bots (search engines).
- **`Disallow`**: The Disallow keyword is used to prevent a specific pattern of URLs from being excluded when indexing.
- **`Allow`**: Allow keyword specifies a specific URL pattern to be indexed.

Here are a few scenarios and how you can configure your **`robots.txt`** for those cases:

- **Allow all URLs to be indexed** - The default configuration of robots.txt is to allow indexing of all URLs. You can see the **`User-agent`** key is set to * and Disallow is empty. This indicates that none of the URLs are to be disallowed.
- **Allow specific URLs** - Some applications where you have both public-facing pages and private pages that are not required to be indexed/ appear in search results. The **`robots.txt`** will be set to the following content for such a case:

```
User-agent: *

Allow: /public/

Disallow: /
```

We can see that only URLs that start with **`/public`** are allowed to be indexed and the rest are disallowed. The same can be reversed to allow only a specific pattern of URLs to be prevented from indexing.

```
User-agent: *

Disallow: /private-path/

Allow: /
```

- **User agent based** - For certain cases, for example, based on the region/ country that your app is being deployed to, you might want to disable indexing in certain search engines and enable the same in other engines. Robots.txt allows you to specify individual configurations for each search engine bot. A list of popular bots is displayed on the robots.txt website here - http://www.robotstxt.org/db.html. Here is how you can configure robots.txt for specific agents:

```
User-agent: Googlebot

Disallow: /


User-agent: *

Allow: /
```

Here we specify a separate configuration just for Googlebot, disabling it to index any URL. Every other bot can index all the URLs. This can be extended to write individual configurations for multiple bots.

When configuring your robots.txt file, you need to understand that when multiple blocks are configured (each block is separated by the User-agent keyword), bots take the first block that matches the condition and fetch their instructions from that. For example, if we have the **Disallow** block for Googlebot after the **User-agent: *** block, bots will not consider the specific Googlebot block, as their condition matches the first block itself.

Configuring robots.txt for each environment

Usually, the **robots.txt** file for each environment will be different. You will not want bots to index your staging environments, but you will want them to index all URLs in your production environment. So the robots.txt will have to be defined separately for the different environments based on your deployment setups. You can name the files based on the environment names, like **robots-prod.txt**, **robots.txt**, and so on. And we can configure the **ember-cli-build.js** file to include the correct file based on the environment as follows:

```
const EmberApp = require('ember-cli/lib/broccoli/ember-app');
const stew = require('broccoli-stew');

module.exports = function (defaults) {
  const app = new EmberApp(defaults, {
    sassOptions: {
      extension: 'scss',
    },

    'ember-bootstrap': {
      bootstrapVersion: 5,
      importBootstrapCSS: false,
    },
  });

  var appTree = app.toTree();
  var env = EmberApp.env();

  if (env === 'production') {
    appTree = stew.rm(appTree, 'robots.txt');
```

```
    appTree = stew.rename(appTree, 'robots-prod.txt', 'robots.
txt');
  } else {
    appTree = stew.rm(appTree, 'robots-prod.txt');
  }


  return appTree;
};
```

We are using a package named **`broccoli-stew`** to find and modify the **`appTree`** during the build time. With this, we can define a specific instruction to index only our production website, and all other hosted environments like **staging and development** can be ignored.

Conclusion

In this chapter, we looked at how we can configure the Ember application for the building and deployment process. We learned to tweak the Ember settings to modify the way the application behaves for each environment; the actions done during the build, and so on. We learnt about the recommended ways to pass secrets and credentials through a **.env** file and why it is a security issue to include these values inside the repository itself. Then we saw the need for a **`.ember-cli`** file and how it provides a single configuration system for multiple developers working on a single Ember project, and not requiring to manually pass the variables while running the application each time.

Next, we learned about Ember's additional extensions for Arrays and how they are used to track changes to Arrays during the runtime of the application. However, just like any other feature in Ember, this can also be configured as per our requirements and we saw how we can disable these extensions and write alternate code in such cases. We looked at deprecations and how they can be handled effectively through Ember addons. We also learned about different ways the application interacts with the browser URL and what their differences are. Then we saw how we can embed our Ember application inside another webpage and the necessary configuration changes required for it.

We saw how we can optionally enable different features that are not publicly enabled in the Ember version we are using. Also, we learned how to specify the list of browsers supported by our application to allow Ember to generate the build effectively. Then we looked at robots.txt and how it can be customized to instruct bots on which pages they can index and which pages they cannot. In the next chapter, we will look in detail at the different types of tests you can write to ensure that your application works as expected and how you can write tests in Ember effectively.

Points to Remember

- Ember provides a wide range of flexibility to configure how the application runs and builds.
- It is not recommended to hard-code credentials in your application and push them to your version control system.
- You can modify the build process based on the environment specified when generating the build.
- `.ember-cli` file can be used to define the parameters passed when running the ember server.
- Ember has built-in extensions to default objects like Arrays for observing changes and updating templates and dependent variables. They can be disabled in the runtime.
- You can define which browser API (hash or history API) Ember uses to interact with the browser URL.
- Ember applications can be easily embedded into other web pages with small tweaks.
- Ember has a list of optional features which can be enabled based on our requirements.
- We can specify the list of browsers supported by our Ember application. The list need not be a hard-coded list of versions, but relative to the latest version.

Multiple Choice Questions

1. Which of the following is not a valid key in the **config/environment.js** file?

   a. `rootURL`

   b. `EmberENV`

   c. `locationType`

   d. None of the above

2. What file is used to specify the parameters passed to the ember server?

    a. `.ember-cli`

    b. `.ember-server`

    c. `.ember-params`

    d. `.ember-config`

3. Which of the following is an extension provided by Ember?

    a. `Ember.DynamicArray`

    b. `Ember.ImmutableArray`

    c. `Ember.MutableArray`

    d. `Ember.StaticArray`

4. What is a valid option for the `locationType` config in the **environment.js** file?

    a. `history`

    b. `hash`

    c. `auto`

    d. All of the above

5. What is the keyword used to enable all experimental flags in the current Ember version?

    a. `ENABLE_EXPERIMENTAL_FEATURES`

    b. `ENABLE_OPTIONAL_FEATURES`

    c. `ENABLE_PRESENT_FEATURES`

    d. None of the above

6. Which of the following is not a valid optional feature shipped by Ember?

    a. `jquery-integration`

    b. `default-async-observers`

    c. `bootstrap-integration`

    d. `application-template-wrapper`

Answers

1. d
2. a
3. c
4. d
5. b
6. c

Questions

1. What are the disadvantages of making an object immutable?
2. What are the differences between hash and history APIs?
3. How do you handle deprecations that are removed in the upcoming version?
4. What are the configurations to be updated for embedding your Ember application into another web page?
5. What are experimental features and the different statuses of these features in a shipped Ember version?
6. What are the optional features shipped in Ember and how do you enable them?
7. What are the different configurations that can be done to `robots.txt`?
8. What is a sitemap?

Key Terms

- **Environment** - Variable used to denote the type of build we are going to generate.
- **App Secrets** - Sensitive information such as credentials to APIs our application interacts with.
- **Deprecation** - A functionality or API in the repository that has been decided to be removed from a future release of Ember.

- **Experimental Feature -** A feature is considered experimental when it is released for the first time in an Ember release. It stays the same manner until the Ember community deems it fit for production use.
- **Optional Feature** - A feature that is shipped as part of the Ember release, but not enabled. We can enable the feature if required by our project.
- **Web Crawler** - A bot (usually part of a search engine) that finds all content available on the internet, downloads and indexes them for providing search results in their engine.
- **Robots.txt** - A file used to define which URLs should be indexed/excluded by a web crawler thereby defining which pages should appear in search results.

CHAPTER 7

Testing Ember.js Applications

Introduction

In the previous chapter, we talked about configuring our Ember application and tweaking the settings to suit our needs. In this chapter, we will look at writing tests for our application to make it robust and secure. First, we will understand what testing is, and why it is important for an application. You will understand the different tools available to test our application. We will learn about the different types of tests that can be written and the advantages of each type.

Then we will look into different approaches to integrating testing with your development process to ensure the application is bug-free. We will look at writing tests for individual modules in Ember like Routes, Models, Helpers and Components. This will ensure that every line of code written by us is tested and secure. At the end of this chapter, you will be well versed in the testing process involved in software development and more specifically how they work with Ember.

Structure

The following topics will be discussed in this chapter:

- Introduction to Testing
- Manual Testing
- Testing Tools in Ember
- Levels of Testing
- Code Coverage

- Unit Tests
- Testing Components
- Testing Controllers
- Testing Helpers
- Testing Routes
- Testing Models
- Application Testing
- Updated Code Coverage

Introduction to Testing

When developing applications at a fast pace, there can be multiple developers working on the project and modifying code from the same file or code written by another developer. This can lead to the following issues:

- We should ensure that the newly developed features work as expected.
- New features written should not break existing features in our project. It can cause problems with existing customers using your application.

In order to avoid these problems, it is mandatory that we have an automated way to ensure every part of our application works as expected. That is where testing comes in. The more your application grows, the more difficult it becomes to track changes and ensure all the connected components still work as expected.

Advantages of Testing

We have seen what software testing is. Now let us look at why we need to spend the time and effort to write test cases for your application:

- **Early identification of defects**: Testing allows us to find out issues as and when they are introduced into the system, instead of going through multiple levels of reviews and merges and complicating the process of fixing them.
- **Improved Customer Satisfaction**: Testing will reduce the number of issues that get past the different steps before the code is deployed to the customer. Thus, the customer's satisfaction with the product increases since they face fewer issues when using the application.
- **Implicit Documentation**: Test cases implicitly serve as documentation on how the application is expected to work. Detailed comments and descriptions in the test cases make it easy for the transfer of knowledge to new people joining the organization/project.

- **Cost and Time efficient**: Finding out bugs early helps identify the cause easily as we can point out the change that caused the issue. Without early testing, it becomes a laborious effort to identify the root cause of the issue especially if the tester is not familiar with the internal code of the application.

Different Ways of Testing

There are different ways of testing an application before confirming its compliance with the requirements and ensuring that existing features are not broken due to new changes. Here are a couple of the most popular ways:

Manual Testing

Manual Testing is the conventional way of testing software without using any tools or libraries. It involves a human doing the testing, assuming the role of an end-user. They will manually go through each page and check if the features are working, just like an end user of the application would. This would mean that the tester will go through not only the flow thought through by the developer, but also workflows that occur rarely and are prone to become edge cases. That is, the tester can do a lot of exploratory testing to identify bugs in areas not encountered during the regular usage of a customer/end-user. A disadvantage of this method is the human component involved, which can cause errors due to human judgment or misses in testing all the scenarios. However, there are a lot of tools available to keep track of test cases and gauge the results of each case before signaling okay on any build.

Automated Testing

Automated tests are code written either by the developer building the feature or by a tester to ensure an application works as expected. This helps developers and reviewers to be confident of the changes done in a specific changeset and the results are instantaneous as the automation mechanisms are usually connected to the CI/CD pipelines of repositories and the code is moved to the review stage only after all the test cases pass. This process gives confidence by running all the test cases in a repository for even a small change made to the code. It drastically reduces the manual effort involved in testing all the cases for each feature developed and has more accuracy as well.

Understanding Manual Testing

There are different ways a tester can manually test an application for defects. Here are some testing methods:

Black Box Testing

It is a testing method where the tester does not have any knowledge of the underlying code of the application that is being tested. The tester simply provides a certain input to the application and verifies the output is received as expected. The way the application reacts to edge cases is also tested. For example, what happens when the values provided are outside the allowed range? How does the application react in case of missing data? and so on.

The advantage of this method is that the testing is done by a person who is not involved in the development process or someone who is not aware of the architecture and internal workings of the application. Thus, it is the closest way to mimic an end user for whom the application is written.

White Box Testing

Unlike black box testing, white box testing requires an awareness of the internal structure and workflow of the application. The tester has access to the source code and creates test cases based on the code. This method requires test cases to be written in the form of code. It is also called **Glass Box Testing or Transparent Testing.** It can be started early in the software development cycle, as it tests the code execution directly without the need for an interface that is required for black box testing.

Through this method, testers can find bugs and provide feedback on the internal code flow rather than just what the user sees on the screen. Viewing the source code means the tester can easily provide detailed test cases that cover the different code paths. However, it is a bit laborious to maintain, as these test cases have to be rewritten to accommodate even small changes in the code base.

Gray Box Testing

Gray Box Testing is a combination of black box testing and white box testing to overcome the disadvantages of both methods. In gray box testing, the tester does not have full knowledge of the internal structure of the system, but they have partial access and awareness of the internals of the application. An example can be, you can test that an authenticated page is not accessible to unauthenticated users. This requires some knowledge of the system to access the URL without clicking through the links in the application, but the tester does not know how the internals work to check if the user is authenticated.

Testing Tools in Ember

Ember being a self-sufficient framework in many senses, offers a wide variety of tools for automating your testing process. It also provides an easy way to integrate the testing in your Continuous Integration process to ensure all builds are tested and bug-free before they are merged.

QUnit

QUnit is a JavaScript testing framework that is part of every Ember application by default. Ember also includes a wrapper for **QUnit** named **QUnitDOM** that helps create tests that are readable and user-friendly. Powered with **QUnitDOM**, you can write tests in Ember that are easy to understand and serve as documentation for reference when trying to learn the expected behavior of a feature.

For example, if we want to check a DOM element has a particular class associated with it, the following is the code in QUnit:

```
assert.ok(button.classList.contains("my-class"));
```

The same functionality can be written in QUnitDOM as follows:

```
assert.dom(button).hasClass("my-class");
```

Based on this, we can see that **QUnitDOM** provides a wrapper that makes test cases more readable.

Running Tests in Ember

There are two ways to run tests in Ember. The first option is to run tests once. We have seen this command when we discussed the list of commands in Ember-CLI:

```
ember test
ember t
```

`ember` t is a short form of the `test` command. In some cases when writing test cases, we will want to run the test cases as and when they are written. Just like how the ember server reloads on each file change, you will want the tests to execute as well. This can be done by passing a simple option to the test command:

```
ember test --server
ember t -s
```

Passing the **--server** command listens for changes to the file and restarts the test server on each change.

Tests interface

Another way to run tests is to visit the URL **http://localhost:4200/tests** while running the server. This will load the test suite and run the tests once. You will receive feedback on the tests that failed as shown in *Figure 7.1*. It shows a summary of the test run with the number of successes and failures. It has a lot of options, like filtering tests from a specific module, showing only failed tests, and even an option to disable try-catch statements inside the application. This also gives you the option to rerun specific tests after you make changes to the code.

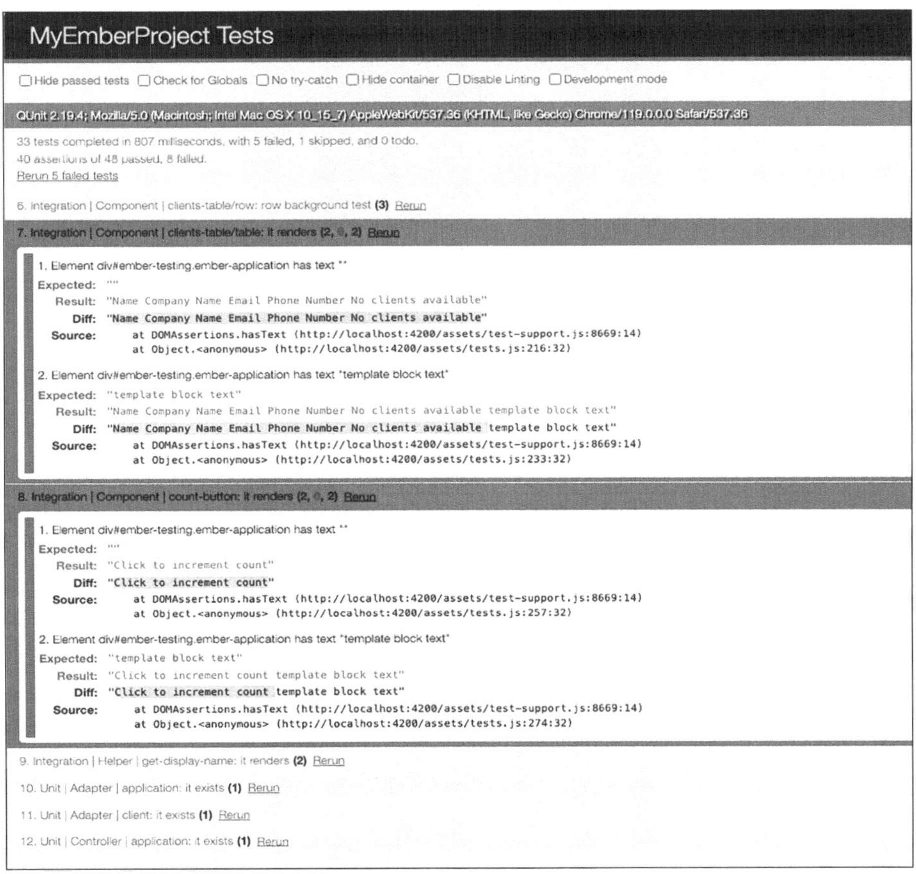

Figure 7.1: Ember Tests UI

Creating Tests in Ember

By default, whenever we create any object in Ember through blueprints, it automatically adds a test file for the object inside the **`tests`** folder of the project. Currently, the tests folder would look something like *Figure* 7.2.

From the example, you can see we have a test file inside the **`unit`** folder for each object we've created in our project. Also, you can see another folder called **`integration`** containing tests for each component and helper. We will discuss what **`unit`** and **`integration`** are later in this chapter.

```
tests
├── helpers
│   └── index.js
├── index.html
├── integration
│   ├── components
│   │   ├── click-tracker-test.js
│   │   ├── clients-table
│   │   │   ├── row-test.js
│   │   │   └── table-test.js
│   │   └── count-button-test.js
│   └── helpers
│       └── get-display-name-test.js
├── test-helper.js
└── unit
    ├── adapters
    │   ├── application-test.js
    │   └── client-test.js
    ├── controllers
    │   ├── application-test.js
    │   ├── clients
    │   │   └── index-test.js
    │   └── clients-test.js
    ├── models
    │   ├── client-test.js
    │   └── salesman-test.js
    ├── routes
    │   ├── about-test.js
    │   ├── clients
    │   │   └── view-test.js
    │   ├── fourohfour-test.js
    │   ├── index-test.js
    │   └── login-test.js
    ├── serializers
    │   └── client-test.js
    ├── services
    │   └── user-reports-test.js
    └── transforms
        └── gender-test.js
```

Figure 7.2: *tests folder*

Apart from this, Ember still provides additional blueprints to generate the test files for each object. Here are some examples of the blueprints:

```
ember generate model-test client
ember generate route-test about
ember generate acceptance-test clients
```

Filtering Tests

We saw options earlier to run tests using the **--server** option to listen for changes and run tests. In those cases, we will not want to run the entire test suite on each change, as it will be time-consuming. We will want to run specific tests that relate to the changes we are making to the application. Before looking into how you can run specific tests, let us look at what a sample test looks like. Let us open an existing test file, the **tests/integration/components/click-tracker-test.js** file. The default test generated for the component would look like this:

```
module('Integration | Component | click-tracker', function (hooks) {
  setupRenderingTest(hooks);


  test('it renders', async function (assert) {
    // Set any properties with this.set('myProperty', 'value');
    // Handle any actions with this.set('myAction', function(val)
{ ... });


    await render(hbs`<ClickTracker />`);


    assert.dom(this.element).hasText('');


    // Template block usage:
    await render(hbs`
      <ClickTracker>
        template block text
      </ClickTracker>
    `);
```

```
    assert.dom(this.element).hasText('template block text');
  });
});
```

The test has two simple steps. In the first step, it renders the component and asserts that it renders without any error. The second time, it renders the component as a block with a sample text in between and checks if the sample text is rendered inside the component.

If you look at the top of this test, there are two things that are used to classify tests and allow us to filter them. Here is how you can use them:

module

The first classification is based on the **`module()`** specification that we see. The module for this test has been specified as **`Integration | Component | click-tracker`**. Inside this module, there are multiple tests we can define. So if we want to run this group of tests, we can use the module filter as follows:

```
ember test --module="Integration | Component | click-tracker"
ember t -m="Integration | Component | click-tracker"
```

Adding this filter will run only the set of tests defined within this particular module.

filter

The second method for filtering and matching uses the **`test()`** or **`module()`** tag. You can see the value for this test to be **`it renders`**. The test filter is more efficient as it allows filtering via substring. For example, if you want to run just all the Component tests, we can do so by the following command:

```
ember test --filter="Component"
ember t -f="Component"
```

This will filter tests across modules and run only modules/tests that match the phrase. An additional functionality is to exclude certain tests based on the module name or test name. For example, to run all tests except for model tests, you can do as follows:

```
ember test --filter="!Model"
```

Test Selectors

In tests, we will want to grab certain DOM elements on a page in order to perform checks on those elements. Just like the normal element selectors we saw in the earlier chapters, we can pull DOM elements using jQuery selectors in Ember tests as well. By installing the **ember-test-selectors** addon Ember tests have functions like **querySelector** and **querySelectorAll** to select DOM elements. In order to select all elements by a particular class, here is an example:

```
this.element.querySelectorAll(".my-class")
```

Or

```
this.element.querySelector("#myElementById");
```

Using this addon, you can use test attributes in your template code by prefixing the attributes with data-test and using the **querySelector** function to filter elements based on the test attribute. The addon ensures that the test attributes are ignored when generating a production build. It is recommended to use data-test attributes instead of CSS selectors in Ember tests, as CSS selectors are bound to change frequently based on how the classes are mapped in your application. That will require your selectors to be rewritten. However, the data-test attributes are constant and need not change based on other dependencies.

Debug your tests

When running your tests, you will face a lot of errors or cases where they do not work as expected. In those cases, we need to find the problem and make changes accordingly to fix the issue. You can add **debugger** to any line in your test or application code. When the code reaches this line, it will pause the execution on that line, allowing you to check the state of each variable to understand where the test fails.

For example, let us add a debugger to the **routes/clients/index.js** file inside the model hook. It will look like this:

```
model(params) {
    debugger;
   return this.store.query('client', {});
}
```

To test this, you can go to the application, open the developer tools by doing a **Right Click > Inspect** on the page and then click the **Clients** tab. This will load the **clients** route and call the model hook, thus triggering the debugger. Your screen will pause and look like this:

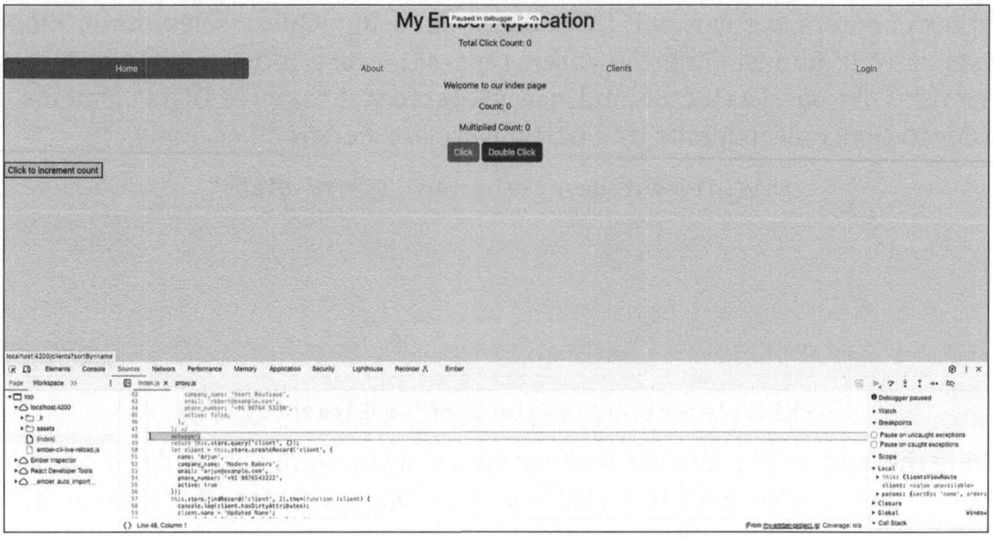

Figure 7.3: Debugger

You can see the code execution pausing at the place where we have added the debugger. At this point, we can look at the state of each variable in the memory now, execute functions, see the response, and so on. You can do that by going to the **`Console`** tab and typing your commands. Let us see what the **`params`** variable contains. Just type params in the console and press enter. You will see the output as follows:

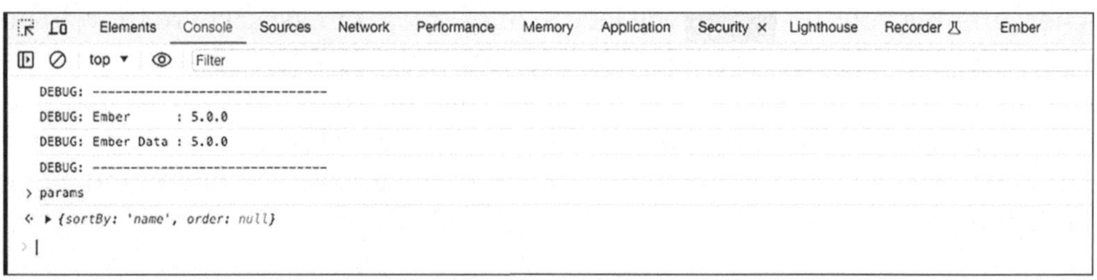

Figure 7.4: Console

pauseTest

Another option specific to Ember tests is to use the **`pauseTest`** function. It can be used only in test code and once you add **`await pauseTest();`** to your test, the code pauses when it reaches this line, very similar to the debugger. Once you are done inspecting the variables, you can enter **`resumeTest()`** in the console and the test continues further.

Levels of Testing

Inside the tests folder, you can see three sub-folders. Each of the subfolders contains tests of each level. We need different levels of testing to ensure all the use cases and code flows are covered in the test flow and the application is bug-free. The levels differ based on what part of the application they concentrate on, their scope of testing, whether they depend on the application being rendered for executing the test, how fast they execute and so on.

Here is a chart of the different levels of testing commonly used in Ember and their hierarchy of execution. We will look at each of them in detail:

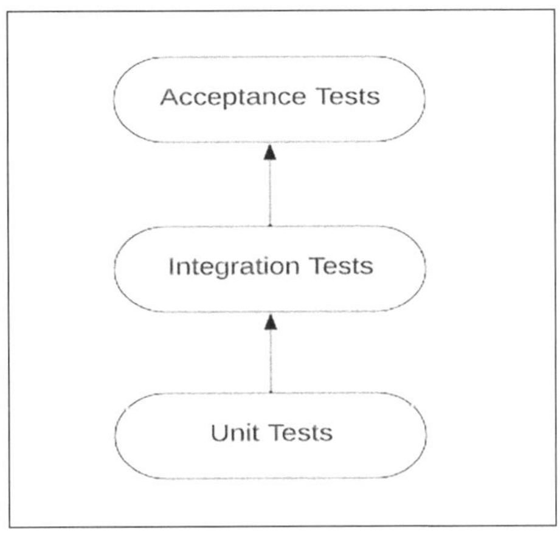

Figure 7.5: *Levels of Testing*

Unit Tests

Unit testing is the basic level of testing individual parts of your application. It will help validate the correctness of individual objects or functions without interference from other objects in the system. Unit tests are made on the smallest testable parts of the system. This will ensure the small parts of the application work as expected. The following are the benefits of unit testing:

- Unit tests are isolated and focus on individual functions. It is easy to debug failures as we can zero it down to the exact object.
- Unit tests allow testing small logics that cannot be tested in big-picture application-level tests.
- Unit tests do not require the application to fully render. Hence, they are pretty fast.

Since unit tests are fast, we write test cases for each and every branching in the code or every scenario that the code is custom-written for. Once we provide 100% code coverage for all the code in these objects, we can be sure that the objects work perfectly as per the requirements and certify the individual objects as bug-free. It also helps us find issues early in the development process, as we can easily narrow down the place and the cause for any issue occurring in the system, as the test cases are written for a specific object and not for the entire application.

The individual test cases will also serve as documentation to understand the various cases handled by this application. This also provides confidence that any change to these objects that affects an existing functionality will immediately be flagged by the failure of the corresponding test cases.

Based on the contents of the **unit** folder in the project, we can understand that we usually write unit test cases for **adapters**, **controllers**, **models**, **routes**, **serializers**, **services**, and **transforms**. We do not need to render the application or the template to test these objects. Hence, they fall under the unit test category.

If you look at any of the existing unit test files, let us say the **tests/unit/services/user-report-test.js** file, you can see the following content:

```
module('Unit | Service | user-reports', function (hooks) {
  setupTest(hooks);

  // TODO: Replace this with your real tests.
  test('it exists', function (assert) {
    let service = this.owner.lookup('service:user-reports');
    assert.ok(service);
  });
});
```

If you look at the contents, the first line below the module declaration - **setupTest(hooks);.** This line can be found in all unit test files. This line allows us to use certain functionalities in the tests like dependency injection. If you look at the first line inside the test.

```
let service = this.owner.lookup('service:user-reports');
```

This line fetches the **user-reports** service to be used in the test. This lookup functionality is enabled by calling the **setupTest** function. This also enables the **pauseTest** functionality we saw earlier.

Rendering Tests

The next level of tests is the rendering test (Integration test). Rendering tests are not restricted to a single object but a combination of objects or components and require some amount of rendering for them to be tested. Unit tests are required to ensure that the objects are individually working as expected. But we also need to ensure that the modules work properly when interacting with each other as well. Rendering tests focus on validating the interactions between different modules and components and verifying that they work as per expectations. So once all objects are unit tested, we run rendering tests to verify that the objects work as expected when interacting with other objects present in the system as well.

From the existing **`tests/integration`** folder, we can see that **helpers** and **components** have rendering tests. This is because helpers and components can be tested only by rendering them on the screen. Hence, integration tests are also called **Rendering Tests**. These tests simulate the rendering of components similar to how they render in the real application, including all the life cycle hooks of the component. You can pass different variables and functions to the component just like you do from inside the application and verify the output.

Similar to how we have **`setupTest()`** in the unit tests, you can see a function call to **`setupRenderingTest();`**. This function calls **`setupTests()`** internally. On top of that, it sets up the rendering engine and allows us to interact with the DOM that is generated. Through this, you can access the DOM using the **`this.element`** attribute. Let us check the **`tests/integration/components/count-button-test.js`** file for example here:

```
module('Integration | Component | count-button', function (hooks) {
  setupRenderingTest(hooks);


  test('it renders', async function (assert) {
    // Set any properties with this.set('myProperty', 'value');
    // Handle any actions with this.set('myAction', function(val)
{ ... });


    await render(hbs`<CountButton />`);


    assert.dom(this.element).hasText('');
```

```
      // Template block usage:
      await render(hbs`
        <CountButton>
          template block text
        </CountButton>
      `);

      assert.dom(this.element).hasText('template block text');
    });
  });
```

From the preceding example, we can see the **setupRenderingTest()** function being called at the beginning and the usage of **this.element** to access the rendered DOM element.

Application Tests

Application tests are the highest level of testing, where the tests simulate the actual loading of the application through routes, triggering all the hooks of the particular route. These tests are very close to the end-user experience. For example, you can visit a URL, and verify that it redirects you to the login page if the user is not authenticated. Then you can fill out the login information and then go back to the first URL and verify we are able to see the contents of the page now. You can also use application tests to verify that the loading and error substates work as expected.

Though rendering tests test the interactions between different components, they do not test the full cycle of loading the entire application and loading multiple unrelated components as part of the page. The application tests, also named **System Tests** do that and make sure the end user does not face any issues when using the application. For that reason, it is slower compared to unit or rendering tests.

You can see from the existing **tests** folder that acceptance tests are not created by default. It is usual behavior to create application tests, one for each route. Acceptance tests can be generated with the following command:

```
ember generate acceptance-test clients
```

You can now see an **acceptance** folder inside tests and a **tests/acceptance/clients-test.js** file with the following content:

```
module('Acceptance | clients', function (hooks) {
  setupApplicationTest(hooks);

  test('visiting /clients', async function (assert) {
    await visit('/clients');

    assert.strictEqual(currentURL(), '/clients');
  });
});
```

You can see the test loads the **clients** route and then checks if the page loads properly. If you look at the first line of the test, you can see **setupApplicationTest(hooks);**. This is similar to the setup functions we saw in the earlier test types. This takes care of setting up the application and helps manipulate the routing of the application and accessing the currentURL, visit functions, and so on.

Code Coverage

Before we modify the predefined test cases or create new ones, we will first go through the process of benchmarking the efficiency of our test suite. Code Coverage is the basic parameter through which we validate the thoroughness of a test suite. This tells you the number of lines of code that are covered by test cases and provides a percentage of the code that is covered in the tests that ran. It is basically the percentage of the code that is executed when you run a full test suite.

A code coverage of 100% is the ideal marker that a repository should aim for. It means every line of code written in the project has at least one test case that executes that line. Code Coverage reports calculate four types of metrics as follows:

- **Function Coverage**: The number of functions defined in the code that is called from the test suite.
- **Branch Coverage**: Out of all the if/else branches present, how many of the branches are called in the test run.

- **Statement Coverage**: Number of statements in the overall code that were called in the test run.
- **Line Coverage**: Number of lines of source code that get executed during the test run. The difference between statement and line coverage is that there can be multiple statements present in a single line separated by a semi-colon (;).

In order to validate the test coverage of our codebase, we will install a package named `ember-cli-code-coverage` with the following command:

```
ember install ember-cli-code-coverage
```

Once installed, we need to do a setup in a couple of places in the application. In the first place, we need to include the plugin in our **`ember-cli-build.js`**. You can do this by adding the following lines to the build file:

```
const app = new EmberApp(defaults, {
  …
  babel: {
    plugins: [...require('ember-cli-code-coverage').buildBabelPlugin()]
  }
  …
}
```

This installs the code coverage plugin, enabling us to use the plugin inside the project. Next, we need to instruct the test code to run code coverage after the tests are completed. You can do that by adding the following lines at the end of the **`tests/test-helper.js`** file:

```
import { forceModulesToBeLoaded, sendCoverage } from 'ember-cli-code-
coverage/test-support';

QUnit.done(async function() {
  forceModulesToBeLoaded();
  await sendCoverage();
});
```

Through these lines, we have instructed the code coverage function to run in the **`QUnit.done`** hook which executes after the tests are done.

Once installed, we can run the tests and generate a coverage report using the following command:

```
COVERAGE=true ember test
```

By passing the **`COVERAGE=true`** environment variable when running the tests, you can see a new folder named **`coverage`** after the test run completes. You can open the folder to see a lot of files inside. Let us visually see the results by opening the **`index.html`** file inside the **`coverage`** folder. It will look like this:

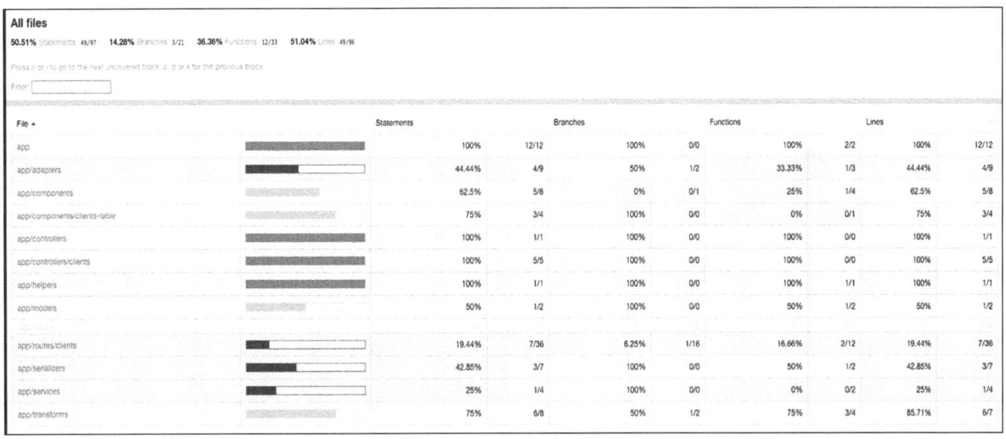

Figure 7.6: *Code Coverage*

From this screen, you can see that we have around 50% of code coverage in our project. And we get the coverage count of each folder in the project as well. You can click on individual folder names and find out the coverage metrics of each of the files inside the folder. For example, we can see that **`apps/components`** have 62.5% statement coverage. Now if you want to see the coverage of each individual component, you can click the folder name and see the coverage result of each component. You can click an individual component name to see red highlights on lines of code that were not touched by the test coverage.

Let us open **`adapters/application.js`** and see the code coverage there. From *Figure* 7.5, you can see that there are no test cases for the **`pathForType`** function that has the type salesman. That is one test case we can add to add coverage to this line. Similarly, we do not have tests for the authentication process as well. Our goal at the end of the chapter will be to increase the coverage as much as possible.

Figure 7.7: *File Code Coverage*

Bug Fixing with Existing Tests

Before writing new test cases, we can first run the test suite and check if there are any failures occurring in our existing test suite and fix them. We can run the tests using the **`ember test`** command, and here is the example of the output you will see:

```
1..25
# tests 25
# pass  17
# skip  0
# todo  0
# fail  8
```

We can see that eight tests are failing in this situation. Let us look at a few scenarios on why they fail and how we can fix them. You can scroll through the output of the test command to find out the issues. Doing this exercise is for us to understand the problems in the code that we have already written and ensure that we do not run into similar issues when writing further code.

tests/unit/serializers/client-test.js

```
not ok 21 Chrome 119.0 - [18 ms] - Unit | Serializer | client: it
serializes records
    ---
        actual: >
            null
        stack: >
           TypeError: Cannot read properties of undefined (reading 'slice')
                at ClientSerializer.serialize (http://localhost:7357/as-
sets/my-ember-project.js:9829:36)
                at Snapshot.serialize (http://localhost:7357/assets/ven-
dor.js:56106:25)
                at Store.serializeRecord (http://localhost:7357/assets/
vendor.js:72381:79)
                at ClientModel.serialize (http://localhost:7357/assets/
vendor.js:60943:41)
                at Object.<anonymous> (http://localhost:7357/assets/
tests.js:3857:62)
        message: >
            Died on test #1: Cannot read properties of undefined (reading
'slice')
                at Object.<anonymous> (http://localhost:7357/assets/
tests.js:3853:21)
        negative: >
            false
        browser log: |
```

This error is in the client serializer we created. As the error states, we are trying to **`slice`** an undefined variable. In our serializer code, we have the following lines:

```
json.data.attributes.phone_number = {
  country_code: phone_number.slice(0, 3),
  phone_number: phone_number.slice(3),
};
```

From the error message, we can understand that the variable **phone_number** is **undefined**, hence the failure. This will cause errors in execution when working with clients without a phone number. So let us update the code to do a slice only when the phone number has a value. The updated code will look like this:

```
if (phone_number) {
    json.data.attributes.phone_number = {
      country_code: phone_number.slice(0, 3),
      phone_number: phone_number.slice(3),
    };
} else {
    json.data.attributes.phone_number = {
      country_code: '',
      phone_number: ''
    }
}
```

Once you make the changes, you can run the test suite again and see that the number of failures is down to seven.

tests/integration/helper/get-display-name-test

```
not ok 7 Chrome 119.0 - [45 ms] - Integration | Helper | get-display-name: it renders
    ---
        actual: >
            undefined <undefined>
        expected: >
            1234
        stack: >
                at DOMAssertions.hasText (http://localhost:7357/assets/test-support.js:8669:14)
```

```
            at Object.<anonymous> (http://localhost:7357/assets/
tests.js:1533:32)
        message: >
            Element div#ember-testing.ember-application has text "1234"
        negative: >
            false
        browser log: |
```

Based on the test code, we can see that the test tries to pass a value to this helper function and checks if that value is present in the generated DOM. This will not suit our case as we expect a client object for this test case and not just a string. For this instance, we will update the test case instead of the code. Let us update the test case to call the helper with an object instead of a string. Since the helper uses the name and email to display, let us update the test code as follows:

```
this.set('inputValue', {'name': 'Test', 'email': 'test@example.com'});
```

Similarly, we should also update the assert statement to check for the actual response that should be returned by the helper. It should be updated as follows:

```
assert.dom(this.element).hasText('Test <test@example.com>');
```

Once these two lines are updated, we now have the test case providing a proper parameter to the helper function and checking for a valid response from the helper function. We can run the test suite now to ensure that the number of failures has reduced to six.

tests/integration/component/clients-table/row-test.js

```
not ok 4 Chrome 119.0 - [49 ms] - Integration | Component | clients-ta-
ble/row: it renders
    ---
        stack: >
            TypeError: Cannot read properties of undefined (reading 'name')
                at getDisplayName (http://localhost:7357/assets/my-em-
ber-project.js:5379:22)
                at FunctionHelperManager.getValue (http://local-
host:7357/assets/vendor.js:27557:14)
                at http://localhost:7357/assets/vendor.js:27518:70
                at http://localhost:7357/assets/vendor.js:31347:37
```

```
            at track (http://localhost:7357/assets/vendor.js:39169:7)
            at valueForRef (http://localhost:7357/assets/vendor.
js:31346:44)
            at Object.evaluate (http://localhost:7357/assets/ven-
dor.js:34877:60)
            at AppendOpcodes.evaluate (http://localhost:7357/as-
sets/vendor.js:32660:19)
            at LowLevelVM.evaluateSyscall (http://localhost:7357/
assets/vendor.js:35822:22)
            at LowLevelVM.evaluateInner (http://localhost:7357/as-
sets/vendor.js:35793:14)
      message: >
         global failure: TypeError: Cannot read properties of unde-
fined (reading 'name')
      negative: >
         false
      browser log: |
         {"type":"error","text":"\n\nError occurred:\n\n- While render-
ing:\n  -top-level\n    application\n      index\n        clients-table/
row\n\n"}
         {"type":"error","text":"\n\nError occurred:\n\n\n\n"}
         {"type":"warn","text":"Attempted to rerender, but the Em-
ber application has had an unrecoverable error occur during render. You
should reload the application after fixing the cause of the error."}
```

For this failure, we can see that the failure is in the **clients-table/row** component. If you look at the test, it calls the component without any parameters. The row component uses the **get-display-name** helper to show the display tag of a client. In the helper, you can see we try to access **client.name** and from the tests, we can see the component being called without a client. There are two ways to fix this:

- Update the **get-display-name** helper to handle cases where the client is not present
- Modify the test case to pass a client from the tests

For security purposes, let us do both. You can update the helper function as follows:

```
export default function getDisplayName(client) {
    if (client)
```

```
            return `${client.name} <${client.email}>`;
        return '';
    }
```

This will check if the client object is present and only then return the display tag. Otherwise, it returns an empty string. Next, let us update the test for the same:

```
test('it renders', async function (assert) {
    this.set('client', {'name': 'Test', 'email': 'test@example.com'});

    await render(hbs`<ClientsTable::Row @client={{this.client}} />`);

    assert.dom(this.element).hasText('Test <test@example.com> (Inactive)
- - View | Edit | Delete');

}
```

Note that to pass an object to the component, you will need to do a **`this.set`** to associate the object to the current test and then pass it to the component using **`this.client`**. The assertion is updated to check for the actual text output generated by this component, stripping out the HTML tags. After updating the test, you can run the suite again and see the failure count reduced to five. You can do the fixes for the remaining tests in the same manner to remove all failures.

Unit Tests

We will now see how we can write test cases for the application. It is recommended that we write test cases for every custom logic or item we write that is custom for our application. Here are some common cases that we will need to write test cases for.

Tracked Properties

We saw earlier how tracked properties are used to update the value of a particular property based on changes to another property. For example, we have a **`count`** variable in our **`user-report`** service. Let us make that a tracked property, and create a **`getter`** function that returns the count multiplied by 2. Here is what the service will look like:

```
import Service from '@ember/service';
import { tracked } from '@glimmer/tracking';
```

```
export default class UserReportsService extends Service {
  @tracked count = 0;

  get multipliedCount() {
    return count * 2;
  }

  …
}
```

Now in our **tests/unit/services/user-reports-test.js** file, let us add a new test for checking if the tracked variable works:

```
test('multipliedCount tracker', function(assert) {
  let service = this.owner.lookup('service:user-reports');
  service.count = 2;
  assert.equal(service.multipliedCount, 4);
});
```

We can run just the service test with the following command. The test passing means that the computed property works as expected.

```
ember test -f="user-reports"
```

Object Methods

Similar to tracked properties, we need to write tests for functions/methods we have written for each object. For example, our **user-reports** service has two functions. **incrementCount** and **getCount**. We will have to write test cases for both. Let us add the following tests for user-reports:

```
test('incrementCount test', function(assert) {
  let service = this.owner.lookup('service:user-reports');
  service.count = 2;
  service.incrementCount();
  assert.equal(service.count, 3);
  service.incrementCount();
  assert.equal(service.count, 4);
```

```
});

test('getCount test', function(assert) {
  let service = this.owner.lookup('service:user-reports');
  service.count = 2;
  assert.equal(service.getCount(), 2);
  service.count = 4;
  assert.equal(service.getCount(), 4);
});
```

From the code, you can see that we set an initial value to the count variable, call the **incrementCount** function twice and ensure the count variable is updated as per expectation every time. Similarly, we set the count variable and ensure that **getCount** returns the value as it is.

Skip Tests

When running the test suite, you will want to skip certain tests from executing because the feature might not have been completed or there is a bug that is not fixed yet. In these cases, You can just change the **test** function call to **skip** and that particular test will not be executed during the test run.

```
import { skip } from 'qunit';

skip('skip this test', function(assert) {
    assert.ok(false);
});
```

Stubbing

When running unit tests, sometimes there will be cases where we will not want to execute the whole code of a function for a few reasons:

- The function could be complex and time-consuming. We would not want the test to take long to execute.
- When testing a function, we will want to restrict the code execution to that particular function so that we can isolate the bugs specific to that particular function.
- There can be third-party API calls from within a function that cannot be executed during test runs, as they can charge you for every API call.

In the preceding cases, it is normal to mimic the execution of a function or an object and make it return a value that you expect the actual function to. This will ensure we know exactly what another function will return and any issues we find are restricted to the actual function we are testing.

Stubbing Functions

Let us say we want to stub the **incrementCount** function in our service to increment the value by two instead of one. Here is the updated test case with the function stubbed:

```
test('incrementCount test', function(assert) {
    let service = this.owner.lookup('service:user-reports');
    service.count = 2;
    service.incrementCount();
    assert.equal(service.count, 3);
    service.incrementCount();
    assert.equal(service.count, 4);
    service.incrementCount = function() {
      service.count += 2;
    }
    service.incrementCount();
    // After the increment, the value should be increased to 6
    assert.equal(service.count, 6);
});
```

By doing this, you can reduce complex functions into simple lines of code to reduce the time and complexity of test cases.

Stubbing Objects

Similar to functions, we will want to mock a complex object in the test as well, with just specific attributes that are required inside the function for testing. A particular object that is used inside a service or component can have complex functions in it, so you might want to simplify them during test execution. For example, in a preceding example, we saw how we passed the client object when calling the **client-table/row** component. There, instead of passing a Client model record, we passed just a sample object. Similarly, we can mimic any object by creating relevant functions within the test code and only attributes/ properties that are required inside the current function that we are testing.

Stubbing Services

Some parts of your application can have multiple services injected into them, and functions from each service can be called from the object. For example, you can have objects that call payment services to make payments or to get your subscription status. In these cases, we would not want the payment API to be called from the tests or the tests failing because of that. So we will need to create a stub for the entire service and the functions inside them. Here is an example of how you can stub it:

```
import Service from '@ember/service';

class PaymentServiceStub extends Service {

  someParam = 'test';
  secondParam = 'example';

  getSubscriptionStatus() {
    return {
      subscribed: true,
      subscriptionId: '123432'
    }
  }

  createSubscription() {
    return { success: true };
  }
}

module('Integration | Component | ClickTracker', function(hooks) {
  setupRenderingTest(hooks);
```

```
  hooks.beforeEach(function(assert) {
    this.owner.register('service:payment-service', PaymentServiceStub);
  });
}
```

You can see that we are creating a dummy service that extends the actual **Service** class. After the **setupRenderingTest** function is called, we call the **hooks.beforeEach** event and register the dummy service we created in place of the original service. Once done, it will replace the service for the entirety of the module. We can be in full control of the service execution and prevent unnecessary API calls.

Testing Components

As mentioned earlier, components are testable via integration/rendering tests that generate the component and allow you to access the generated DOM to test for HTML elements and their attributes/values. We can use this to test whether DOM generation works as expected and the component HTML is generated as per requirements.

Testing DOM attributes

For example, we have the **client-table/row** component that adds a green background if the client is active, and gray if the client is inactive. We can add a test for the same using the following code:

```
test('row background test', async function(assert) {
  this.set('client', {'name': 'Test', 'email': 'test@example.com',
'active': false, 'id': 1});
  await render(hbs`<ClientsTable::Row @client={{this.client}} />`);
  assert.dom('.my-custom-class').hasClass('bg-gray');

  this.set('client', {'name': 'Test', 'email': 'test@example.com',
'active': true, 'id': 1});
  await render(hbs`<ClientsTable::Row @client={{this.client}} />`);
  assert.dom('.my-custom-class').hasClass('bg-green');
});
```

In this test, we are rendering the component twice, once with each case that we want to test. After each render, we find the element using the class name

my-custom-class, which we have added to the **clients-table/row** component already. After fetching the element, we check if the element has the proper class name attached to it based on our requirements. We can use this to check if certain attributes are present for the element as well. We can check if the element has the proper ID based on the ID of the client. You can do the check as follows:

```
assert.dom('.my-custom-class').hasAttribute('id', 'client-1');
```

Testing User Interactions

In components, we will need to test that user interactions are triggering actions and making changes to the DOM accordingly. For example, in our **click-tracker** component, we have two buttons that increment count by one and two, respectively. We need to write tests to click the button and confirm if the count increases as expected. Ember tests offer a **click** function that allows you to simulate a button click inside a test case. Here is how it works:

```
import { click, render } from '@ember/test-helpers';


test('increment count', async function (assert) {
    await render(hbs`<ClickTracker />`);
    assert.dom('.count').hasText('Count: 0');
    assert.dom('.multiplied-count').hasText('Multiplied Count: 0');

    await click('.btn-primary');
    assert.dom('.count').hasText('Count: 1');
    assert.dom('.multiplied-count').hasText('Multiplied Count: 2');

    await click('.btn-success');
    assert.dom('.count').hasText('Count: 3');
    assert.dom('.multiplied-count').hasText('Multiplied Count: 6');

});
```

In this test, we are rendering the component and verify the initial state of the component by checking if the count and multiplied count are set to 0. Then we simulate the button click by using the **click** function of Ember tests. We click each button once and check if the DOM elements are updated with proper values, as expected. It ensures that the corresponding action is called when the button is clicked and the values are updated in the DOM immediately.

Testing Actions

When calling components, you can pass actions from a parent component or controller to the child component, and the same can be called from the child component. Even though we can test the action separately in the parent component, we will need to check that the action is being called from the child component in this case. It can be done by altering the stubbing mechanism we saw previously in this chapter.

For example, let us consider a component that expects a **dummyFunction** as a parameter and calls that function when a button is clicked. The test will need to pass a stub of that function when rendering the component and then clicking the button. After that, we need to check if the stubbed function was called. Here is how we can do it:

```
test('dummyFunction call check', async function (assert) {
    assert.expect(1);

    this.set('dummyFunction', (param) => {
      let expectedParam = 10;
      assert.equal(param, expectedParam, 'dummyFunction is called with
the expected param');
    });
    await render(hbs`<MyDummyComponent @dummyFunction={{this.dummyFunc-
tion}} />`);

    await click('.dummy-trigger');
});
```

We create a sample **dummyFunction** inside the test. Inside the function, we create a variable containing the value you expect this function to be called with. In this example, we expect the function to be called with the parameter 10. We do an assertion on the same. Then we pass this function to the component and simulate the click of the button that triggers the **dummyFunction**.

Notice the **assert.expect(1)** at the beginning of the test. It notifies Ember that it needs one successful assertion for the test to be considered a pass. By this, we can be sure that the function is called, and the assertion is triggered from inside the function, for the assertion count to match.

Testing Controllers

Testing Controllers are similar to testing components. But Controllers tests are unit tests, as we test only the functions and actions in the controller rather than checking on the rendering of the page and rendering the components called from inside the controller. That is because the components are individually tested and the interactions among them are tested in the acceptance tests. So, unit tests for controllers are to ensure that all the functions and actions in the controller are working as expected.

When testing components, we tested actions by the results that they produced in the DOM. But here we cannot do that as we do not have a DOM in these unit tests. We will need to call the action and test its execution based on the updates it does to properties inside the controller. Let us consider a sample controller that has an action which updates a property in the controller as follows:

```
import Controller from '@ember/controller';
import { action } from '@ember/object';


export default class SampleController extends Controller {


  testProp = '';


  @action
  updateTestProp(updatedValue) {
    this.testProp = updatedValue;
  }
}
```

To test this controller, we can write a test that checks the value of the prop on load, then calls the action to update the value and finally checks if the prop is updated. Here is how it will look:

```
test('sample controller test', function(assert) {
    let controller = this.owner.lookup('controller:sample');
    assert.equal(controller.testProp, '');
```

```
    controller.send('updateTestProp', 'update');
    assert.equal(controller.testProp, 'update');
});
```

The action is called from the test using the **send** function in the controller, which eventually updates the **testProp**.

Testing Helpers

When testing helpers, we need to ensure that we write test cases for every combination of arguments that this helper can accept. This will help us ensure that the helper is working for all cases and will not raise an issue irrespective of whether the helper is called with or without the correct set of parameters.

For example, in our get-display-name helper, we tested that it succeeds and returns the expected data when passing the client object. But what if there is no parameter passed to this function? Let us add a test case for that by adding the following lines to the existing test case in the **tests/integration/helpers/get-display-name-test.js** file:

```
await render(hbs`{{get-display-name}}`);
assert.dom(this.element).hasText('');
```

This ensures that even if the helper is called without any parameters, there is no error and the helper renders with an empty string. Note that helpers can also be unit-tested, by simply calling them like a function and checking the response, instead of rendering the helper.

Testing Routes

Routes are an integral component of the application that connects the different modules in the application. But for the test suite to be thorough and for us to validate each functionality, it is required to test the individual or lifecycle hooks of each router. However, some of them can only be tested via Application Testing (like transitioning to a different route). Here is what a simple route test will look like:

```
import { module, test } from 'qunit';
import { setupTest } from 'my-ember-project/tests/helpers';

module('Unit | Route | index', function (hooks) {
```

```
  setupTest(hooks);

  test('it exists', function (assert) {
    let route = this.owner.lookup('route:index');
    assert.ok(route);
  });
});
```

The test just fetches the route and checks if it loads okay. We saw in earlier chapters about the different lifecycle hooks in an Ember Route like **`beforeModel`**, **`afterModel`**, **`error`**, and **`loading`** states. We can also set controller variables from within the router using the **`setupController`** method. We can test each of these hooks by calling them directly from the test and checking if a particular value has been updated in the controller.

Testing Models

Models can be unit tested by isolating them from the Store service, making the model just like any other object in our application. Without the involvement of the store, there are a few functionalities we can test:

Default Values

When defining the model, we usually specify a default value for items when the value is not specified in the API or not specified when creating the model object in the Ember application. Such behaviors have to be tested by creating a dummy model object. We can modify the default test case created for the model as follows:

```
module('Unit | Model | client', function (hooks) {
  setupTest(hooks);

  // Replace this with your real tests.
  test('it exists', function (assert) {
    let store = this.owner.lookup('service:store');
    let model = store.createRecord('client', {});
    assert.equal(model.date, new Date());
  });
});
```

Model Functions

The next type of testing is for model functions. We will need to check if each of the functions returns data exactly as expected. For example, our client model has a function named **displayTag** which returns a formatted name and email. Here is how we can test it:

```
test('displayTag test', function (assert) {
    let store = this.owner.lookup('service:store');
    let model = store.createRecord('client', {name: 'Test', email:
'test@example.com'});
    assert.equal(model.displayTag, 'Test <test@example.com>');
});
```

As an exercise, you can write test cases for different cases like empty names, empty emails or both fields being empty.

Relationships

We saw different ways in which models can be related to each other. In tests, we will need to ensure they are related to the correct model with the correct type of relationship. In our project, we have a relationship between the user model and the salesman model. We can test the relationship as follows:

```
import { get } from '@ember/object';


test('relationship test', function (assert) {
    let client = this.owner.lookup('service:store').modelFor('client');
    let clientRelationship = get(client, 'relationshipsByName').
get('salesman');


    // Assert the name of the related model
    assert.equal(clientRelationship.key, 'salesman');


    // Assert the type of relationship
    assert.equal(clientRelationship.kind, 'belongsTo');
});
```

We fetch the relationship object from the model and check that the field is linked to the correct model and that the type is as expected as well. A similar check can be done for the salesman:

```
test('relationship test', function (assert) {
    let salesman =
this.owner.lookup('service:store').modelFor('salesman');
    let salesmanRelationship = get(salesman, 'relationshipsBy-
Name').get('clients');


    assert.equal(salesmanRelationship.key, 'clients');
    assert.equal(salesmanRelationship.kind, 'hasMany');
});
```

Application Testing

Application Testing or **System Testing** is for checking if the entire application loads properly and redirections happen as expected. Ember provides a set of functions to help us judge the current status of the application like the **`currentURL`**, **`currentRoute`**, and so on. Here are some of the actions that you can do in the application tests:

- **`visit`**: The visit function can be used to load the application with a specific URL. We discussed earlier in our generated acceptance test how this works.
- **`click`**: This function can be used to simulate a click on any element present in the DOM.
- **`fillIn`**: When there are input elements present on the page, we can use this method to enter values into this input field. You can select input elements either through their id or class or through their name or the **`data-test`** attribute of the element. Here is an example:

  ```
  fillIn('[data-test-field="Name"]', 'Fill Value');
  ```
- **`triggerEvent`:** This function can be used to trigger any DOM event like a mouse click, hover, blur, and so on. Here is an example of how you can use it:

  ```
  triggerEvent('#id-of-element', 'hover');
  ```
- **`triggerKeyEvent`**: Similar to **`triggerEvent`**, this function can be used to trigger any key-based event like **`keyUp`** and **`keyDown`**.

These functions are asynchronous and return a promise that resolves once the action is performed. As seen in the preceding examples, it is required to use **await** when calling these helpers. Similar to this, there is a set of synchronous functions that return data about the state of the application immediately:

- **currentURL**: Returns the current URL that is loaded in the application
- **currentRouteName**: Returns the route that is loaded in the application
- **find**: Enables you to fetch a single element from the DOM that matches the selector passed to this function
- **findAll**: Allows filtering multiple elements in the DOM that match the selector

Setting up Mirage

By default, Mirage is not enabled during tests. It is disabled by default to prevent accidental third-party calls so that tests are executed only based on data provided to each test. We will have to consciously enable Mirage in those specific tests where we want the application to contact Mirage. Here is how you enable Mirage in tests:

```
import { setupMirage } from 'ember-cli-mirage/test-support';


module('Acceptance | clients, function (hooks) {
  setupApplicationTest(hooks);
  setupMirage(hooks);
});
```

Testing Redirections

A main part of Application Testing is to verify redirections between routes. In our case, we have a restriction about redirecting the user back to the clients list page, when the client is inactive. Let us generate an acceptance test for **clients/view** route and add the following test to check the redirection:

```
import { module, test } from 'qunit';
import { visit, currentURL } from '@ember/test-helpers';
import { setupApplicationTest } from 'my-ember-project/tests/helpers';
import { setupMirage } from 'ember-cli-mirage/test-support';
```

```
module('Acceptance | clients/view', function (hooks) {
  setupApplicationTest(hooks);
  setupMirage(hooks);

  test('visiting /clients/view', async function (assert) {
    await visit('/clients/1');

    assert.strictEqual(currentURL(), '/clients/1');
  });

  test('visiting inactive client', async function (assert) {
    await visit('/clients/2');

    assert.strictEqual(currentURL(), '/clients');

  });
});
```

Here we have two test cases. From the Mirage data, we know that the client with id 1 is active and the client with `id` 2 is inactive. So we first load the client with id 1 and ensure the application stays in the same route. Then we load the client with id 2 and check that the user is routed back to the clients list route.

Updated Code Coverage

In the entirety of this chapter, we have written a variety of test cases to make our code more secure. Let us quantify the results by running the code coverage via the command **`COVERAGE=true ember test`**.

Here is the updated code coverage:

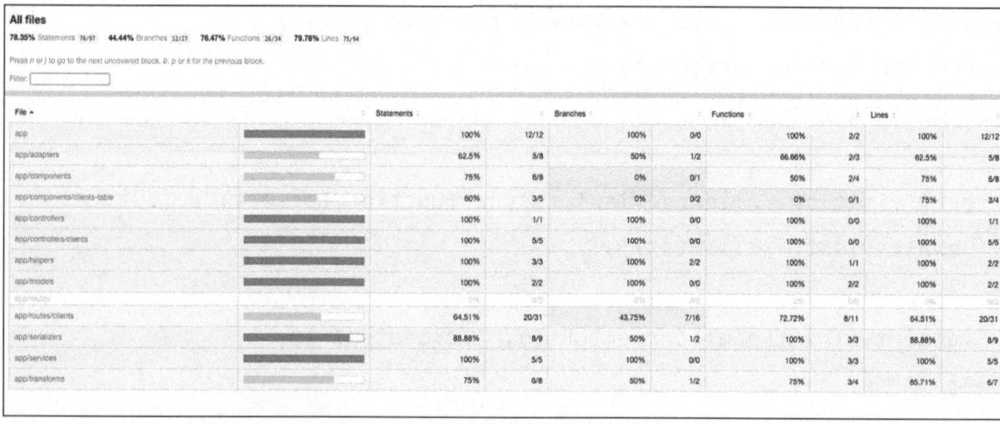

All files

78.35% Statements 76/97 44.44% Branches 12/27 76.47% Functions 26/34 79.78% Lines 75/94

Press *n* or *j* to go to the next uncovered block, *b*, *p* or *k* for the previous block.

Filter:

File	Statements		Branches		Functions		Lines	
app	100%	12/12	100%	0/0	100%	2/2	100%	12/12
app/adapters	62.5%	5/8	50%	1/2	66.66%	2/3	62.5%	5/8
app/components	75%	6/8	0%	0/1	50%	2/4	75%	6/8
app/components/clients-table	60%	3/5	0%	0/2	0%	0/1	75%	3/4
app/controllers	100%	1/1	100%	0/0	100%	0/0	100%	1/1
app/controllers/clients	100%	5/5	100%	0/0	100%	0/0	100%	5/5
app/helpers	100%	3/3	100%	2/2	100%	1/1	100%	2/2
app/models	100%	2/2	100%	0/0	100%	2/2	100%	2/2
app/routes	0%	0/0	0%	0/0	0%	0/0	0%	0/0
app/routes/clients	64.51%	20/31	43.75%	7/16	72.72%	8/11	64.51%	20/31
app/serializers	88.88%	8/9	50%	1/2	100%	3/3	88.88%	8/9
app/services	100%	5/5	100%	0/0	100%	3/3	100%	5/5
app/transforms	75%	6/8	50%	1/2	75%	3/4	85.71%	6/7

Figure 7.8: *Updated code coverage*

Through our efforts, we have improved the code coverage from around 50% to more than 78%. We can visibly see the red color bars in the previous image turn to yellow or green in the new one. The goal of our test suite and an exercise for you is to convert this 78% to 100%.

Conclusion

In this chapter, we went through in detail about what testing is and how it is done for software applications. We discussed the different methods of testing, the advantages and disadvantages of each of them, and the efforts involved. We discussed individual testing methods like manual and automation testing and learned how they can be classified based on who does the testing and the technical knowledge required for the testing. We also discussed the different levels of testing, their scope and why each level is required to make the application robust and secure.

We then moved towards testing in Ember and how we can run tests, and configure the application to support plugins for testing purposes. We also looked at how we can debug our tests in the runtime. After that, we went through some of the auto-generated test cases that were failing and gained knowledge about how we could fix those test failures. This gave you hands-on experience working with an existing code base and fixing bugs in them.

We then discussed individual modules in the application and how we can write test cases for each of them. We also learned about the general use cases the tests can concentrate on to make sure we get a very high code coverage. We also saw how we can mock/stub functions or objects to reduce the complexity of the tests. In the end, we saw around a 28% increase in the code coverage of our application.

In the next chapter, we will dive into detailed runtime debugging through the **Ember Inspector tool.**

Points to Remember

- Tests are important for an application to make sure the features work as expected and the new code does not break any existing feature.
- Testing can be classified into Automated and Manual Testing.
- Tests in Ember have three levels - Unit, Rendering and Application tests.
- Unit tests check on a specific object/function in an isolated environment.
- Integration/Rendering tests test the rendering of a component or the interaction between different components in the application.
- Application tests check the working of the entire application by loading the application from an end-user point of view.
- We need to mock/stub objects and functions to reduce the complexity of tests.
- Application tests can be used to test redirection/transition between routes.

Multiple Choice Questions

1. Which of the following does not require any knowledge of the internals of the application that is being tested?

   a. Black Box Testing

   b. White Box Testing

   c. Gray Box Testing

   d. Automated Testing

2. Which of the following is a level of testing provided by Ember?

   a. Unit

   b. Rendering

   c. System

   d. All of the Above

3. What is the keyword used to pause the execution of a test during runtime?
   a. **`debug`**
   b. **`debugger`**
   c. **`pause`**
   d. None of the above
4. Which of the following modules can be unit-tested?
   a. Component
   b. Model
   c. Helper
   d. Template
5. What is the name of the test that simulates an end-user perspective?
   a. Unit
   b. Rendering
   c. Application
   d. Global
6. Ember Mirage is enabled by default in tests.
   a. true
   b. false

Answers

1. a
2. d
3. b
4. b
5. c
6. b

Questions

1. What are the different types of Manual Testing?
2. What is Code Coverage and how do you improve it in an application?
3. Why are different levels of testing important?
4. How do you test the different lifecycle hooks of a route?
5. What are the points to note when coming up with test cases for your application?
6. How do you connect your test suite to your CI/CD process?

Key Terms

- **Testing**: A process for ensuring the application works as expected before deploying it to customers.
- **QUnit**: A JavaScript framework testing framework that forms the core of Ember's tests.
- **Module**: A group of tests that targets a specific part of the application.
- **Code Coverage**: A metric that specifies the percentage of your code base that is covered when running your test suite.
- **Stub**: A dummy object or function that mimics a function defined inside the code to reduce the complexity when running tests.

CHAPTER 8

Ember Inspector

Introduction

In the previous chapter, we discussed writing tests to keep your application secure and complying with your requirements. In this chapter, we will look at the next step towards production readiness, which is to ensure the application is scalable and does not have memory issues when navigating between routes or keeping the application loaded for a long time in the browser.

Ember Inspector is a very useful tool provided by the framework to debug and keep track of the running state of the application. We will explore the tool in detail in this chapter. We will look at how you can install the application, look at the object inspector to view individual data present in the application and how you can inspect each module of the application. This tool is necessary for you to track the memory and data usage of your application and ensure it does not spiral out of control in any case. This helps you track memory leaks in the system that can cause the page to hang in the browser.

Structure

The following topics will be discussed in this chapter:

- Introduction to Ember Inspector
- Installation
- Version Info
- Object Inspector
- Component Tree
- Inspecting Routes
- Inspecting Data

- Performance Monitoring
- Debug Promises
- Handling Deprecations
- Troubleshooting

Introduction to Ember Inspector

Ember Inspector is a browser add-on that allows you to inspect and read information about an Ember application, and look at the routes, components and data loaded in the browser at a particular time. It helps you visually understand the application better and easily debug the application in the runtime. Ember Inspector is used for the following cases:

- Visually map out the routes in the application
- View the data loaded in the Ember store at any time
- View the status of promises
- Monitor the application for performance issues and detect memory leaks

Installation

Ember Inspector is available as a browser extension for Firefox and Google Chrome. For other browsers, you can install it directly through a bookmarklet application. Let us look at the installation steps:

Google Chrome

The Chrome extension of `Ember Inspector` is available at the following link: https://chrome.google.com/webstore/detail/ember-inspector/bmdblncegkenkaciei hfhpjfppoconhi

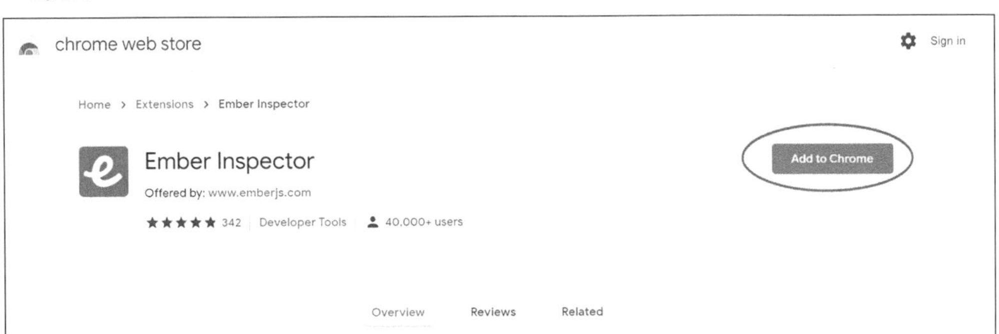

Figure 8.1: *Ember Inspector Chrome*

You can click the **`Add to Chrome`** link to install the inspector in your browser. Once installed, you can now see the inspector by opening the developer tools. There you will see a new tab named **`Ember`** now, as shown in the following figure:

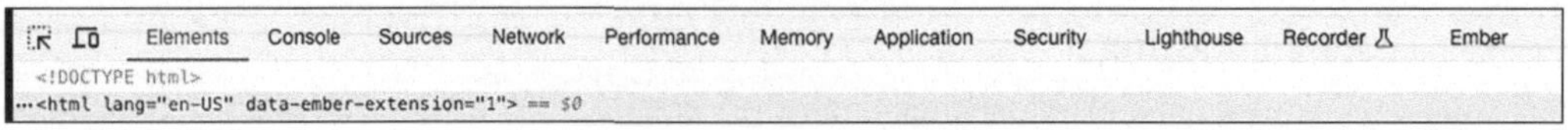

***Figure 8.2**: Ember Inspector Tab*

Display Ember Favicon

In order to be alerted when you are visiting a website that uses Ember, you can enable an option in Ember Inspector to display the ember favicon on such sites. You can do so by visiting **`chrome://extensions`** in your browser, selecting **`Details`** on Ember Inspector and clicking **`Extension Options`**. It will open a popup with an option to enable the favicon:

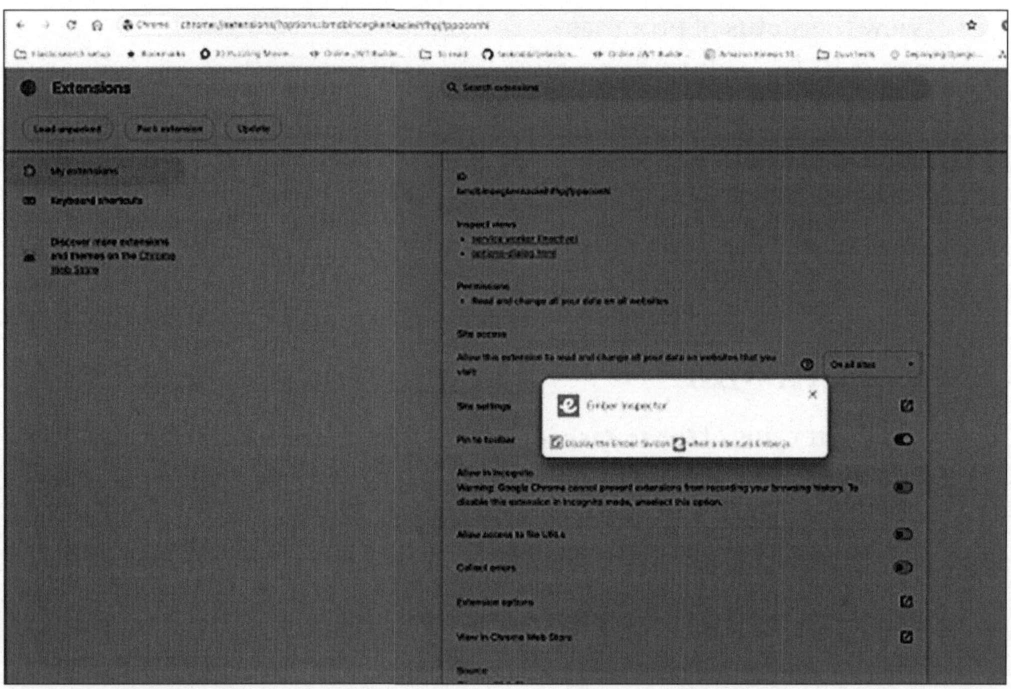

***Figure 8.3**: Ember Inspector favicon*

Once enabled, you can see an Ember favicon as illustrated in *Figure* 8.3. The favicon is grayed out by default and whenever you visit a website that uses Ember, the favicon lights up to notify the same.

Firefox

Firefox extension can be found here - https://addons.mozilla.org/en-US/firefox/addon/ember-inspector/

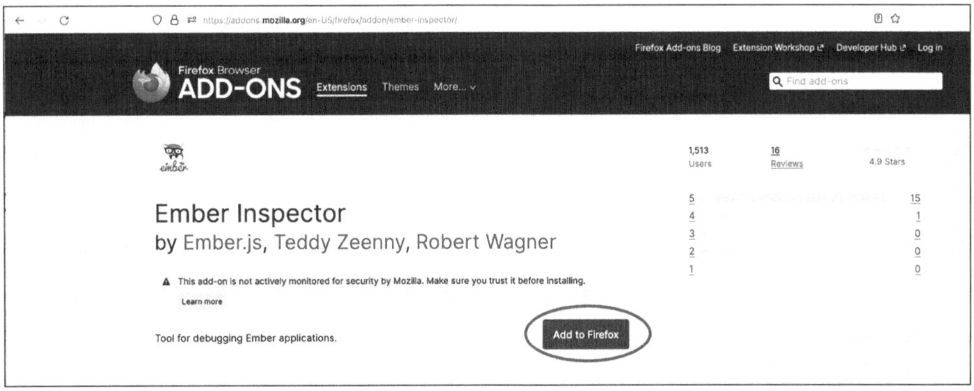

***Figure 8.4**: Ember Inspector Firefox*

Once installed, the Ember tab will be available in developer tools similar to Chrome. You can also enable the favicon in the URL bar by visiting **`about:addons`**, selecting Ember Inspector in the **`Extensions`** list and enabling the checkbox for **`Display the Ember Favicon`**.

Bookmarklet Application

For browsers other than Chrome and Firefox, the Ember Inspector is easily accessible via a URL, which can be bookmarked in your browser. You can visit the extensionusingthefollowingURL:https://ember-extension.s3.amazonaws.com/dist_bookmarklet/panes-3-16-0/index.html?inspectedWindowURL=https://guides.emberjs.com

This will load the Ember Inspector in a separate browser tab.

Mobile Devices

When testing your application on mobile devices, you might want to inspect the elements there and detect issues. Ember Inspector is available for that as well, through an addon: https://github.com/joostdevries/ember-cli-remote-inspector

Once the addon is installed, you can open the inspector in any browser by visiting http://localhost:30820 and then open the application through the default http://localhost:4200 in any other browser/mobile device to see the remote inspector in action.

Version Info

The first thing you can see in the Ember Inspector is the list of versions used in the project. The version of Ember, Ember-CLI, Ember Data and other dependencies used in the project. You can see this information by visiting the **`Info`** tab in the Inspector. Here is how it will look for our project:

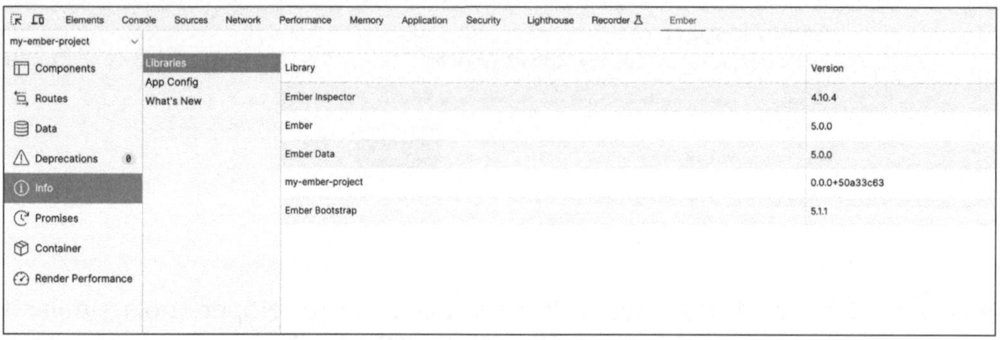

***Figure 8.5**: Version Info*

You can see that along with the list of addons, you also see our project name on the list. It is because by default we use the **`ember-cli-app-version`** addon, which adds the current project and version details found in the **`package.json`** file on this list.

App Config

Along with the version details, the Inspector also reveals some configuration values we have set up for the project.

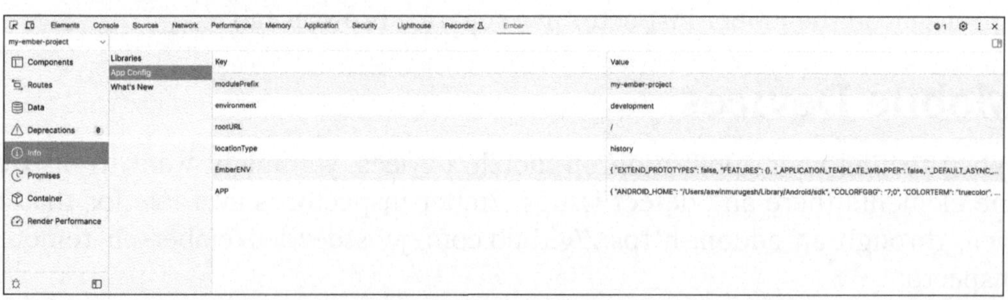

***Figure 8.6**: App Config*

Even though this information can be retrieved through general debugging or inspecting the code, Ember Inspector compiles and tabularizes important information to be easily checked when someone is debugging the application. *Figure* 8.6 shows what you can see by clicking the **App Config** sub-tab in the **Info** tab.

You can see that important configuration information like Environment Variables, APP config, the root URL, and so on can be seen from this tab itself.

Object Inspector

The Object Inspector provides detailed information on each object we have in our application. The Object inspector can be loaded by clicking the **Container** tab in the Inspector. This will give you an overall list of objects present in the application, as follows:

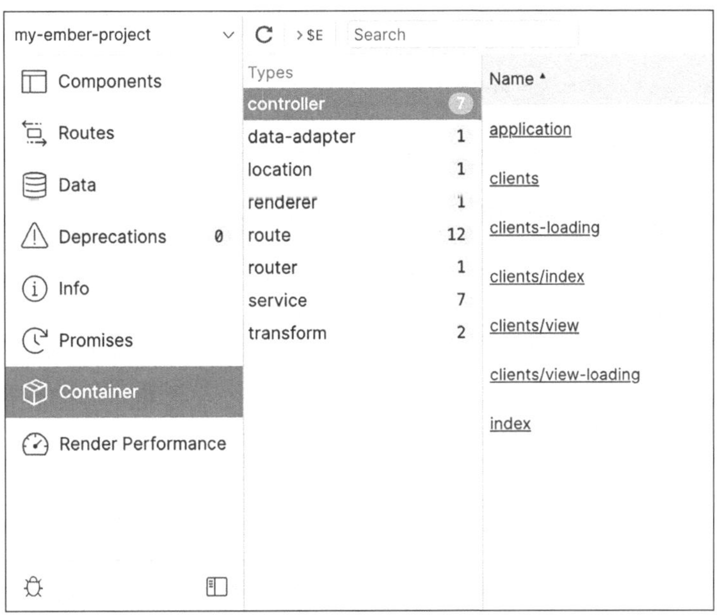

Figure 8.7: *Object Inspector*

You can see from this list the different types of objects and the number of objects we have created/used in our application for each type. If you click any type, you can see the list of objects we have in this type. For example, in *Figure* 8.7, we can see that our application has seven controllers and the names of the individual controllers. When you click an individual object, you will see the list of properties defined in the object and the list of actions and functions defined in the object. Here is how it looks when you click the **clients/index** controller:

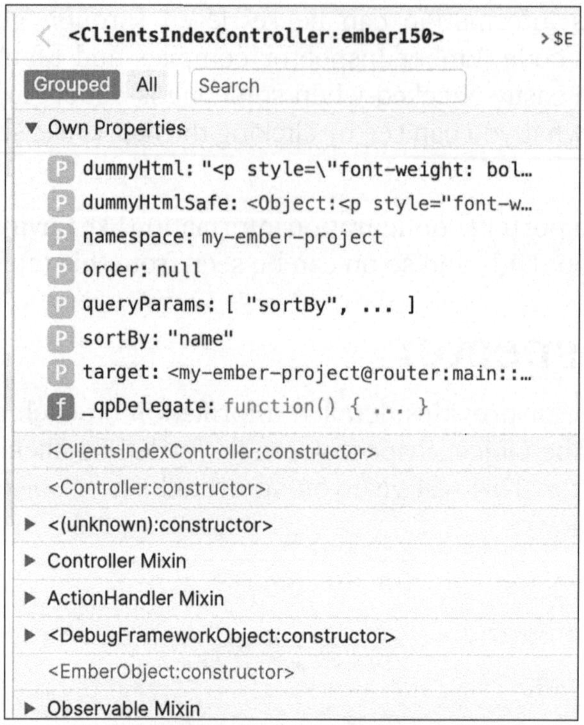

***Figure 8.8**: Object Inspector Detail*

The inspector not only shows properties defined inside the object but also the attributes inherited from the parents. You can also see the value of each property (both inherited and defined). The values displayed in the Inspector are consistent with the values present in the application. So, if the value of any attribute changes after you load the inspector, the value will be updated in the Inspector then and there. The binding is also two-way. Meaning, you can click any string value to edit the value of a particular attribute. The changes will be immediately reflected in the application.

We can see that the items are grouped by their types (`Own Properties`, `Action Handler`, `Constructor`, `ActionHandler`, and so on). Each property/item defined in this list will be prefixed with an icon and a letter notation defining the type of notation. You can hover over the icon to see more details on what it denotes. Here are some notations:

- **P** - Property
- **F** - Function
- **T** - Tracked Property
- **G** - Getter function

Sending Objects to Console

Sometimes it would be easier to inspect the object in the console rather than seeing it in the Inspector. Inspecting it on the console will allow you to drill down on the options to multiple levels at the same time. To make that process easier, we can ask the Ember Inspector to send an entire dump of the selected object to the console. You can do that by clicking the **`>$E`** icon you see on the top right of the Object Inspector:

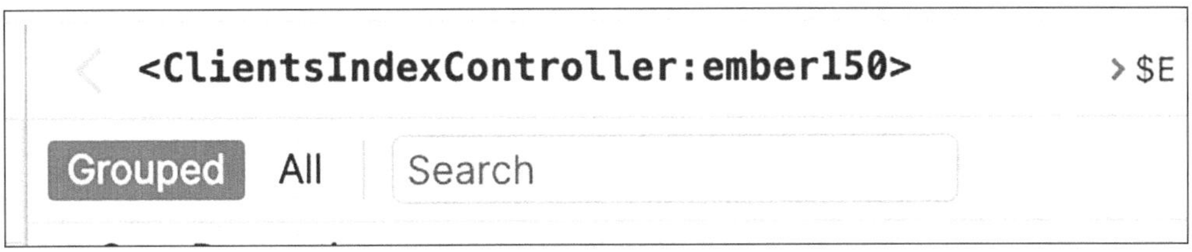

Figure 8.9: *Send to Console*

If you send the **`clients/index`** controller to the console, here is what the object will look like when you go to the **`Console`** tab:

Figure 8.10: *Console Dump of Data*

You can see all the information provided in the Inspector, with the additional capability of interacting with the object and viewing values at multiple levels at the same time.

Instead of dumping the entire object in the console, you can also send individual properties or functions to the console by clicking the **`>$E`** icon appearing when you hover over a particular element. By sending individual functions to the console, you can see the source code of the functions.

Console to Inspector

Similar to sending objects from Inspector to the Console, you can also add new objects to the Inspector from the Console. You can use the **`EmberInspector.inspect`** function to send the object to the inspector:

```
let obj = Ember.objects.create({'test': true})
EmberInspector.inspect(obj)
```

Navigating through Objects

Along with viewing the values of each property/attribute, complex Ember object values can be inspected further by clicking them. For example, the model of a controller/route will contain either a single model object or a list of model objects. When you click one of those objects, Ember Inspector will automatically open the particular model object in the Object Inspector for you to debug/change the values of the model object in the runtime. There is also a back array (<) provided on the top left of the Object Inspector that allows you to go back to the previous object that you were viewing.

Component Tree

The Component Tree section provides a view of the Ember components that are loaded into the application at the moment. This provides a tree view similar to what we see in the **`Elements`** tab of the Developer Tools, but the tree is made up of Ember components present in the application instead of normal HTML tags. You can view the tree by clicking the **`Components`** tab of the Inspector. Here is how the tree looks for our application's index page:

Figure 8.11: *Component Tree*

In this tree, you can see the hierarchy of Components present in the application, along with details on which route calls this component, so that it is easy for us to find the code and debug. From this figure, we can see that the navigation components are called from the application route that is common for all the routes, and the index route contains only the **click-tracker** component. You can click any component to see the **Object Inspector** for that particular component. You can use this to dynamically change the values of attributes in the component and test different scenarios instead of making changes to the code or performing the test steps multiple times. Here are some functionalities present in this part of the Inspector:

View Component

When you hover over each component in this tree, you will see two icons. One of an eye and the other representing code (</>).

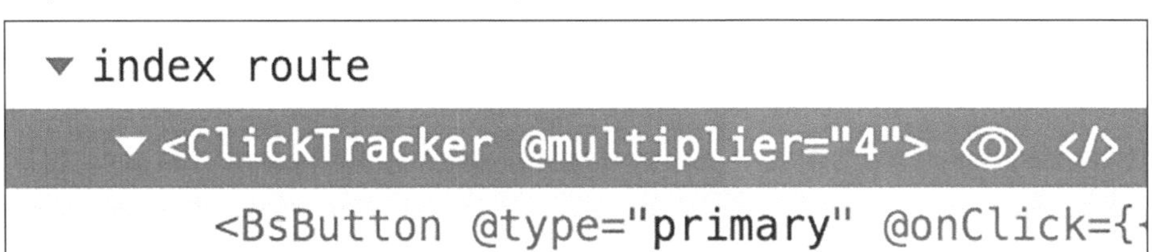

Figure 8.12: *View Component*

The eye icon will scroll to make the selected component visible. So, if you do not know where the particular component appears on the page (if there are CSS issues and you cannot see the component on screen), this icon will scroll the component to the visible section of the DOM and highlight it, making it easy for us to identify.

The code icon (`</>`) does the same, but opens the root HTML element for the particular component in the **`Elements`** tab. This will be used to identify the parsed HTML code for any given component.

Search Components

When the page grows larger in size, it might be cluttered with a lot of Components and it would become difficult for us to locate a specific Component in our tree. You can easily find out the component you are looking for by searching the Component by its name in the search bar present in the Component Tree module:

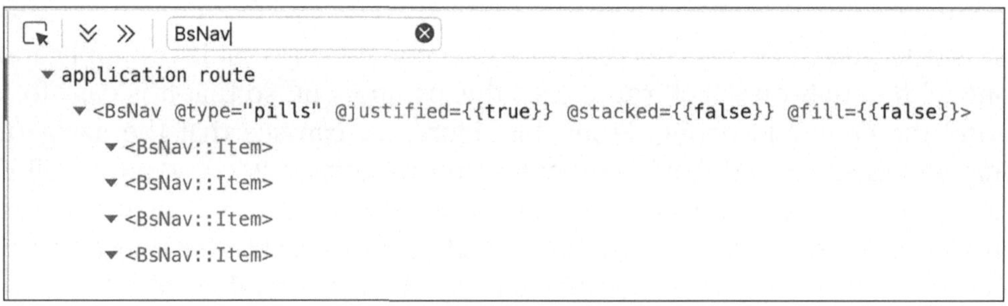

***Figure 8.13**: Component Tree Search*

Locate the Component of an Element

Sometimes you might see an element in the DOM which you do not recognize or want to inspect the particular Component that this element belongs to. You can use the arrow icon present on top of the Component tree to do that.

***Figure 8.14**: Locate Component*

Once you click this option, you can then go around the DOM and hover on any element in the DOM to see the corresponding Component highlighted in the

Component Tree. You can click any element to select the Component in the Tree. This method makes it easier to locate a Component in the tree compared to searching and finding it.

You can also use the arrow icons seen in *Figure* 8.14 to collapse and uncollapse the tree.

Inspecting Routes

The Routes tab provides a detailed list of Routes configured in the application along with their hierarchy. Here is what the content looks like:

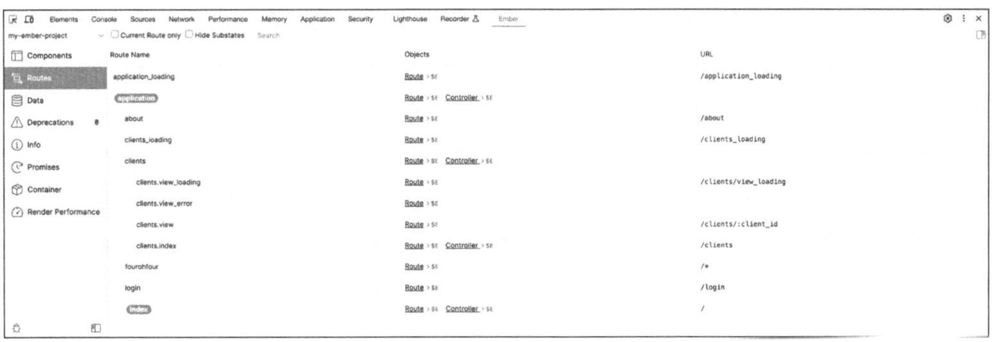

***Figure 8.15**: Routes*

You can see the list of all routes we have in the application, along with the loading and error substates of each route. You can also see a hierarchy of the children of each route clearly. In the second column of this table, you can see two links - **`Route`** and **`Controller`**. Clicking any of those links will open the particular Route or Controller associated with that Route in the Object Inspector. Ember Inspector also provides the **`>$E`** icon to dump the state of any object into the console. The URL associated with the particular route can be seen in the third column of the table.

Let us take a look at some of the options we have in this tab:

Search Bar

The Search Bar can be used to locate any Route by searching for its name. This will be useful when the application grows large and scrolling through the list to find a specific route becomes difficult.

Current Route Only

In the normal view, you can see that the Current Route that is loaded in the application is highlighted with a blue background. The Current Route only checkbox hides all other routes and displays only the Route that is loaded in the application, along with its parents.

Hide Substates

By default, you can see the loading and error substates as individual entries in the Routes table. The Inspector provides a specific option to hide these substates so that you can see only individual routes and not the substates.

Inspecting Data

You can notice that in the Container tab, we could see Controllers, Adapters, Routes, Services and even Transforms, but not Models. This is because the Models and their data are shown specifically in a separate tab in the Inspector. You can see that in the `Data` tab of the Inspector. The Data tab shows the list of models for which records are loaded into the store, along with the number of records of each model type that have been loaded.

When you load the clients-index route, you can see the Data tab contains two objects of the client model:

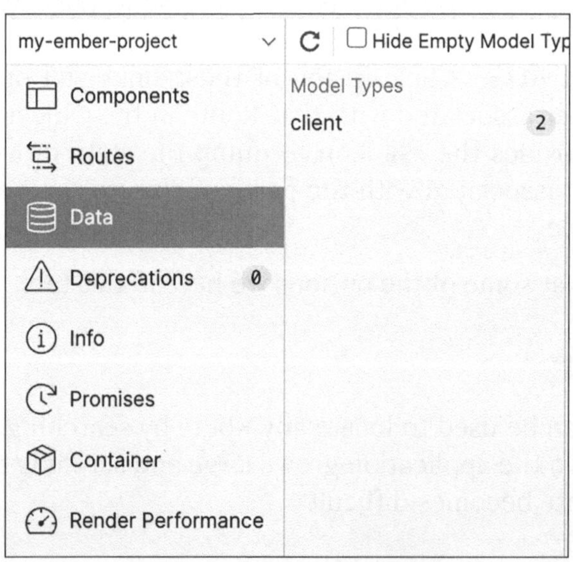

Figure 8.16: *Data tab Models list*

When clicking each model type, it will open a table with the list of objects that are loaded for the selected model type. This table will provide the value of each object for every column the model contains.

***Figure 8.17**: Data tab Model Objects*

You can click any row and it will open the particular Model Object in the Object Inspector. From the Object Inspector you can edit any property and the same will be reflected on the screen immediately.

Filters

The **`Data`** tab provides four filter options to view Model Objects based on their current state in the store. Here are the filters:

- **All:** View all the records in the store for this Model.
- **New:** View records that were created in the store, but not pushed to the API yet.
- **Modified:** View records that are present in both the Store and API, but were modified after the last push/after last loaded from the API. This will show the list of records whose values are different from what was last synced from the store.
- **Clean:** View records that are up to date with the store and have no modifications.

Inspect Store

The **`Data`** tab has a button on top for Inspecting the Store. Clicking this button will open the **`Store`** service in the Object Inspector. This can be used to see the different functions and customizations we have done to the Store service. The Store service can also be located in the **`Services`** section of the **`Container`** tab.

Performance Monitoring

An important functionality of the Ember Inspector is to allow the developers to debug and figure out the performance timings of each Route/Component. When the application becomes larger, the page load times are bound to increase due to loading and interaction between Components and so on. This section of the Inspector helps you see the time taken for each route to load. Through this, we can identify the sections of the page that cause delays in loading the page and reduce the delays or inefficiencies in the particular component.

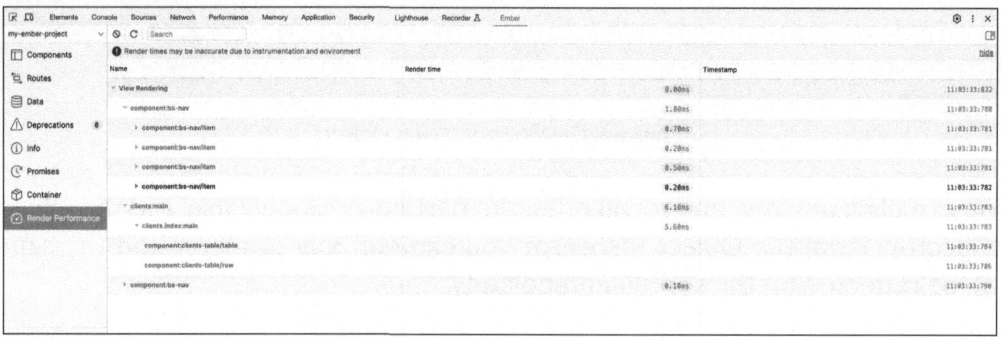

***Figure 8.18**: Rendering Performance*

From the **`Render Performance`** section, you can see the list of Components and the time taken for each of them to load. The **`clients/table`** and **`clients/row`** Components do not have a time shown for them as they are too negligible.

There are two buttons on this panel along with the default search bar. The clear button can be used to clear the existing logs you see, and the reload button will trigger and track load times of Components at the application boot time. Do note that tracking the performance using the Ember Inspector itself will create a small delay in code execution, so these numbers are not an exact representation of the rendering times in the production setup. But you can use these numbers to compare the rendering times and find out the bottlenecks involved in the load process. Components taking a long time to load because of making multiple unnecessary API calls, the same Component being called multiple times, or memory leaks in a Component are scenarios that can be found using the Performance section of the Inspector.

Debug Promises

We have seen how Promises are used in the Ember application when making API calls through the store or for services that have external API interactions. The

Promises tab in the Inspector lists all the Promises created in the application and the state of each of them. You can see the details of the state of the promise, the resolved value, the time it took to resolve/error out and so on.

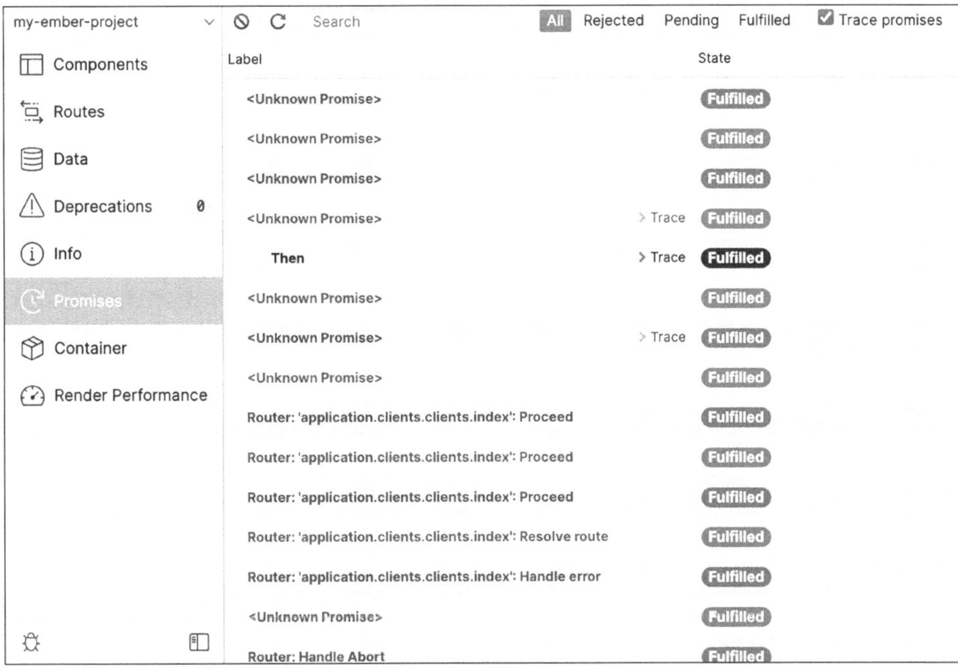

Figure 8.19: *Promises*

As you can see from this image, you can filter the Promises based on the following states:

- Fulfilled
- Pending
- Rejected

If the fulfilled value of a Promise is an Ember object (like a model) or an Array of Ember objects, the values are displayed in this tab and you can open those objects in the Object Inspector to understand the values returned by the Promise. When a promise fails, you can find an option to send the error stack trace to the console as well, to debug why the Promise was rejected.

Trace Promises

You can see a checkbox on top that says **`Trace Promises`.** This can be used to keep track of the stack trace of each Promise made from the application and through the **`Trace`** link you see in each row, the stack trace/call trace of the particular Promise will be printed to the console for us to exactly identify where the particular Promise was generated from.

Handling Deprecations

Earlier we discussed what Deprecations are and how you can handle and resolve them in your Ember application. Ember Inspector also provides options for viewing the Deprecations, locate them and provide links to Transition plans that can be used to fix the deprecation.

The **`Deprecations`** tab in the Inspector has a count denoting the number of existing Deprecations in this application. Clicking it will list all the deprecations in the application:

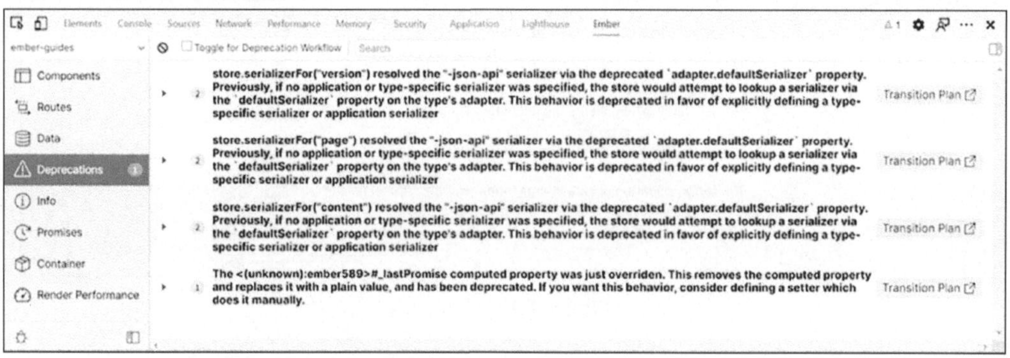

Figure 8.20: *Deprecations*

When you have Source Maps enabled in your application, this list will provide links to the exact places where this Deprecation is used. You can use these to locate your deprecations and fix them. The Inspector also provides an external link when clicking the **`Transition Plan`**, which will take you to the particular deprecations' documentation that contains the steps to fix the deprecation.

Troubleshooting

When opening Ember Inspector in existing applications, the Inspector may not load for these applications for some reason. Let us look at a few of them:

Ember Application Not Detected

This is a common error you see when loading the Inspector for older Ember applications. The Ember Inspector may not be able to detect your Ember application for a few reasons:

- The URL you have visited does not use Ember at all.
- The application uses a very old Ember version, not compatible with the current version of your inspector.
- The Ember application is sandboxed or embedded into another URL.
- You are using a protocol other than HTTP/HTTPS to load the application (like opening the HTML file directly).

In those cases, you will see the following error in the Inspector page:

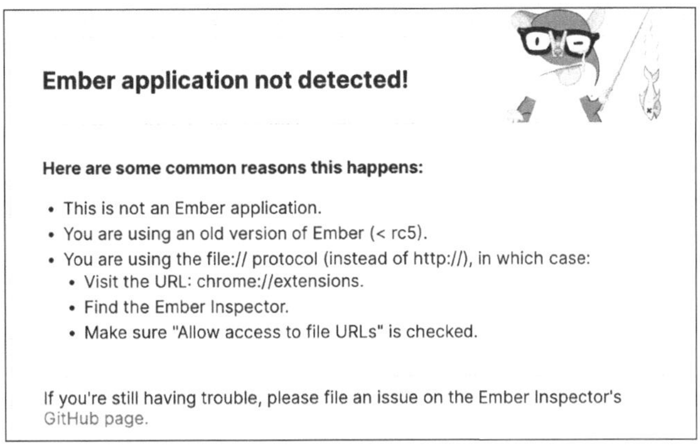

Figure 8.21: *Ember application not detected*

Promises not detected/Missing

Sometimes, Promises that were created before the inspector was loaded will not be visible. So you might see some Promises missing from the logs. A simple click of the reload button will usually fix the error and load all Promises. But sometimes, there can be an error with loading the Promises in the Inspector itself. This could be because of using a very old Ember version, as Promise tracking was added only in Ember versions greater than 1.3.

Conclusion

In this chapter, we learnt in detail about Ember Inspector. We discussed the uses of Ember Inspector, the installation process and the options available in it. First, we saw how to view the versions of libraries used in the project and a list of configuration values supplied for this build. Then we looked at inspecting individual objects, how you can look at the values of each variable in the object and so on. We then looked in detail about the Object Inspector, how you can edit values of an object in the runtime and see it reflected on the screen immediately.

Then we viewed the workings of the Component Tree and how it can be used to locate and drill through Components that are rendered on the current page, and how you can search for components and inspect the Components for values stored in them. We then saw the Routes tab that shows all the routes in the application and how we can filter only the route that is currently loaded along with its parents. Next, we saw how you can look at the model records loaded in the store, inspect them and change their values in runtime. We also looked at understanding the rendering performance of the application and how the numbers can be used to make the application more efficient. After this, we saw how we could handle Deprecations through the Inspector and finally saw a couple of commonly occurring errors and ways to solve them.

In the next chapter, we will discuss deploying the application to different cloud storage providers and making our application live.

Points to Remember

- Ember Inspector helps debug and improve the efficiency of the application
- You can find a comprehensive list of all objects defined in the application
- Ember Inspector provides a two-way binding on the values of every attribute defined in any object of our application
- The Component Tree provides a tree structure of the Components loaded on the current page
- You can see the individual model records loaded in the store and edit them in real-time through the Inspector
- The inspector provides options to handle Deprecations introduced into the application

Multiple Choice Questions

1. Which of the following is Ember Inspector used for?

    a. View Routes in the application

    b. View Components loaded for the current Route

    c. View Model objects loaded into the store

    d. All of the above

2. Which of these browsers does not have a dedicated extension for Ember Inspector?
    a. Chrome
    b. Firefox
    c. Safari
    d. None of the above
3. Which of the following is a valid filter option for an Ember model?
    a. New
    b. Fulfilled
    c. Modified
    d. Clean
4. Ember Inspector provides options for viewing data from resolved Promises.
    a. True
    b. False

Answers

1. d
2. c
3. b
4. a

Questions

1. What is the purpose of Ember Inspector and how is it different from the default debugger in the browser?
2. How do you load the Ember Inspector in browsers other than Chrome or Firefox?
3. What are the steps to figure out slow loading Components in the application?

CHAPTER 9

Build and Deployment

Introduction

In the previous chapters, we looked at how you can create Ember applications, develop the pages you need using the different modules provided by the framework, how you can interact with third party APIs from the application and how you can test the code and the features. In this chapter, we will look at the last step remaining in the pipeline of getting your application live for everyone to access the application from the comforts of their browser.

We will also look at how you can automate your deployment process and connect it with your version control management system in order to reduce the manual effort/errors involved in the deployment process.

Structure

In this chapter, we will cover the following topics:

- Building the Application
- `ember-cli-deploy`
- Deploying to AWS
- Deploying to GCP
- Deploying to Azure

Building the Application

Building your application is the first and most important step before deployment. Building is the process of compiling and generating static files from your Ember application that can be used by the browser to run the application. When running the Ember server, a development build is generated, and that build is served by the server with an additional functionality of automatic reloads when the code changes.

But the server is unnecessary in the production environment, as we do not need the auto reload functionality and the additional web socket connection used to implement the auto reload functionality. Hence, we create a build and simply host it in a file storage service that serves the build files to the browser on demand. Let us look at how we can build the application:

```
ember build --environment=production
```

Generating the build will create a static output of the Ember application and place it inside a **dist** folder created in the project. You can customize the folder of output to a different folder by passing the --output-path parameter passed to the build command.

Now that the build is generated, it is all about uploading the build files to an online directory that can serve the files on demand. There are different cloud hosting providers that we can use to serve the files. We will go through a few of them and see how the application can be set up online.

ember-cli-deploy

In order to deploy the application automatically to any of the cloud hosting providers, we will need the **`ember-cli-deploy`** plugin that takes care of interfacing with the APIs of different providers and programmatically upload our build files into the specified locations. We can install **`ember-cli-deploy`** with the following command:

```
ember install ember-cli-deploy ember-cli-deploy-build
```

ember-cli-deploy is a base plugin and it will need additional plugins based on the hosting provider to interface with the APIs of that particular provider. We will look at how you can set up the plugin for each provider when we discuss in detail the deployment steps for each provider. We also need to install the **`ember-cli-deploy-build`** plugin alongside to automatically create a build before deploying it to the specific provider.

Deploying to AWS

The first provider we are going to see is Amazon Web Services (AWS). Amazon provides a huge variety of services to deploy and manage your cloud applications. We are going to use the S3 service of AWS to deploy our application.

For this, you will need to create a free AWS account by visiting https://portal.aws.amazon.com/billing/signup. Once created, let us go through the setup process:

Creating a Bucket

The S3 service allows you to create directories called `Buckets` inside which we can upload our files and manage who can access them. Once logged in to your AWS account, you can search on the top bar for S3 and go to the S3 service. Inside the S3 dashboard, click the `Create Bucket` option. We need to provide the following information for creating the bucket:

- `Bucket Type`: The Bucket Type can be `General Purpose`, since we are going to use this as a deployment container for our website.
- `Bucket Name`: Any bucket name you prefer. Usually for hosting websites, it is preferred to name the bucket the same as the domain name you will be applying to this bucket.
- `Object Ownership`: Since this is going to be an Ember application, we will need public access to all the files present in the bucket. Hence, we need to select `ACLs Disabled.` ACL means Access Control List. ACL can be enabled when you want to provide different access permissions for individual files/folders in the bucket. For example, when you want users to access only folders that are in their name, an ACL can be set for each folder. In our case, we will be using bucket policy to determine who can access the data. We will discuss that next.
- `Public Access:` The bucket is going to contain a frontend application and hence it has to be opened for anyone to access. For that purpose, we are going to uncheck the `Block all Public Access` checkbox. That will require you to acknowledge that everyone can access the files using another checkbox below that field.

The remaining items can be left as the default values and the bucket can be created. Once created, you will be redirected to a list page containing the list of buckets in your account. Select our newly created bucket to view its files. Once inside the bucket, you can use the `Upload` option on the top right section of the bucket. In the upload page, select `Upload Folder` and upload all the contents from the dist folder, or simply drag and drop the contents of the dist folder into the upload space and click the `Upload` button. Once uploaded, the bucket will look like this:

Figure 9.1: *AWS Bucket*

We can see all the contents of our dist folder listed in the bucket. But still, it is not accessible for everyone. To make it accessible, we need to do two things as follows.

Enabling Static Website Hosting

We need to change the setting in the bucket to notify that the bucket will serve as a static website. For that, we need to go to the **`Properties`** section seen in the list of tabs, and scroll to the end of the section to see a card named **`Static Website Hosting.`** You can see that it is disabled by default. You can enable it by clicking the **`Edit`** button in the section and clicking the **`enable`** radio button. When you click enable, it will ask for a few options:

- **`Hosting Type`**: We are going to host a static website.
- **`Index Document`**: This field determines which file should be the default file when a request is made to this bucket. Since **`index.html`** should be served for all the requests, we will put that as the **`Index Document.`**
- **`Error Document`**: Usually, when a request is made to an S3 bucket, AWS looks for the specific file relative to the root of the bucket. For example, if the URL is some-bucket.aws.amazon.com/my-folder/test, then it looks for a folder called **`my-folder`** in the root of the bucket and a file named **`test`** inside that folder. Since our application is not going to provide individual files for each URL, AWS cannot find these files when looking for them. In those cases, the Error Document specified will be served by AWS. In our case we want **`index.html`** to be served for all requests. So we will set that as the Error Document.

You can click **Save Changes** after providing the discussed values. Once saved, you can see the Static Website Hosting enabled and a URL associated with the bucket. It will be similar to what you see in the following figure:

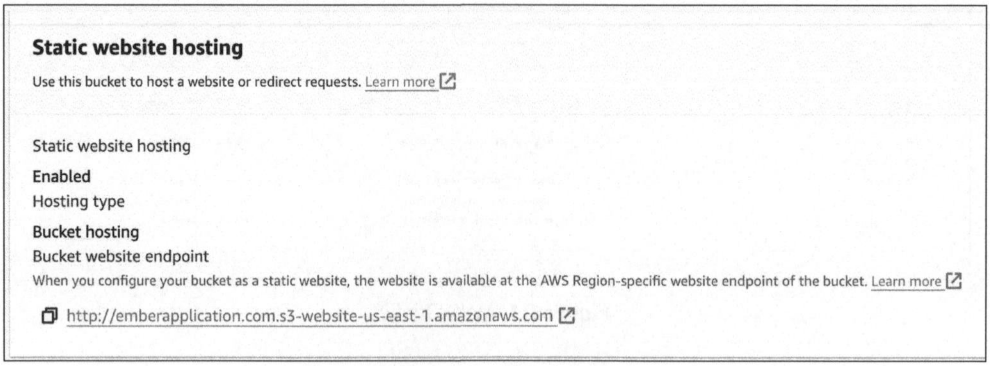

Figure 9.2: *AWS Static Website Hosting*

Enabling Public Access

Even though we can see a URL for our website, when you visit the URL you will be seeing a **403 Forbidden** error. It appears so because we have not configured public access for our files and AWS does not allow unauthorized people from accessing the files. Let us remedy this by enabling public access.

In order to enable public access, we need to go to the **Bucket Policy** section of the **Permissions** tab in the bucket. The Bucket Policy section can be used to define who can access which folder/file in the application. Since our use case requires public access to all our files, here is what we will set in our Bucket Policy:

```
{
    “Version”: “2012-10-17”,
    “Id”: “MyPolicy”,
    “Statement”: [
        {
            “Sid”: “PublicReadForGetBucketObjects”,
            “Effect”: “Allow”,
            “Principal”: “*”,
            “Action”: “s3:GetObject”,
            “Resource”: “arn:aws:s3:::emberapplication.com/*”
```

```
            }
        ]
    }
```

Based on the policy JSON we added, we are simply stating that we will allow any request to our resource, which falls under **`s3:::emberapplication.com/`** folder. This will mean all the files inside the bucket are publicly accessible. Once you add the Bucket policy and save, you can wait a minute for these changes to take effect and then visit the bucket hosting URL to see our Ember application in action. Now that we have set up the application, we will look at a way to automate the deployment process instead of manually uploading files like we did just now.

Create Programmatic User

For setting up automated deployments, we need to create a programmatic user that has access to the S3 bucket. Here are the steps:

1. Search for the **`IAM`** section in the top bar to go to the **`User Management`** section of AWS.
2. Inside IAM, select the **`Users`** menu item from the left menu.
3. Click **`Create User`** to set up our user.
4. Provide a name for our user. For example, **`my-application-programmatic-access.`**
5. You can see a checkbox that says **`Provide user access to the AWS management console`** - This checkbox should be selected if the user we are creating should be able to login to the AWS portal that you are using now. Since that is not required, we leave the checkbox disabled.
6. Next, we need to provide permissions for the user. Since the user is going to interact only with S3 for now, we will provide only S3 access to the user.
7. Select **`Attach Policies Directly.`**
8. In the provided list of policies, search for **`S3FullAccess`** and add only that policy to the user.
9. By doing this, we are allowing the user to only access S3 and no other service. If needed, we can even create policies that will allow the user access to only the bucket that we wish, instead of the entire S3 service.

10. Click **Create User** after selecting the policy. Now the user is created and ready to use.
11. Since the user is programmatic, we will need an **Access Key** and **Secret** combination to access AWS APIs on behalf of the user.
12. For creating the credentials, go to the particular user's page, click the Security **Credentials** tab and go to the **Access Keys** section.
13. Click **Create Access Key** and in the use cases list, select **Command Line Interface** option and click Next and **Create Access Key.**
14. Make sure to Download the CSV of the generated keys, as the secret cannot be seen anymore once you move out of this screen.

ember-cli-deploy-s3

ember-cli-deploy-s3 is a plugin specific for deploying Ember apps to S3. We will install it using the following command:

```
ember install ember-cli-deploy-s3
```

Once installed, we need to add the following configuration inside the **config/deploy.js** file:

```
ENV.s3 = {
    accessKeyId: process.env.AWS_ACCESS_KEY_ID,
    secretAccessKey: process.env.AWS_SECRET_ACCESS_KEY,
    bucket: process.env.AWS_BUCKET,
    region: process.env.AWS_REGION,
    acl: false
}
```

Note that we do not specify any credentials within our code and we simply fetch it from the **process.env.** Notice that we have specified the configuration inside the **production** environment because we might have a different provider for our staging environment or we will have to deploy to a different bucket for staging and hence we will use a different set of keys for the bucket. We have also specified **acl: false** because our bucket does not support ACL and we have an overall configuration for the files.

We can supply the data to **process.env** by adding the following to our .env file:

```
AWS_ACCESS_KEY_ID=<Your Access Key>
AWS_SECRET_ACCESS_KEY=<Your Secret Access Key>
AWS_BUCKET=emberapplication.com
AWS_REGION=us-east-1
```

In order to test if the process works, you can make some small change to the application and run the following command:

```
ember deploy production
```

Running the mentioned commands will create a new build and deploy that build to the specified S3 bucket. We can see the changes by refreshing our bucket URL.

Deploy to GCP

Google Cloud Provider (GCP) is Google's infrastructure and cloud management service. You can access the Google Cloud Console using your existing Gmail/Google account by visiting https://cloud.google.com and clicking the **`Console`** menu on top. Once you go into the console, there is an additional step in creating and activating a billing account in GCP. https://cloud.google.com/billing/docs/how-to/modify-project mentions the steps needed to enable the billing setup for your project.

Creating a Bucket

Similar to S3, GCP offers a service called **Google Cloud Storage (GCS).** We will follow the same procedure as AWS to create a bucket. Go to GCS by searching for **`Cloud Storage`** in the search bar on top of the page.

In Cloud Storage, you can create a new bucket using the **`Create Bucket`** button. In the create bucket form, the following details have to be entered:

- **`Name:`** Provide a name for your bucket. It is good practice to name the bucket to be the same as your domain name.
- **`Storage type:`** We can select the Auto storage class since we don't need a specific class of storage.
- We will need to set up Access Control for the files. We will select **`Uniform`** as we will need the same permission set for all the files.

Once the bucket is created, we can upload all the files from the dist folder into the bucket by clicking the **`Upload Files`** button in the **`Objects`** tab of the bucket. Now that the files are uploaded, we will make changes to the bucket setup to enable public access and Static Website Hosting to the bucket.

Enable Public Access

For enabling public access, you can follow these steps:

1. Go to the **Permissions** tab in your GCS bucket.
2. Inside the Permissions tab, go to the **Public Access** pane and we can see that public access is disabled. In order to enable it, click the **Remove Public Access Prevention** button you see at the top of the pane and click Confirm.
3. Once you've enabled public access, you can then share the files by clicking the **Grant Access** button in the same pane.
4. Here, we will enable access for all users to read the files in the bucket. In order to do that, enter **allUsers** in the **New Principal** field.
5. **allUsers** in this section defines any request coming to this bucket (both authenticated and unauthenticated requests)
6. In the **role** dropdown field, we need to select **Storage Object Viewer** as the role. It means that for all the requests we will allow viewing the objects in this bucket.
7. Click the **Save** button and confirm the same by clicking the **Allow Public Access** button.

Now we will have public access enabled for this bucket.

Enable Static Website Hosting

For enabling Static Website Hosting, we need to set up the **Index Document** and **Error Document** that we specified in AWS. Follow these steps:

1. Go to the buckets list page in Cloud Storage.
2. Click the three dots specific to our bucket and select **Edit Website Configuration.**
3. In the dialog that opens, specify **index.html** in both the Main page and the Error page.
4. Click **Save.**

You can now access the application by clicking the URL associated with the **index.html** file in the bucket. Unfortunately, GCP does not allow creating a generic URL for the bucket like AWS. It requires us to set up a domain and map the domain to GCS to access the application. Hence, for the scope of this book, we will load the application by loading the **`index.html`** file.

Create Programmatic User

Next, in order to automate the deployment process, we will need to create a programmatic user who can access the GCP from our command line. Such users are named as **`Service Accounts`** in GCP. Create a service account through the following steps:

1. Search for **`Service Account`** in the top search bar.
2. In the Service Account dashboard, click **`Create Service Account.`**
3. Provide a name for your service account and click **`Next.`**
4. In **`Grant Service Account access to this project`** section, we will provide it with access to our Cloud Storage. Select the role **`Environment and Storage Object Administrator.`**
5. Click **`Done`** to complete the setup.

Once the service account is created, you can see the account is identified by an email address. We need to generate a key to allow access to GCP services via this service account. Let us do so using the following steps:

1. Inside the newly created service account, go to the **`Keys`** tab.
2. Click **`Add Key`** and **`Create New Key.`**
3. In the key type, select **`JSON`** and click **`CREATE.`**

A JSON file will be downloaded with the credentials required for this user. We will use the **`Private Key`** field in that file as a credential to access the application.

ember-cli-deploy-gcloud-storage

The Gcloud Storage plugin of **`ember-cli-deploy`** allows us to deploy our application into the GCS service. To test this, let us deploy our staging setup to GCP. In the **`config/deploy.js`** file, let us add the following to the staging environment.

```
if (deployTarget === 'staging') {
  ENV.build.environment = 'production';
```

```
ENV['gcloud-storage'] = {
    credentials: {
        private_key: process.env.GCLOUD_PRIVATE_KEY,
        client_email: process.env.GCLOUD_SERVICE_ACCOUNT_EMAIL,
    },
    projectId: process.env.GCLOUD_PROJECT_ID,
    bucket: process.env.GCLOUD_STORAGE_BUCKET,
  }
}
```

We do not hardcode the credentials in the code here as well. The corresponding values will be added to our .env file to be taken during the deployment process. The **`projectId`** can be fetched by clicking the project name that you see on top of the cloud console (to the left of the search bar).

Once the .env file is updated, you can run the deployment using **`ember deploy staging`** to see the files getting uploaded to your GCS bucket.

Deploy to Azure

Azure is the Cloud Infrastructure Management tool offered by Microsoft. You can create a free account here - https://azure.microsoft.com/en-in/free/. Once you have created an account and entered your card details to enable the account, the process is pretty simple in Azure.

Azure offers an inbuilt integration with Microsoft's github.com to provide a hassle free deployment setup of your Ember application. In order to facilitate the integration, let us first set up the GitHub repository for our project.

ember-cli-azure-deploy

We will install the **`ember-cli-deploy`** plugin specific for Azure:

```
ember install ember-cli-azure-deploy
```

Setup GitHub Repository

Create an account on **github.com** if you do not have one already. Create a repository with the following steps:

1. Click the **+** Button on the right side of the navbar and select **`New Repository`**

2. Provide a name to your repository and click **`Create`**, leaving all other options to default

Your repository will be created with setup instructions for the project. In your local setup, you can run.

```
git status
```

Git status allows you to see the list of uncommitted files in the repository. Since we have not configured any repository yet, all the folders/files in the root directory of the repository will show up in the list. We need to add our newly created repository to this project using the following command:

```
git remote add origin git@github.com:aswinm/sample-ember-application.git
```

Replace the repository link with the specific link you see for your project in the GitHub repository configuration section. Before we push the files to the repository, we need to ensure that our credentials in the .env file are not uploaded to the repository for security reasons. In order to confirm that, let us open the **`.gitignore`** file in the repository and add **`.env`** to the end of the file.

Next, let us upload the repository files into GitHub.

```
git add .
git commit -m "Initial Commit"
git push origin main
```

Through the preceding commands, we are adding all the files (excluding the ones specified in .gitignore) and committing it to the repository and pushing it to the main branch.

Create Static Web App

Azure provides a service named **Static Web Apps** for deploying front-end-frameworks. This static web app can be integrated with your GitHub repository directly.

1. Search for the **`Static Web Apps`** service in the search bar on top of the console.

2. Inside the **`Static Web Apps`** section, click **`Create +.`**

3. Provide a name to your application.

4. In the deployment source section, select **`GitHub`**

5. It will then ask you to provide access to your GitHub account.
6. Click the link and enable access to your GitHub account
7. Then it will allow you to select your repository and branch.
8. Select the newly created repository and the default branch main.
9. Click **`Create.`**

Once the static web app is created, Azure automatically does a few changes to your GitHub repository:

- Adds a new file inside your repository for the deployment workflow
- Adds a deployment token into your GitHub Actions configuration

You can go to the **`Actions`** section in your repository to see the CI/CD pipeline created by Azure. But we can see that the latest deployment failed. You can see an error similar to this:

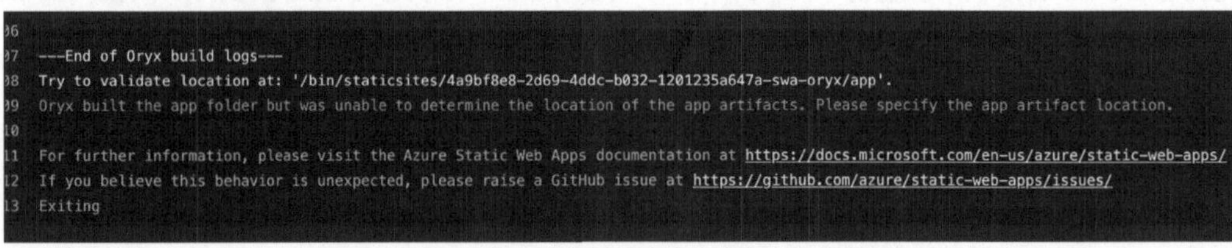

***Figure 9.3**: GitHub Actions failure*

This error occurs because we have not configured the folder in which the build files will be stored. Our Ember application stores the output files into the **`dist`** folder. We need to specify this in our github workflow file. Pull the latest code containing the commit made by Azure into your local by doing:

```
git pull origin main
```

Once pulled, you can see a file named **`.github/workflows/<some-random-name>.yml`**.

This file is a **`GitHub Action`** file, containing the steps for automatically deploying the code to your Azure Static Web App. Inside the file, you need to look for a line named **`output_location`**, which will contain an empty value. Replace the line with the following:

```
output_location: “dist”
```

We can now push these changes just like we did earlier and see the github actions succeed. The GitHub Actions is a CI/CD pipeline that automatically deploys your branch into the specified environment (Azure Static Web App in this case) by simply adding a commit to the specified branch of our repository (We have configured the **`main`** branch in our Static Web App). Next, we can visit the Static Web App URL available on the Static Web App overview page.

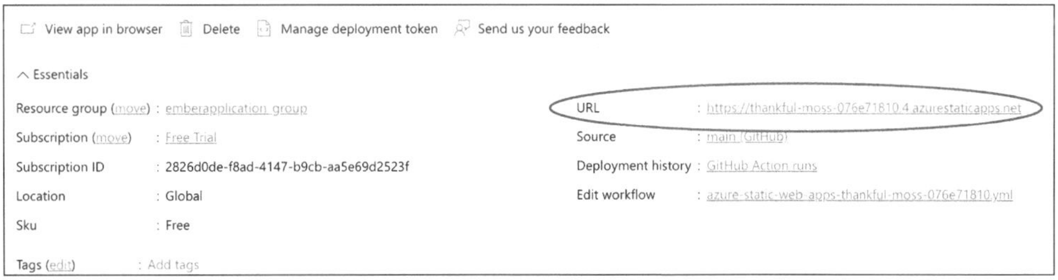

Figure 9.4: *Azure Static Web App URL*

You can click the URL to visit our web application hosted as an Azure Static Web App.

Adding Environment Variables to GitHub

In the previous setups, we initiated the deployment process from our local terminal. Hence, the required ENV variables were being fetched from the .env file we have inside our project. But in this case, we are doing the deployment from the **Github Actions** environment. We have intentionally not pushed our .env file to the repository, for security reasons. So how will the build process access the environment variables in that case? We will need to specify them in the repository settings in GitHub.

1. Go to the **`Settings`** tab of the repository.
2. In the settings page, expand the **`Settings and Variables`** menu in the left navbar and select **`Actions`** inside it.
3. In the Actions section, we can already see the **`AZURE_STATIC_WEB_APPS_API`** key configured to supply the Azure authentication token into the Github Action. This is how GitHub authenticates to upload the files to their portal.
4. Here, click **`New Repository Secret`** and provide the name and value for each secret that we have in our **`.env`** file that we want to expose to the GitHub Actions runtime environment.

We can see that the values are not visible once uploaded. This makes it secure from even people who can access the Settings page of the repository. The values uploaded can only be seen during the upload time and even when editing, the old value will not be displayed.

This completes our automatic deployment setup to push our application as an Azure Static Web Application.

Conclusion

In this chapter, we have discussed how you can create a production build that can be pushed into online environments in order to make it accessible for everyone. We saw how to generate a build and how the build is made to work in the Ember production environment. We then learned how you can deploy the application into different cloud hosting providers of unicorn companies like Amazon (AWS), Google (GCP), Microsoft (Azure). We saw how the credentials should not be exposed anywhere inside the code or uploaded into any online repository. We learned the workarounds of using the **`process.env`** object to access secure variables.

When setting up Azure, we saw automated deployments using GitHub actions, how it automatically pushes the code into the Azure environment when we add a commit to our main branch. We also discussed adding dynamic environment variables in a secure manner using the **`Secrets and Variables`** section of the GitHub settings, thus exposing our credentials only to the **`Github Actions`** environment.

In the next chapter, we will summarize everything we have learned throughout the book and discuss some of the best practices and workflows followed by the Ember Community.

Points to Remember

- Ember builds the code into static CSS and JS files
- The build folder can be uploaded and served just like any static HTML site
- The browser downloads the static files and the JS files in the build activate the Ember environment in the browser
- Once the build is generated, we can upload the build files in any of the preferred online cloud hosting providers.
- Credentials should never be hardcoded into the application's code

Multiple Choice Questions

1. What is the best way to serve an Ember application in a production environment?
    a. Run the **ember server** and access it through port 4200
    b. Generate a static build and upload it to a cloud environment
    c. Both
    d. None of the Above
2. Which of the following is not a cloud hosting provider supported by ember-cli-deploy by default?
    a. AWS
    b. GCP
    c. Azure
    d. Digital Ocean
3. What is the AWS service that allows Static Web Hosting?
    a. S3
    b. S4
    c. Static Hoster
    d. None of the above
4. What is the GCP service that allows Static Web Hosting?
    a. Compute
    b. Cloud Functions
    c. Cloud Storage
    d. Cloud File System

5. What is the Azure service that can be used for deploying a Static Web Application?
    a. S3
    b. Static Web Apps
    c. Websites
    d. Compute

Answers

1. b
2. d
3. a
4. c
5. b

Questions

1. How does the Ember build process work internally?
2. What are the advantages of generating a static build?
3. What is a CDN and how does it help in serving our static website?

Key Terms

- **Static Build:** An easily deployable version of our Ember Application that can be downloaded and run in any browser with ease
- **AWS:** Cloud Hosting Solution provided by Amazon
- **GCP:** Cloud Hosting Solution provided by Google
- **Azure:** Cloud Hosting Solution provided by Microsoft
- **Secrets:** Credentials that cannot be hardcoded into our codebase. They have to be configured and supplied separately.

Chapter 10
Conclusion

Introduction

So far, this book has given you a basic introduction to what Web Applications are, how they are different from websites, the components present in a web application, and some of the popularly available frontend and backend frameworks. We have covered the process of installing Ember.js into your system, creating a new application, developing the pages based on our requirements, testing the changes and deploying them.

Our discussions and exercises will help you gain knowledge of the framework and build your confidence as an Ember.js Developer. Instead of just focusing on the development process, you have end-to-end knowledge of the development, testing and deployment of the application.

In this final chapter, we will summarize the items we have learned so far and then talk about some best practices in Ember.js. We will also discuss how you can become a contributor by writing code for this widely used framework.

Structure

In this chapter, we will discuss the following topics:

- Ember.js
- Ember-CLI
- Developing your Ember Application
- Testing your Ember Application
- Deploying your Ember Application
- Maintaining your Ember application
- Writing and deploying an addon

- Best practices in Ember.js
- Contributing to Ember.js

Ember.js

From our understanding of the framework with what we have gone through so far, we can clearly state that Ember.js is a robust and scalable frontend framework for building web applications. We have also discussed the popular frameworks used around the world and how Ember is different from all of them. It is designed in such a way to build large applications that can handle big amounts of data in them.

Convention over Configuration

Ember follows the **Convention over Configuration** design flow by default. This reduces the number of decisions the developer has to make during the development process. It simplifies the job of beginners and guides them in following the best practices of the framework, like naming conventions, folder structure of the application, and so on. This helps anyone to get the basic application that follows the default conventions up and running very fast.

Even though it follows strict conventions, it is flexible enough to allow configuring the application as per our needs. By this methodology, the framework is easy enough for beginners to set up and get the application working in a secure manner even though the developers are not fully aware of the internal workings of the framework. Making the application do something that deviates from the conventions of the framework requires the developer to read and understand the framework and the conventional changes they are making to the application.

Application Architecture

Ember is built using the MVC (Model, View, Controller) model. It clearly defines different modules in the application and what should be contained in each module. By defining this, Ember can easily connect the different modules internally based on its conventions so that the developer needs little effort to handle the coordination between different modules in the application. Even though we do not have an explicit View module in Ember, based on the definition, a View is part of the application that handles interactions with the user (without containing any business logic within itself) like displaying data or allowing the user to enter information. Templates are the parallel for views in Ember. Hence,

Ember's architecture model is sometimes referred to as **MTC** (Model, Template, Controller). Here is what each component in the architecture model refers to:

- **Model**: The model represents the JavaScript object representation of the data present in the application.
- **View/Template**: Handles the interactions of the application with the end user. This takes care of the user interface, aesthetics, look and feel of the application that the user sees.
- **Controller**: The controller part of the application contains the core business logic and takes care of connecting the Model and View. It also handles any external interaction of the application with APIs or third-party services.

Ember applications are built using the **Component-Service strategy**. The business logic and connectivity of the application are split and written into modularized Components and Services as much as possible, allowing us to reuse the same code in multiple places in the application. It also uses **Two-way data binding**, which means any change to the data in the View gets immediately reflected in the controller and vice versa.

It provides you with a few optional features which can be enabled in the application quickly based on your needs. Features like allowing usage of jQuery inside your application are present in the framework by default but require you to manually enable them if and only when required.

Ember-CLI

Ember Command Line Interface (Ember-CLI) is a wrapper on the main framework, thus creating an interface for developers to interact with and manage their Ember application. Following are some of the functionalities of the CLI:

1. Create a new Ember application/addon with the proper folder structure.
2. Install Ember addons into your project and run the blueprints configured in the addon.
3. Run the Ember development server with Watchman, so that any change in the code will immediately alert the browser and trigger a page refresh.
4. Generate different modules in the application like Routes, Components, Models and generate the boilerplate code for the same based on configured blueprints. There are also options to destroy the modules created with the generate command.

5. Run tests on the application.
6. Build the application to generate static files that can be hosted easily.

Ember-CLI is a huge part of the framework as it handles the complex jobs of creating the application, installing the dependencies, running, testing, building and deploying the application. It also allows us to configure the development server in such a way that it is accessible from remote machines as well. The simplicity of the interface encapsulates all these functionalities and makes them available to developers in the form of simple commands. Each of those commands supports a wide variety of parameters to configure anything you want with your application.

Ember-CLI requires **Node.js** to be installed in your system and available to access from your terminal. It supports usage of both `yarn` and `npm` as package managers and you can choose one based on your convenience when creating the Ember application.

Developing your Ember Application

The Ember application is fully modularized with specific conventions of where each module is placed and how they interact with each other. Here are the core modules/concepts in an Ember application:

- **Route Handler**: Route handler is the first part of the application that interacts with the user. When the user enters a URL in the browser, the Route Handler decides which route should be called based on the URL and loads the particular Route.
- **Route**: A Route is a piece of code that directly links to a URL in the browser. The Route can handle dynamic parameters in the URL like id. It takes care of fetching the data (model) related to the route and loading the template associated with the route. It contains a wide range of hooks like `beforeModel`, `afterModel`, and `setupController` to execute any logic at any given point of the Route's lifecycle.
- **Model**: A Model is the JavaScript representation of real-time data that is loaded into the application. The model and the underlying Ember Store take care of interacting with the backend API to load data into the application and convert them into JavaScript objects.
- **Template**: A Template is the part of the application that the user sees on screen. The Ember Template allows for displaying dynamic data on screen using the `{{ }}` and `{{{ }}}` syntax. It provides options to introduce a lot of dynamicity using conditions and loops. The Template

is also responsible for the aesthetics of the screen (CSS). Template files are represented in the repository using the `.hbs` extension, as Ember templates use the syntax of the `Handlebars.js` templating library.

- **Controller**: A Controller is an intermediary between the Route and the Template. The model data or any parameter fetched from the Route is passed to the Template only through the Controller. There can be a maximum of only one Controller per Route. It is not necessary for a Controller to be present for each Route and the Ember blueprint does not generate it by default. Ember uses a pre-generated default Controller whenever the application does not provide an explicit Controller for a particular Route.
- **Component**: Components are the basic building blocks of Ember.js. It is the smallest reusable piece of code in the application that can be called from any Template in the application. Each Component contains two files - an HTML (`.hbs`) file for templates and a JavaScript (`.js`) file for business logic. The JavaScript file is not generated by default and can be created for each Component based on requirements.
- **Service**: A Service is a Singleton object that lives through the lifecycle of the application. Services can be injected into any object like Component, Controller, Route or even other Services. Services usually contain logic that is not part of any particular page, like making third-party calls to interact with other applications like payment systems and so on.
- **Helpers**: Helpers are reusable JavaScript functions that can be called from Templates. A Helper can receive any number of parameters and the response is rendered directly in the Template. Helpers support named arguments that allow us to understand the code better by seeing what data is being passed to a Helper along with the parameter name.

We have discussed in detail about each of these modules in the previous chapters, about how they work and interact with each other. The Ember application is a modularized yet tightly knit collaboration between all these modules. The framework handles the internal communication among the modules, thus letting the developer worry only about building the application rather than facing the hassle of getting the basics to work.

Testing your Ember Application

Once the application is developed, it is important to have automated tests written for your application. Automated tests allow you to ensure that the features in the application are working as per the requirements and that new changes do not affect any existing modules in the application. By doing so, it gives a lot of confidence even when the application grows large. Ember Tests are built on top of the `QUnit` JavaScript framework. Here are the different levels of tests that are present in Ember:

- **Unit Tests**: These tests cover the basic modules of the application and test their behavior in solitary environments. Unit tests are written for Routes, Models, Templates, Controllers and Services. Running a unit test does not render the application.
- **Rendering Tests**: Rendering/Integration tests are for testing modules or a combination of modules, and their interactions with each other. It requires at least a part of the application to be rendered and hence the name Rendering tests. Components and Helpers are tested using rendering tests.
- **Application Tests**: Acceptance tests are for testing the application from the user's point of view. It allows you to open a particular URL in the browser, enter data in the forms, click buttons, and then track the transition between routes and so on. Acceptance tests trigger all the lifecycle routes of each module, just like it happens when the user loads the page in the browser.

We had discussed in detail how each level is different from the other and the scenarios where each of them is useful. We also looked at how we can find issues based on auto-generated tests and how they can be fixed. The important part we discussed was about writing tests for each module in the application, thereby increasing our code coverage.

Code Coverage

Code Coverage is a vital benchmark in rating the exhaustiveness of your test suite. The `ember-cli-code-coverage` add-on tracks the lines of code that are called when running the test suite and generates a report on the percentage of your code that is covered during tests. The primary goal for a test suite to be perfect is to have 100% test coverage. From our small exercise in *Chapter 7: Testing Ember.js Apps*, we were able to improve the coverage from around 50% to more than 78%.

Deploying your Ember Application

Once the application is developed and tested, it can be deployed for everyone to access from their browsers. Deploying the Ember application consists of two steps:

1. Generating the build files for your application.
2. Copying the build files to a hosted environment for serving it to others on demand.

Build Process

The build process of an Ember application takes the individual modules of the application and combines them into a single JavaScript file that can be expanded and activated by any contemporary browser. Generating a static build in Ember involves the following steps:

- **Transpiling**: The Ember application may contain modern JavaScript code that is not directly supported by all browsers. For example, using arrow notations for functions is not supported by default in a few browsers. So Ember converts these notations into basic JavaScript code that is readable by all supported browsers.
- **Minifying**: In order to reduce the size of the output file, Ember CLI renames variables and functions in the code, thus improving the performance of the code in the browser as well.
- **Bundling**: Once minified, the multiple files are combined into a single file for easy sharing.
- **Fingerprinting**: For every build, the output files generated are suffixed with a random set of characters and numbers. This fingerprint is used to uniquely identify a build and prevent browsers from loading old files from the cache, even after a new deployment. The fingerprinted file names are updated in the index.html file generated for the new build.
- **Testing**: To ensure the build is generated properly, Ember CLI runs the tests against the build.
- **Linting**: Linting is the process of checking code semantics. This ensures that there are no potential errors and bugs like using a variable without defining it, and so on.

Deployment

Once the build files are generated, the deployment process is simple. We discussed how we can integrate with different cloud hosting providers and how the **`ember-cli-deploy`** package can help us efficiently deploy the application with a single command. We had gone through the process of deploying to AWS, GCP and Azure in detail.

Maintaining your Ember Application

After the application is developed and deployed in the production environment, maintaining the application is an important task. Even though the application might not have any changes to the requirements or any new features, it is recommended to keep the application version up to date and prevent the usage of outdated packages. There are two steps to the maintenance process:

Handling Deprecations

We have discussed the different techniques available in Ember to filter out the deprecations and modify them before upgrading to a newer version. Deprecations are functions or properties that are flagged to be removed/renamed from the framework in a future release. So it is important to keep our application deprecation free and updated so that release upgrades are easy to do.

Upgrading packages and Ember

The Ember.js community keeps releasing new versions of the framework with updated technical and security features. The new versions also take into account the current browser support and improve the performance of the application based on the latest available browsers. So it is necessary to run your application using the **Latest Stable Version** (LTS) of Ember. The details about the latest releases of Ember can be found at https://blog.emberjs.com.

Along with Ember.js, the dependencies of your application will also have to be upgraded, so that any updates regarding the usage of the addon are incorporated into the system. When upgrading either Ember.js or any package, we need to look for breaking changes in the packages that might affect the existing code and deploy only after the necessary changes are made in our code accordingly. Ember provides the `ember-cli-update` package to make this process easier. You can install this package and then run `ember update.` This will download the latest version of Ember (or the version specified when running this command) and check the changes between the two versions. Once the update is run, we need to run the following command:

```
ember update --run-codemods
```

The mentioned command will make any syntactic changes required for upgrading from your current version to a new version. It might be a function name that is changed, the way variables are declared and so on. If there are some changes that Ember is not sure about and wants you to intervene, it will raise them as merge conflicts and you can decide which changes to keep and what to delete.

Writing and Deploying an addon

We have looked at creating and deploying Ember applications. In this section, we will discuss how you can create your own addon, and get it deployed to the Ember Observer website (https://emberobserver.com/) so that everyone can look at your addon and install it in their applications. Here are the steps involved in building and deploying your addon:

Generating an addon

Creating an addon is a simple process similar to creating an Ember application. We can run the following command outside the current Ember project. We have to create a new addon:

```
ember addon my-new-addon
```

This will create a folder named **`my-new-addon`** just like **ember new**. But you can see the differences in the folder structure with a new **`addon`** folder inside the project.

Adding Content

Adding content into the addon is similar to how you do for an Ember project. Let us create a new Component in this addon to print some text. Let us generate a component with the following command:

```
ember generate component title-displayer
```

Let us say this component will get the title from the calling template and display the title in a specific styling format. The preceding command will have created a few files in both the **`app`** folder and the **`addon`** folder inside our project. You can open the **`app/components/title-displayer.js`** file to see that it references the file inside the **`addon`** folder. This means this component is rendered by default by our addon. Let us add the following code to our **`addon/components/title-displayer.hbs:`**

```
<h1>{{@title}}</h1>
```

So this component will simply get the title from the calling template and display it inside h1.

Linking the addon to our existing project

Once the addon is ready, next we can try using it in our local project to ensure it works as expected. Here is how you can link/import our new addon into our current Ember application:

1. To ensure all dependencies of the addon are properly installed, we should run **`yarn install`** from inside the addon directory.
2. In order to expose our addon to projects available locally, we will run **`yarn link`** so that the local yarn manager will be notified to fetch the addon files from this folder when someone tries to install this addon.
3. Next, we need to call the addon from our Ember application directory. From inside the Ember application directory, run **`yarn link my-new-addon`**.
4. Once linked, we need to add our addon to the **`package.json`** file in the Ember project. Since we do not have any version constraints as of now, we add the following line to the devDependencies section of the Ember project: **`"my-new-addon": "*"`**
5. Now yarn will treat the addon as a new dependency and we will install it by running **`yarn install.`**
6. The setup process is complete and now we can call our addon from anywhere inside the application using the Camelized name of the addon. Let us add the following to our index template:

```
<MyNewAddon @title="Testing my new Addon" />
```

You can now refresh your browser to see the text reflecting in a h1. Thus we have successfully tested our addon in our project.

Pushing to Ember Observer

After your addon is tested and ready to deploy, you can publish it as an npm package by following https://docs.npmjs.com/creating-and-publishing-scoped-public-packages which provides the instructions for publishing an npm package. Some steps are recommended before publishing:

- Creating a website for your addon. There is already an existing package **`ember-cli-addon-docs`** which helps you design a webpage for your addon.
- Your addon should contain a **`README.md`** file that explains in detail about the addon and how it works.

- A `CONTRIBUTING.md` file for informing people if they can contribute to building this addon and the steps for the same.

Once published, you can share the link to your addon website on Ember Observer and then developers will start noticing your addon and start incorporating your addon in their projects.

Best Practices in Ember.js

Best practices are framework-level conventions that are not enforced upon us but are good to have in your application. Here are some of the best practices to be kept in mind when developing your application:

- URLs with nested Routes should be named in plural (for example, clients, users).
- Model names should be named singular (for example, client, salesman, user).
- All variable names should be camel-cased. Class Names should start with a capital letter whereas functions and variables should start with a small letter.
- Use Components and Component actions as much as possible instead of Controllers and Controller actions.
- **Data down, actions up**: When nesting Components, it is always preferred to abstract the data handling and pass the information from a parent Component to the child Component. But when you want to update a particular property or information passed from a parent Component, it is recommended to call a function in the parent Component to update the data instead of updating the data directly in the child Component.
- Always keep in mind that Controllers are singleton objects and the property declarations inside the Controller are not automatically reset when the application transfers from one Route to another. So, it is better to ensure any property of the Controller that is updated should be reset back to default using the `resetController` function in the Route.

Contributing to Ember.js

Ember.js is a community-driven framework and as a developer, you can do your duty to the developer community by helping build Ember.js. The core repository of Ember.js is present at https://github.com/emberjs/ember.js. You can contribute to Ember through the following methods:

- You can create an issue in the Ember repository to report any bug you find in the latest version or any enhancement you would like to add to the framework.
- You can take a look at existing issues and submit a Pull Request with the changes to the same. You should look at the **`CONTRIBUTING.md`** file in the Ember GitHub Repository for guidelines on how to submit a Pull Request to Ember.
- If you find any typos in the Ember documentation or API guides, you can update the relevant documentation and submit Pull Requests to the Ember repository.

More information can be found in the **`CONTRIBUTING.md`** file present in the Ember.js GitHub repository.

Conclusion

Thus, we have covered the basics of Ember.js and through this book we have gone through the process of creating your first Ember application, adding different pages to your application, and configuring, testing and deploying the application. With a core understanding of the basics, you will be able to apply this in creating any scalable application for large-scale use.

It is now time for you to close this book and open yourself up to the world of opportunities presented by this wonderful framework. Being used by some of the top tech companies in the world, Ember.js Developer is one of the most in-demand roles, with a constant need for new developers joining the community. My best wishes for your journey with Ember and the community looks forward to your contributions to this esteemed framework.

Index

Symbols

A

B

C

F